PROCEEDINGS OF THE BATTLE CONFERENCE ON ANGLO-NORMAN STUDIES

III · 1980

PROCEEDINGS OF THE BATTLE CONFERENCE ON ANGLO-NORMAN STUDIES

III · 1980

Edited by R. Allen Brown

THE BOYDELL PRESS

First published 1981 by The Boydell Press, an imprint of
Boydell & Brewer Ltd, PO Box 9, Woodbridge, Suffolk IP12 3DF and of
Boydell & Brewer Inc., PO Box 41026, Rochester, NY 14604, USA

Reprinted 1990

British Library Cataloguing in Publication Data

Battle Conference on Anglo-Norman Studies
  (3rd: 1980)
  Proceedings of the Battle Conference on
  Anglo-Norman Studies III, 1980.
  1. Great Britain—History—Norman period,
  1066–1154—Congresses
  I. Brown, Reginald Allen
  942.02   DA195

  ISBN 0-85115-142-6

The cover illustration is from BL MS Cotton Domitian AII f. 21, and is reproduced by kind permission of the Trustees of the British Library.

Photoset in Great Britain by
Rowland Phototypesetting Limited
Bury St Edmunds, Suffolk
and printed by St Edmundsbury Press Limited
Bury St Edmunds, Suffolk.

Contents

List of plates

List of figures

List of Maps

Preface

The third Battle Conference in Anglo-Norman Studies was held between 25 and 30 July 1980 at Pyke House in Battle. Because Pyke House may be closed hereafter, and because the retirement of its warden, Mr Hobson, is regretably certain, it is more important than ever to emphasize how much the annual conference has owed to its agreeable and hospitable *venue*. We are also again indebted to the British Academy for a generous grant towards the expenses of bringing distinguished speakers from overseas.

The present third volume of the *Proceedings* contains the text of the papers given at the conference and substantially as read. Unfortunately Dr Margaret Gibson is unable to publish here her communication on the Norman library of Christ Church, Canterbury. On the other hand the volume contains Mr Ifor Rowlands' paper on the Norman settlement in Dyfed held over from last year. The volume also contains the extra item of a note on Chichester cathedral, which was the principal objective of our Outing this year, by Dr Richard Gem who conducted the visit. Since its inauguration in 1978 the conference has been fortunate in being able to inspect the current excavations at Battle Abbey directed by Dr John Hare for the Department of the Environment, and we are very glad to be able to publish on this occasion the first fruits, so to speak, of his labours there.

It remains to thank all those who contributed greatly to the undoubted success of the 1980 conference—the East Sussex County Council (our sponsors) and especially Mrs Gillian Murton and Mr David Thornton; the Department of the Environment and Mr Jonathan Coad; Miss Parker, the Headmistress of Battle Abbey School, for her kind cooperation and especially for allowing us again to have our opening reception in the Abbot's Hall; the Warden and staff of Pyke House, as above; Dr Richard Gem, as above; and Mr Ian Peirce for his indefatigable help, not least in connection with our now traditional inspection of the battlefield of 'Hastings'. Many would think it appropriate also to add the landlord of the 'Chequers' to this list. Finally, I must express my particular gratitude to Mr Richard Barber of the Boydell Press for his work, help and skill in seeing this volume through the press.

R.A.B.

Thelnetham, Suffolk
12 November 1980

Abbreviations

ASC	*Anglo-Saxon Chronicle*
BIHR	*Bulletin of the Institute of Historical Research*
BL	British Library
BN	Bibliothèque Nationale
BT	*The Bayeux Tapestry* ed. F. M. Stenton, 2nd ed. London 1965.
Carmen	*The Carmen de Hastingae Proelio of Guy bishop of Amiens* ed. Catherine Morton and Hope Muntz, Oxford Medieval Texts, Oxford 1972.
De gestis regum	William of Malmesbury, *De gestis regum Anglorum libri quinque*, ed. W. Stubbs, RS 1887.
Domesday Book	*Domesday Book, seu liber censualis . . .*, ed. A. Farley, 2 vols, Record Comm., 1783.
Eadmer	*Historia novorum in Anglia* ed. M. Rule, RS, 1884.
EHD	*English Historical Documents* i ed. & tr. D. Whitelock, London 1955; ii ed. & tr. D. C. Douglas, London 1953.
EHR	*English Historical Review*
Gesta Guillelmi	Guillaume de Poitiers, *Gesta Guillelmi . . .*, ed. R. Foreville, Paris 1952.
Historia Novella	William of Malmesbury, *Historia Novella*, ed. K. R. Potter, Nelson's Medieval Texts, Edinburgh 1955.
Hollister	C. W. Hollister, *Anglo-Saxon military institutions on the eve of the Conquest*, Oxford 1962.
Huntingdon	Henry of Huntingdon, *Historia Anglorum*, ed. T. Arnold, RS 1879.
Jumièges	Guillaume de Jumièges, *Gesta Normannorum ducum*, ed. J.Marx, Société de l'histoire de Normandie, 1914.
MGH	*Monumenta Germaniae Historica*, Scriptores
ns	New Series
Orderic	Ordericus Vitalis, *Historia ecclesiastica*, ed. M. Chibnall, Oxford Medieval Texts, Oxford 1969–.
RS	Rolls Series, London
ser.	series
Trans.	Transactions
TRHS	*Transactions of the Royal Historical Society*
VCH	Victoria County History
Vita Eadwardi	*The Life of Edward the Confessor*, ed. and tr. F. Barlow, Nelson's Medieval Texts, London 1962.

Wace   Wace, *Le Roman de Rou*, ed. A. J. Holden, 3 vols, Société des anciens textes français, Paris 1970–3.

Worcester   Florence of Worcester, *Chronicon ex Chronicis*, ed. B. Thorpe, English Historical Society, London 1848–9.

The Battle of Hastings

R. ALLEN BROWN

I had thought of beginning with an explanation of my temerity in presenting to this assembly a paper in which there is little new beyond what I wrote in my book some years ago,[1] but, finding myself, like the Normans in the generally accepted version of the battle, in grave difficulties in the Malfosse at the end thereof, I now know there is no time for any lengthy *apologia*. Suffice it to say, therefore, that I thought we should have an account of Hastings on our agenda and in our *Proceedings*, for others to alter later if they wish or can, and that I was selfish enough to want to write it myself.[2]

There must be, however, an introduction which places the Battle of Hastings in a treble context. The broadest is the context of medieval military history, more specifically its neglect and, worse than neglect, the travesty which is generally made of it. Of course there are honourable exceptions,[3] but, neglected for the most part by serious historians, the subject tends to fall into the hands of antiquarians, amateurs and, not least, retired military gentlemen with whom an admittedly valuable military experience is no substitute for historical knowledge and scholarship. Such neglect is amazing, for war is one of the fundamentals of history and as such is far too important to be left to military historians as I have unhappily defined them. Michael Howard, on the first page of his *Franco–Prussian War*,[4] observed of the French defeat at Sedan in 1870 that it was 'the result not simply of a faulty command but of a faulty military system; and the military system of a nation is not an independent section of the social system but an aspect of it in its totality'. Yet while we are told often enough that feudal society is society organized for war, there is no Michael Howard for the so-called Middle Ages. In his absence, what we know in London as the myth of medieval warfare, or more specifically of the feudal period, has become established and appears ineradicable. It is represented in English historical literature by Sir Charles Oman's *A History of the Art of War in the Middle Ages*,[5] which was first written as an undergraduate prize essay in 1884 and thereafter, expanded but only slightly ameliorated, went on to become the standard work which it has ever since remained. Moreover, the first, and worst, edition was quite recently reissued by the Cornell University Press,[6] without a word of warning (quite the reverse) to the student for whom it is intended. In that edition the young Oman wrote, amongst many other outrageous travesties of the truth, that while 'arrogance and stupidity combined to give a certain definite colour to the proceedings of the average feudal host', nevertheless 'a feudal force presented an assemblage of unsoldierlike qualities such as have seldom been known to coexist'.[7] I will not go on, but here is the myth of feudal warfare as disorganized and amateur chaos in all its unbelievable absurdity. Further it is not, of course, confined either to this country or to Oman, for the erudite works of Spatz[8] and Delbrück,[9] invariably cited in footnotes as authorities for Hastings, are little or no better in their conviction that contemporary warfare was, above all, lacking in discipline—a point to which we shall assuredly return.

The second context, with some apology, is feudalism and the origin of feudalism in this country. It is a sharp indication of the fundamental importance of military history properly understood and properly studied, that the 'military' question of whether Old English armies in the eleventh century used cavalry or not—which even Maitland thought only a matter of tactics as opposed to anything fundamental[10]—is basic to the larger question of the presence or absence of feudalism in England on the eve of the Norman Conquest. No cavalry, no knights, we may say; and no knights, no feudalism. Yet in the virtual absence of any serious study of military matters by serious historians, the old arguments seem never to be ended, and it is well-known that one of the few recent studies of 'English Warfare in 1066', by Mr Richard Glover,[11] argues for the use of cavalry by Old English armies, though not at Hastings itself—and without, unless I am mistaken, ever seeing the profound social implications of what he was saying. To this we shall obviously have to return, albeit as briefly as possible. And, lastly, all this brings me to my third context of this or any study of the Battle of Hastings, for which I do not so much apologise as express my profound regret. I refer, of course, to that controversy, leading to or even based on prejudice, which still does vitiate the study of almost every aspect of the Norman Conquest of England, and not least, of course, any study of that most famous of victories on Saturday, 14 October 1066. Pots call kettles black and the disinterested pursuit of truth is lost in the fog of war and forgotten in the heat of battle. Freeman himself, for whom the defeat of clean-limbed Liberal Englishmen on that occasion was an agony to be explained away only by the foreign use of Dirty Tricks like horses and archery, would have stood in admiration at that latest study of the battle which comes as close as it is possible to get to making Hastings an English victory and attributes what little credit there is for the real victors to participants called the French and not the Normans.[12]

The contexts thus delineated, let us approach our actual subject with the observation that we probably have more information and potential knowledge about Hastings than any other medieval battle—appropriately, and fortunately, enough, since it is also one of the most decisive battles in Western history. This observation remains true, I hasten to add (lest I be thought out of date), even if R. H. C. Davis has successfully dismissed the *Song of the Battle of Hastings* from the canon of early or contemporary and acceptable texts for the study of the Norman Conquest[13]—as I am inclined to think that he has, though we shall in some respects miss it—and even if Eleanor Searle has dismissed the Conqueror's vow before the battle, to found an abbey on the site of his victory if God granted it, to the realm of monastic myth—as, again, I am much afraid she has.[14] For we are left with the long and detailed account of William of Poitiers, who had every qualification to write it save that of an eye-witness, including that of having first been a knight in the service of the duke before he became his chaplain. We have also the near-miraculous survival of the Bayeux Tapestry, more than one quarter of whose length is explicitly devoted to the battle and whose patron, it is now generally agreed, was Odo bishop of Bayeux, the Conqueror's half-brother and certainly present on the field.[15] To these two outstanding sources we add, of course, the briefer testimony of other con-temporary and near-contemporary accounts in William of Jumièges, the Anglo-Saxon Chronicle and Florence of Worcester; and to these we add in turn, though with increasing scholarly caution, the accounts and traditions recorded in such later sources as William of Malmesbury, Henry of Hunting-don and even Wace (who may give us the correct number of ships in the Norman fleet[16])—and here I would add also those local traditions which survive to be enshrined, for example, in the *Chronicle of Battle Abbey*, and indeed survive, alive and well, even today. Further, the mention of local tradition brings me to that other type of evidence, topographical, even archaeological, which we are so fortunate as to possess for the Battle of Hastings. We know the site of the engagement (Fig. 1): we know with an unusual degree of precision where it was fought, and thus, with the aid of the generous literary and artistic evidence, we have a good chance of knowing *how* it was fought also. The Normans like others in this period were adept at putting great buildings on difficult sites, as witness Mont St Michel, but such dramatic undertakings require a good reason, usually religious or military. If the Conqueror's vow before the battle to found his penitential abbey on the battlefield is now discredited, there remains no reason at all to disbelieve the tradition preserved at Battle of his eventual determination to build his church with its high altar on the spot where Harold fell, and only this can satisfactorily explain its awkward architectural position, on a hill requiring artificial levelling, and without water. The first monks from Marmoutier and the lush valleys of the Loire were appalled when they initially surveyed the site, and promptly chose a better one, north-west of the present abbey, which was still marked in the 1180's. The king when he heard of this was exceeding wrath, and sweeping aside all difficulties 'ordered them to lay the foundations of the church speedily and on the very spot where his enemy had fallen and the victory been won . . . And so at length, the foundations were laid of what was in those days thought an outstanding building, and they prudently erected the high altar as the king had commanded, on the very place where Harold's emblem, which they call a "standard" [*sic*], was seen to have fallen'.[17] (Which spot, incidentally, according to the chron-icle, had been carefully marked at the end of the battle.[18])

All save the very narrowest military historian of the old school would accept

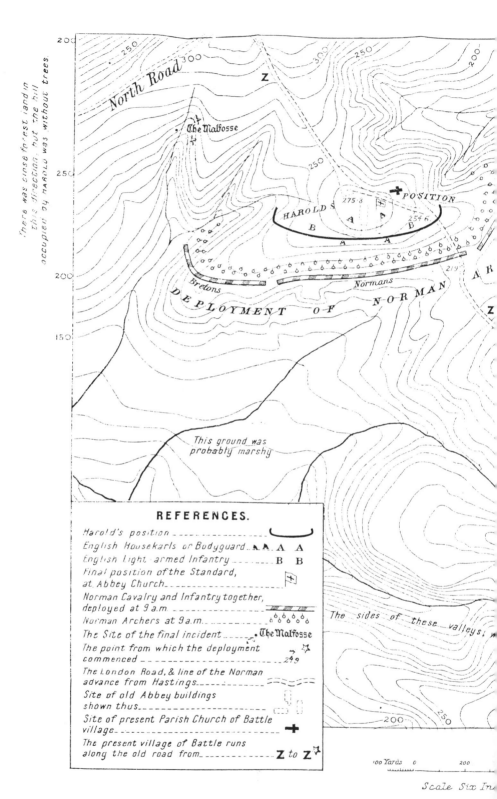

Map 1. Map of the Battle of Hastings by General E. Renouard James, from F. H. Baring, *Do...*

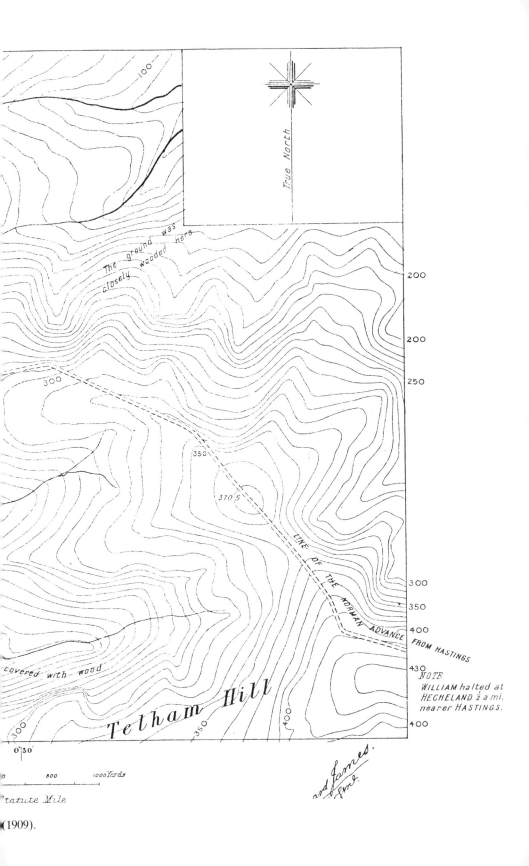

True North

The ground was closely wooded here

100

200

200

250

300

350

310.5

LINE OF THE NORMAN ADVANCE FROM HASTINGS

300

350

400

430

covered with wood

T e t h a m   H i l l

300

350

400

400

NOTE
WILLIAM halted at
HECHELAND ½ a mi.
nearer HASTINGS.

0°30'

800   1000 Yards

Statute Mile

and James.
Sc.

(1909).

that military history must deal with something more than battles, and that at least the preparations leading up to them and the campaigns of which they form a part must be included. Certainly we must spend some time on the process of bringing our contenders together on the battlefield and the preliminaries of the battle, for several important matters arise therefrom. I must unfortunately pass over briefly the impressive preparations in Normandy, many of which are graphically portrayed upon the Bayeux Tapestry and all of which illuminate Norman military might and the quality of the Conqueror's leadership.[19] They began at once on the speedy receipt of the news of Edward's death and Harold's coronation, and included a series of great councils, the building of a fleet and the assembly of an army including many volunteers from overseas (if we now exclude the *Carmen* from the canon we must also exclude Normans from southern Italy, who always were unlikely), the maintenance of that great force in good order through more than six weeks of weary waiting, first at Dives-sur-Mer and then at St Valery-sur-Somme.[20] They also included a veritable diplomatic offensive, to which for whatever reason Harold made no answer, and which obtained the support both of the Papacy and, so to speak, of the public opinion of most of Latin Christendom for the Norman cause. When at last the Conqueror got the wind we are told he prayed for, the rapid and ordered embarkation of the Norman army must also be admired, and so, of course, must be the transportation of the horses across the Channel. There is also one other point that I would add. Because, owing to the nature of our sources, events may often seem to happen in the so-called Middle Ages out of the blue without explanation, it is silly to suppose that they did so in reality; and so here it really will not do to suppose that on the evening tide of 27 September 1066 the Conqueror set sail in the general direction of England without knowing where exactly he was going. Hypothesis is as dangerous as it is unavoidable in any account of the whole business of the Norman Conquest, but it is surely reasonable to suppose that duke William, after such careful preparations on such a scale as this, made his landfall at Pevensey the next morning also according to plan. And in this connection I would call attention to a searching paper given by A. J. Taylor at the Château-Gaillard Conference at Battle in 1966, suggesting that both Pevensey, which the Normans first occupied, and Hastings, to which they soon afterwards repaired as a better base, were Old English boroughs in 1066.[21] At both places, of course, they raised castles—but we have quite enough to discuss in this paper without involving ourselves in that other quasi-military controversy, *viz* the origin of castles in England, equally significant though it is for the nature of society.

On the English side of the Channel there are three points concerning Harold's preparations that seem to me to require emphasis, and also further investigation. First, that the logistical problems, if anything on a lesser scale than those which duke William triumphantly overcame, proved too much for him. Harold had first mobilized his forces in May against the renegade Tostig, and thereafter kept them in the south-east against the expected invasion from Normandy throughout the summer, the fleet with the king himself off the Isle of Wight and the fyrd 'everywhere along by the sea'. But, says the 'C' version of the Chronicle, 'in the end it was no use. When it was the Feast of the Nativity of St Mary (8 Sept.), the provisions of the people were gone, and nobody could keep them there any longer'.[22] In short, the army had to be dismissed and the ships sent back to London (with losses on the way). The potentially disastrous incident calls out for explanation from Anglo-Saxon military historians, and must throw light on the Old English military organization and its efficacy in the situation it had to face in 1066. My second point to call for emphasis and investigation is the striking ease with which Old English leaders, not only the king, are able to raise fleets in this period, whether it be, for example, Tostig in 1066 or the Godwinsons in 1052. On the broadest interpretation, I should like to think this reflects the essentially Anglo-Scandinavian nature of our Old English society, but, if so, it throws into sharper contrast the situation in Normandy, the land after all of the Norsemen, where a fleet—or at least a suitable fleet—had to be constructed for the invasion. Perhaps in feudal society, with its emphasis upon horses, knight service and chivalry, navies were taken less seriously. Third and last, it has always seemed to me amazing that Harold should have had no foreknowledge or expectation of Harold Hardrada's impending invasion from Norway; yet all military preparations of his own that we hear of are in the south-east against Normandy, and the 'C' version says specifically that 'Harold, king of Norway, came *by surprise* north into the Tyne', the English king being informed at the very moment of disembarking at London from his fleet returned from the Isle of Wight.[23]

Harold's dramatic reaction to the news of the Norwegian landing, compounded as it soon was by the defeat of the northern earls Edwin and Morcar at Gate Fulford on 20 September, is well known—his assembly of an army, his great and impressively rapid march north, his muster of his forces at Tadcaster on 24 September. Then on the morning of the 25th he 'went right on through York' to take Harold Hardrada, now with his ally Tostig, 'by surprise' at Stamford Bridge and win a great victory.[24] One would dearly like to know how these things were done precisely, in terms of the raising of troops, and of what kind, and of their movement; but again there are three points for us of particular relevance to the subsequent engagement at Hastings. The first is Richard Glover's recent resurrection of the credibility of Snorri Sturluson, whose *Heimskringla* contains the only detailed account of the battle, as evidence for the Old English use of cavalry at it.[25] Glover, of course, does not seek to argue for the use of cavalry by Harold at Hastings, which in the light of the abundant evidence to the contrary would be impossible; but in a somewhat unnecessary defence of Old English armies against their detractors who are nowadays few if any, he seeks to show that they could use cavalry when they wished but did not so wish at Hastings because it was for them a defensive action. The latter proposition is merely a misguided hypothesis, and the former, dependent exclusively upon Snorri Sturluson's thirteenth-century account of Stamford Bridge of demonstrable unreliability, is simply unacceptable. There is more than sufficient contemporary evidence to show that Old

English armies habitually fought on foot, and so did their time-honoured opponents, the Danes and the Norse.[26] In this at least Freeman was right, and Stamford Bridge was the last major battle fought on English soil in the ancient manner, hand to hand and axe to axe.[27] Our next point must be that of course the engagements of Gate Fulford and Stamford Bridge, fought within a week of each other (20 and 25 September) must have seriously affected Harold's strength at Hastings three weeks later. And the third point is that Harold's brilliant success at Stamford Bridge and the manner of it—the rapidity of movement, the thundering march north (190 miles from London to York) and the taking of the Norwegians by surprise—surely determined his conduct of his next and immediate campaign against the Normans. Of that I wrote in my book of 'reckless and impulsive haste'[28] and I think I still stand by it, though the qualification should be added that the ravaging by duke William of Sussex, the very patrimony of the house of Godwin,[29] would, according to contemporary notions of honour, demand immediate retaliation to demonstrate and defend one's lordship. Nevertheless, in terms of military appreciation, we are also surely right to see in Harold's movements before Hastings the intention to repeat the strategy and tactics which had given him such success at Stamford Bridge. Within two weeks or thirteen days at most from his receipt of the news of William's landing (on or soon after 1 October and traditionally at York) he had repeated his great march, this time in the reverse direction from York to London, delayed in the latter city for what was clearly the minimum time to make his final preparations and raise more troops, and made another forced march over the fifty-seven miles from London to Battle to engage his enemy.[30] William of Jumièges and William of Poitiers followed by Orderic Vitalis all state that Harold's intention was to take William by surprise, the last two adding even the possibility of a night attack.[31]

In the event it was not to be, but before we proceed to duke William's counter measures it may surely be urged that all this precipitate speed was as unwise as it was unsuccessful. For time, like the homeland, was on Harold's side and ran against the Norman duke, at the end of a long and hazardous line of communications across the Channel (Poitiers followed by Orderic—and the *Carmen* for what it is worth—say that Harold sent a fleet to cut off the Normans[32]), in an alien country, and not even knowing at first who his opponent would be, Harold or Harold Hardrada. And certainly Harold's haste brought material disadvantages: fatigue must have been amongst them, though I know of no contemporary source to say so, and lack of numbers on the scale he might have had is another. For that, the 'E' version of the Chronicle explicitly states that the king fought with William 'before all the army had come',[33] and Florence of Worcester is both more emphatic and more detailed. Commenting on Harold's haste, he writes 'and although he knew very well that some of the bravest men in all England had fallen in the two battles [*i.e.* Fulford and Stamford Bridge], and that half his army was not yet assembled, yet he did not hesitate to meet his enemy in Sussex as quickly as he could, and nine miles from Hastings he gave them battle, before a third of his army was drawn up'.[34]

On the second of those two seemingly cumulative statements by Florence we shall have occasion to comment again in a moment, but meanwhile there seems a case here for bad generalship for anyone who wants to take it up.

Although according to the Oman myth of medieval warfare reconnaissance was seldom if ever practiced by commanders in the feudal period, it is clear that duke William at Hastings, unlike Harold Hardrada at Stamford Bridge, learnt of Harold's approach in ample time to prepare his counter measures and put them into practice. Further, while the night before the battle is not explicitly mentioned by William of Poitiers, it is quite clear from his account supplemented by William of Jumièges that the news was received the day before the battle, *i.e.* on Friday, 13 October. In Poitiers the mounted patrols return to report Harold's rapid advance while the greater part of the Norman army is out foraging,[35] while in Jumièges the duke orders his army to stand to arms from dusk to dawn in case of a night attack, and at day-break moves off in the known direction of the enemy.[36] From Hedgland on Telham Hill, according to the local tradition in the Battle Chronicle,[37] the scouts of the advancing Norman army first saw the English on the Battle ridge two miles away, and the battle itself began at 'the third hour' or 9 a.m. according to Poitiers, Jumièges and Florence of Worcester.[38] From Hastings to Battle there are some seven miles to be covered by foot as well as horse. The decisive speed of all this is impressive enough as it is: clearly we cannot envisage the report of the English approach being received that morning as well, as has sometimes been maintained,[39] and to the accumulated evidence and argument we may cautiously add the later traditions (most memorably written up, of course, by Wace) of how the two armies passed the night before the battle, the Normans in prayer and the English in whooping it up.[40] No contemporary source in fact gives us any details of how Harold spent the night before his last engagement, but though William of Jumièges has him marching through the night to appear on the battlefield in the morning,[41] he must surely have rested his troops, presumably not far from the modern Battle and its ridge, from which he evidently first saw the Norman host advancing[42] and upon which he then arrayed his troops. If this reconstruction of events be accepted, two points follow. The first is that far from succumbing to a surprise attack, William (by good reconnaissance) turned the tables upon Harold, seized the initiative, and took his opponent by surprise; and the second is that Harold cannot possibly have selected the place of battle well in advance, as Freeman insisted and others have since suggested.[43] The one version of the Anglo-Saxon Chronicle which is contemporary explicitly states that 'William came against him [Harold] by surprise before his army was drawn up in battle array',[44] and Florence, as we have seen, has Harold engage the Normans 'before a third of his army was drawn up'.[45] If, as thus seems certain, Harold lost the initiative and was constrained to fight at that place and time by William's advance from Hastings, then all the more credit to him for selecting on the spur of the moment a site so admirably suited to the defensive tactics which alone he could offer—but yet it was not perfect. There was no way of withdrawal save the narrow isthmus which is now Battle High Street and along which he had come, while the space on the ridge was so confined that according to Florence many deserted before the action began.[46] Finally, in view of what has been written one should at least suggest that, far from 'supine loitering' on the Sussex coast (the phrase is Richard Glover's[47]) the Norman duke, since his landing at Pevensey, had achieved one of the most difficult strategic intentions, of drawing his opponent to give him the decisive action which he wanted, and that as soon as possible and without leaving his beach-head and his fleet. In this the ravaging of the countryside about Pevensey and Hastings, which William of Poitiers cites as one reason for Harold's haste,[48] may well have been a deliberate and calculated provocation—as may indeed have been the landing in Sussex in the first place.[49]

If the *Carmen de Hastingae Proelio* is to be dismissed, then we are confined for detailed contemporary information about the Battle of Hastings itself to William of Poitiers and the Bayeux Tapestry. Generous as both sources are, hypothesis is inevitable, but it must be informed by a knowledge of the warfare of the period. Later sources must be used with discretion since tradition and even myth soon gather about so famous and even elegiac an occasion. Something of a modern consensus puts the numbers of each army at some 7000 men.[50] On the English side one assumes this number to have been made up of the quasi-professional housecarls[51] of the king and of the households of his brothers and other great lords, well-armed thegns (if the distinction be allowed) who had ridden with Harold from London or even from York or come in since, together with less well-armed levies from neighbouring shires. The élite of housecarls is not mentioned specifically, *eo nomine*, in any contemporary source, though the two-handed battle-axe, their weapon *par excellence*, is much in evidence in the account (it is *hache norresche* in Wace and *haches danesches* in Benoit de Sainte-More[52]). William of Malmesbury seems to vouch for their predominance when he states[53] that Harold had with him mostly stipendiary troops *(stipendiarios et mercenarios milites)* and comparatively few from the provinces *(ex provincialibus) i.e.* the local levies, *vulgariter dicitur* 'fyrd', and it seems to me that in this connection more attention than is usual should be paid to William of Poitiers' unique remark that abundant help *(copiosa auxilia)* had been sent to the English from their kith and kin in Denmark.[54] The king planted his standard and took up his own position thereby on the highest point of the ridge, where the high altar of the abbey church was later to be placed.[55] According to William of Malmesbury his two brothers were with him there,[56] but since Gyrth and Leofwine were killed early in the battle[57] and long before Harold they were presumably in a different part of the line, and presumably with their own contingents—which in turn may be further reason to suppose that the housecarls were disposed along the entire English front and not massed in the centre as some commentators have argued.[58] The English position comprised the whole crest of the ridge facing south towards the Normans and extending for some 6-800 yards, *i.e.* 400 yards to the west or right of the king and standard, where the ground falls steeply away, and 2-400 yards to the east or left, where it ended roughly opposite the present 'Chequers' inn or somewhere between the junction of the Hastings and Sedlescombe roads and the school on the latter.[59] (Fig. 1) The entire English host, from the king downward, were dismounted to fight on foot. Of this there is not a shadow of doubt and all sources, contemporary and later, are agreed[60]—though one may and should add that this fact only makes it extremely improbable that Old English armies ever fought in any other manner. To a complete absence of cavalry, it seems there has to be added a more surprising deficiency of archers[61]—because, one can only surmise, Harold's rapidity of movement eliminated most of those who had to march on foot. We do not know how many ranks composed the line, but we do know that they stood in very close order, so close, wrote William of Poitiers, that the dead could scarcely fall and the wounded could not remove themselves from the action.[62] This, then, was the famous formation of the 'shield-wall', the 'war-hedge' of the Song of Maldon,[63] though an element of poetic licence must be allowed it, for clearly the shields must part for the weapons to be wielded and the great two-handed battle-axe especially required space on either side (it also, as Wace pointed out, left the warrior raising it dangerously off his guard.[64] Doubtless we must assume experience, training and team-work, all of which are as necessary for the effective use of ancient hand weapons as they are for modern military technology).

Against this seemingly impregnable position, at the foot of the steep slope of the ridge, the Norman duke deployed his forces in three lines, archers and, less certainly, crossbow-men in front,[65] heavy infantry, some at least with mail coats, next, and the heavy cavalry of knights and esquires not, as is sometimes said, in reserve but in the rear, to deliver the hoped for *coup de grâce* of their irresistable shock charge.[66] Such are the dispositions listed by William of Poitiers.[67] In the absence of the *Carmen* we have to be less confident than heretofore on the three lateral divisions (*i.e.* each in the above formation) of Bretons on the left (west), Normans in the centre and French on the right (east), though Poitiers later refers to the Bretons being on the left, and has duke William in the centre of the knights—and thus we may assume with Norman contingents—where he could direct operations by voice and gesture.[68] The presence of large numbers of well-armed infantry, who were given an important rôle to play, in the Norman army should remind us that Hastings was a battle of cavalry against infantry only in the sense that the English had no cavalry, not that the Normans had no infantry. It should also dispel another lingering Oman myth that infantry was despised by the commanders of the feudal period.[69] Nevertheless, the tactics of their enemy at Hastings were a source of some wonder to the hard-riding Norman and Frankish cavalry and their writers. 'It was,' wrote William of Poitiers, 'a strange kind of battle, one side attacking with all mobility, the other withstanding, as though rooted to the soil.'[70]

At Hastings, however, the battle having opened with a terrible sound of trumpets on both sides, the Norman infantry went in first until, having achieved no marked success, they were followed by the knights, spurring their horses up the hill. And thus, writes William of Poitiers, the last became first. Again, there was no success, which failure Poitiers carefully explains by the superiority of the English position on the hill-top, their dense ranks and close order, and the effectiveness of their arms (presumably their axes), which could easily cleave both shield and armour (presumably hauberk).[71] At this point in his narrative Poitiers proceeds to the first and real retreat of the Norman forces and the first climax of the battle.

But at this point we must pause to consider the true use and tactics of the Norman heavy cavalry of knights at Hastings—or indeed of Frankish chivalry anywhere else in this age—in the light of Richard Glover's tendentious remarks.[72] Seeking, as we have noted, to upgrade the Old English military capacity, and thus seeking to show that they could use cavalry when they wished, he turns, in the most unforgivable section of his monograph, to denigrate the Norman, so to achieve, by levelling up on the one hand and levelling down on the other, a kind of double equality. In any case, runs his argument, there was nothing to the Norman use of cavalry in this period, anyone could do it; and he goes on to speak of 'infantile' Norman cavalry tactics, and of Norman knights at Hastings as mere 'mounted javelineers' while citing yet others without horses as 'happily mixing it in on foot'. All this is said to be based on the evidence of the Bayeux Tapestry, but, to dismiss the last allegation first, I can find only one or two [*sic*] candidates for dismounted knights on the Tapestry[73] and they and any others there may have been in a similar predicament are likely to have had their horses killed under them (and to have been thus anything but happy)—as duke William had three horses killed under him that day according to William of Poitiers.[74] As for the infantile cavalry tactics, one must read above all D. J. A. Ross on these matters.[75] While we have the unimpeachable testimony of Ordericus Vitalis for the throwing of spears from the saddle as a knightly skill to be practiced,[76] it was obviously not very effective in battle and it is accordingly very difficult indeed to find certain instances of it in the Bayeux Tapestry's depiction of Hastings.[77] Those many knights on the Tapestry apparently brandishing their lances above their heads, and whom Mr Glover assumes to be about to throw them, are in fact about to strike over-arm in the manner most likely against infantry,[78] the two methods of using the lance on horseback inherited from antiquity being the overarm and underarm[79] thrust (Pl. 1, 2). Already at this date, however, what is to be the classic medieval usage of the couched lance was being developed, whereby with a heavier lance, no longer a spear, locked under the rider's arm, the whole momentum of horse and armoured horseman is concentrated in the point, to make possible the shock tactic of the charge. This is what Anna Comnena had in mind when she wrote of the Frankish chivalry of the time of the First Crusade that the charging knight would pierce the walls of Babylon.[80] Some of the Norman knights depicted on th Tapestry are quite clearly couching their lances,[81] (Pl. 3) and the fact is all the more remarkable in that the new tactic was developed on the Continent for the unhorsing of horsed opponents of whom there were none at Hastings. All the relevant evidence of the Tapestry,

Plate 2 Norman knights at Hastings: the lance used overarm (B.T. Pl. 63)

properly understood, points in the same direction, *viz* of the Norman chivalry in the van of the new developments: the hevier lances in some cases clearly shown,[81] the gonfanons on lances which are obviously not meant therefore to be thrown away,[83] the built-up saddle-bows to hold the rider in his seat at the shock of contact, and the very long stirrup leathers to afford the same security.[84] In the literary sources, including William of Poitiers, it is true that the *arme blanche* of the sword is more prominent than the lance, but this is presumably because the latter was liable to break at the first contact (thereafter to be renewed), and it is significant that in Poitiers' account of Hastings William the Conqueror is found at the end of the battle with the stump of a broken lance in his hand.[85]

To revert to the progress of the battle as recounted in the narrative of William of Poitiers,[86] after the failure of the initial hard-pressed assaults to make any significant impression on the English line, the Bretons and other auxiliaries on the Norman left, both horse and foot, began to fall back. The movement spread as such movements will, fanned by an ugly rumour that the duke was dead—though this alone, Poitiers assures us, could have caused the Normans themselves to yield. Some of the English forces, with or without orders,[87] began to advance down the hill in pursuit—and we reach one of the two best known incidents in the battle, dramatically depicted on the Tapestry,[88] as the duke himself stops the rot. Galloping in front of his retreating troops, 'shouting and brandishing his lance', he lifted his helmet to reveal himself and harangued the faint-hearted. 'Look at me. I am alive, and, by God's help, I shall win. What madness puts you to flight . . .' etc. On the Tapestry count Eustace of Boulogne on the right points to the living, gesticulating duke (who in this scene bears a mace) while on the left bishop Odo, also with a mace 'comfortat pueros', *i.e.* turns back the young men, the *tirones*, the esquires, who are about to ride off the field.[89] The duke himself, sword in hand, then led a counter attack and the Normans, enflamed, surrounded and cut down those who had pursued them down the hill.

After this crisis the general assault upon the English position was renewed by the knights especially, any breaches made being followed up by the men of Maine and Aquitaine, the French and the Bretons, 'but above all by the Normans with a courage beyond compare'. Thus William of Poitiers,[90] who goes on to praise the exploits in particular of the young lordling or *tiro*, Robert, the son of Roger de Beaumont, who in this his first battle particularly distinguished himself at the head of his contingent over on the right wing. But, Poitiers continues, 'the Normans and their allies, realizing that they could not overcome an enemy so numerous and standing so firm without great loss to themselves, retreated, deliberately feigning flight'—*terga dederunt, fugam ex industria simulantes*—remembering what success had attended their counter-attack upon the pursuing English after the recent real retreat.[91] And so we reach the second of the best-known incidents of the battle, the feigned flight, according to William of Poitiers twice repeated, and very well attested by all the principal sources for Hastings, contemporary and later, save only, perhaps,

Plate 3 Norman knights at Hastings: the lance couched and the overarm thrust (B.T. Pl. 65)

Plate 4 Pl. 67 from the Bayeux Tapestry, *with the caption 'Hic ceciderunt simul Angli et Franci in prelio'*

the Bayeux Tapestry, whose medium scarcely lent itself to its depiction.[92] Further, the attested manoeuvre was triumphantly successful, so much so that William of Malmesbury, the historian, in his *Gesta Regum* (*c.*1125) presented it in his account as the turning point of the battle and the chief reason for the eventual Norman victory.[93] Each time numbers of English were tempted to break ranks and drawn down from the ridge in pursuit, to be cut down as the knights wheeled their horses (*regiratis equis*[94]). Yet most modern commentators and *soi-disant* military historians have doubted the feigned flight to the point of its rejection.[95] For this they have no reason whatever save the persistent and persisting myth of Oman and others to which I have so often, and necessarily, referred. The feigned flight, so the argument runs, cannot have happened because it could not have happened; and it could not have happened because it would have required to a high degree discipline and training which feudal armies, and most especially the exhibitionist knights who formed them, notoriously did not possess. The truth is, of course, that our Frankish knights and Norman knights were as professional as the age could make them, born and bred to war and trained from early youth, in the household which is the contingent of a lord, in the art and science of horsemanship and arms. Not only do we have entirely acceptable, one might almost say overwhelming, evidence for the tactic of the feigned flight employed at Hastings, but we also have further evidence of its practice on other occasions by other knights of this generation—by the Normans at St Aubin-le-Cauf near Arques in 1052-3 and near Messina in 1060, and by Robert le Frison of Flanders at Cassel in 1071.[96] If this is not enough, then we can find much earlier references to the manoeuvre, which was thus evidently a well-known *ruse de guerre*, in *e.g.* Nithard under the year 842, over two-hundred years before Hastings, and in Dudo of St Quentin writing in the first decades of the eleventh century.[97] Clearly of all the arguments which surround the Norman Conquest and Hastings, this one at least must stop. If some military writers, blind in the arrogance of their ignorance, still demur, the key to understanding the feigned flight in practice is the *conroi*,[98] the comparatively small unit of the feudal host, presumably to be identified with the contingents and military households of individual lords, each marked out by the *gonfanon* of its leader. Such units, trained together over long, arduous years, and bound by the companionship of expertise, had ample discipline and the capacity not only to work and fight together but also to combine with other similar units. One need not, if one does not wish to, envisage the entire Norman cavalry at Hastings, or even very large sections of it, executing the feigned flight *en masse*—though personally I would not put it past them.

Still those many of the English who were left stood firm, 'still a formidable force and extremely difficult to surround'. Thus William of Poitiers,[99] and the last words are significant as presumably indicating that no part of the ridge had yet been taken. There follows, as the English at last seem to begin to weaken, what in the event becomes the final Norman all-out assault with horse and foot. Poitiers' prose rises to the occasion as in his poetic onomatopoeia one can almost hear the shock and thud of battle—*sagittant, feriunt, perfodiunt Normanni. Sagittant* is perhaps important here as a possible source for the later tradition of arrows shot on a high trajectory at this stage in the battle. It is not otherwise mentioned by Poitiers and appears first in Henry of Huntingdon to be worked up by Wace, which means its credentials are not very good.[100] And so we approach the final scenes of the battle, admittedly blurred, as the fog of war descends and the autumnal daylight wanes, as king Harold is slain and the English at length give way. It seems appropriate to quote William of Poitiers,[101] in the absence of the *Carmen* the nearest of our sources to the events he describes. Again he achieves a poetic and this time elegiac note in a paragraph admirably beginning *Jam inclinato die . . .* 'Now as the day declined the English army realized beyond doubt that they could no longer stand against the Normans. They knew that they were reduced by heavy losses; that the king himself, with his brothers and many magnates of the realm had fallen; that those who still stood were almost drained of strength; that they could expect no help. They saw the Normans not much diminished by casualties, threatening them more keenly than in the beginning, as if they had found new strength in the fight; they saw that fury of the duke who spared no one who resisted him; they saw that courage which could only find rest in victory. They therefore turned to flight . . . some on looted horses, many on foot; some along the roads, many across country.'

For the victorious Normans only the matter of the Malfosse remained, but for us there are two matters and the first is the death of the king. It is notable that no details at all of the manner of Harold's death are given by William of Poitiers, and the same is true of William of Jumièges who makes, indeed, a rare mistake in having him slain by lethal wounds at the beginning instead of the end of the battle—in which he was to be followed by Ordericus Vitalis.[102] It is perhaps strange, too, that there is no tradition of the matter in the Chronicle of Battle Abbey (where Harold is slain by a chance blow[103]), though it was certainly not the business of the monks there to contribute to any cult of the dead king and usurper. The Bayeux Tapestry, however, as our second detailed and contemporary source after William of Poitiers, has its famous scene, labelled '*Hic Harold rex interfectus est*', where *Harold* is written above the figure with an arrow in the eye and *interfectus est* above the falling figure being cut down by a mounted knight whose sword is against its thigh.[104] In recent years it has been fashionable to say that contemporary artistic convention prevents both figures from being Harold, that only the second one is (*interfectus est*) but the first is not, and that therefore the tradition of Harold's being slain by an arrow in the eye is false, derived probably from a misunderstanding of the Tapestry. In 1978, however, Dr N. P. Brooks in a paper given at the first Battle Conference and entitled 'The authority and interpretation of the Bayeux Tapestry'[105] re-examined the whole question and showed beyond reasonable doubt that the Tapestry *did* intend both figures to represent the stricken king. The tradition therefore—perhaps one of the best known facts in all English history after the date 1066 itself—is thus restored to something more than respectability as derived from no less an authority than the Tapestry, before taking off via Baudri de Bourgueil, William of Malmesbury, Henry of Huntingdon and, inevitably, Wace.[106] Perhaps matters should be left there, but the lack of detail in William of Poitiers especially remains curious and may prompt two further comments. The first is that William of Malmesbury's account, though close to the Tapestry, may yet provide some explanation. There, Harold is first lethally struck by a chance arrow which pierced his brain and then slashed on the thigh by the sword of a knight as he lay prostrate—for which cowardly and shameful act the unfortunate knight was subsequently stripped of his knighthood by William *(militia pulsus est)*. Here then are no feats of arms to be celebrated by the victorious duke's biographer. But what cannot be accepted is the version of the death of Harold given by the *Carmen* and its interpretation by its recent editors, wherein there is no arrow but the king is slain by four knights led by duke William himself.[107] Had William, duke of the Normans, with only three companions, attacked the heavily defended headquarters of the English army—which is what the alleged exploit amounts to—to kill the king and thereby take the crown, far from being hushed up as Morton and Munz will have it, the feat of arms would have been bruited abroad in every court and *chanson* in Latin Christendom and beyond. Meanwhile, as it seems to me, the whole improbable incident recorded by the *Carmen* goes far to condemn that source itself.

And so we come finally to the Malfosse incident, by which of course I mean what we all think we mean, the well-known incident at the end of the battle— more precisely, *after* the end of the battle—in which the Norman knights, hotly pursuing the fleeing English, ride pell-mell in the gathering gloom and broken countryside into a deep fosse or ravine with heavy and tragic losses. The dilemma is, however, that for this incident there is very little if any contemporary evidence; most modern commentators, with no excuse at all after Marx's edition of 1914, having confused Ordericus Vitalis' interpolations in William of Jumièges with William of Jumièges himself.[108] The story (and perhaps we must use such a word) clearly has its origins in William of Poitiers, yet in his version there is no Malfosse in the generally accepted sense of the Normans riding into it.[109] Some of the fleeing English are encouraged to make a stand by 'a broken rampart or entrenchment [the word used is *vallum* with its suggestion of a man-made obstacle] and a labyrinth of ditches'. Duke William comes galloping up, armed only with the stump of a broken lance, intent on attacking even though he assumes they are English reinforcements. He meets, already there, count Eustace of Boulogne with a contingent of fifty knights, all of whom are withdrawing. Eustace advises the duke also to withdraw, and even as he speaks is severely wounded between the shoulder blades by a missile and has to be helped away. The duke, nothing daunted, equating caution with defeat, presses on and tramples his enemies underfoot *[sic]*. We are given no military details of the brief action save the statement that a number of Normans lost their lives because their prowess was inhibited by the difficult country. For anything else and more familiar we have to wait until Ordericus Vitalis'

Interpolations in William of Jumièges, dating from before 1109 to after 1113.[110] There[111] we are told that 'when the Normans saw the English fleeing from the battlefield they pursued them relentlessly through the whole night until Sunday [evidently one may detect elements of exaggeration in this] but to their own harm. For by chance long grasses concealed an ancient rampart *(antiquuum aggerem)* and as the Normans came galloping up they fell, one on top of the other, in a struggling mass of horses and arms'. There then follow some sentences on casualties (15000) and God's judgement on both sides, which must surely relate to the whole battle. Here, then, is a recognizable Malfosse incident, but we do not get, so to speak, the full version until Ordericus Vitalis' *Ecclesiastical History* where, in his Book III finished in the early 1120's,[112] in his account of the battle which in general follows William of Poitiers very closely, he awkwardly combines William's passage on the post-battle affair with his own seemingly independent version from the Interpolations.[113] Both are given more or less verbatim but cut into each other, to produce a combined version which seems to me to have given Orderic much trouble. The result of all this is that pursuing Normans ride into an *antiquum aggerem*, as in the Interpolations. The English, encouraged by this, and also by the *praeruptum uallum* and labyrinth of ditches as in William of Poitiers, make a stand and inflict severe losses. Next we have the passage from the Interpolations on casualties on both sides, wherein Engenulf castellan of Laigle is named amongst the Normans[114] and which is now much more ambiguous than before as to whether it relates to the Malfosse incident or the whole battle. Finally we have the advent of duke William, his meeting with count Eustace and his dealing with the situation, as in William of Poitiers.

After Orderic there is nothing, so far as I can see, until the Battle Abbey Chronicle of the late twelfth century, where, at the end of the battle, 'a final disaster was revealed to the eyes of all'.[115] A little ambiguously we are told that 'just where the fighting was going on, and stretching for a considerable distance, an immense ditch yawned'. Hidden by brambles and thistles it engulfed great numbers, especially of pursuing Normans—'For, when, all unknowing, they came galloping on, their terrific impetus carried them headlong down into it, and they died tragically, pounded to pieces'. The author goes on to say that the place of the disaster (which now becomes a 'deep pit') is known in his day as the *Malfosse*. He does not, unfortunately, identify it on the ground—and nor am I going to try to do so, partly because, as I think you will have anticipated, in my essentially literary approach there is more, and worse, to come. Meanwhile it is rather alarmingly clear that the literary credentials of the well-known *Malfosse* incident *after* the Battle of Hastings—which henceforward we had best call Version A—are not very good. This Version A may well begin in William of Poitiers, *i.e.* one of our two best and contemporary sources; but he says nothing of its best-known feature of knights riding into a ditch—he says nothing, in short, of the *Malfosse*. For that we have to wait until Ordericus Vitalis (who may have had his own source, which may have been the family of Engenulf castellan of Laigle[116]), and after him there is nothing until the local

Battle Chronicle of *c*.1180—where and when, incidentally, we meet for the first time the word, the name, *Malfosse*. The situation is equally alarming in negative terms; that is to say, these are the only sources to relate Version A, which does not appear in others. The negative side of the dilemma is best emphasized by stressing that Version A does not even appear in Wace who, though not in my view a source altogether to be despised for the Norman Conquest, is certainly not a man ever knowingly to omit a good story.

Let us therefore turn to what I will call Version B, wherein a Malfosse incident occurs not at the end but in the middle of the Battle of Hastings. For this, too, it appears we can begin with one of our two best, contemporary sources, this time the Bayeux Tapestry, and I refer back again to that enigmatic scene—artistically magnificent—labelled *Hic ceciderunt simul Angli et Franci in prelio*[117] (Pl. 4). It occurs in the middle of the battle, and, more specifically, immediately between the scene representing the death of Harold's brothers Gyrth and Leofwine and that representing the real retreat of the Norman forces, *i.e.* the scene of bishop Odo's turning back the retreating young men or esquires and of duke William's bearing of his head to show he is alive. I have previously suggested that this possibly may be the Tapestry's representation of the feigned flight[118] (which, in that case, would precede and not follow the real retreat), but what matters to us now is what is actually shown, namely a group of Stenton's 'half-armed peasants'[119] making a stand upon a hillock, at the foot of which, and in a marsh or bog,[120] Norman cavalry are in grave difficulties. If one has studied all the sources for the Battle of Hastings one cannot but be reminded by this scene of the Malfosse incident and, more important, William of Malmesbury in his *Gesta Regum* of *c*.1125 thus interpreted it. Evidently knowing his Tapestry, and following it closely here as he does for the death of Harold,[121] having told us how, unable to force an issue any other way, duke William ordered the feigned flight with devastating effect, he goes on to say that the English nevertheless took their toll by frequently making stands. Thus for example, 'getting possession of a hillock *(occupato tumulo)*, they drove down the Normans . . . into the valley beneath where, easily hurling their javelins and rolling down stones upon them, they destroyed them to a man'. Then he adds, 'Besides, by a short passage, with which they were acquainted, avoiding a deep ditch *(fossatum quoddam praeruptum*, wherein we may have an echo of William of Poitiers, whose account of the battle William of Malmesbury also uses), they trod under foot such a multitude of their enemies in that place that they made the hollow level with the plain by the heaps of carcasses'. Here, then, is certainly a Malfosse incident in the middle of the battle. Henry of Huntingdon, writing at much the same date (*c*.1125-30?), also has a Malfosse incident in the midst of the battle, and as part of the feigned flight,[122] in which the Normans ride into a great but concealed ditch *(quandam foveam magnam dolose protectam)*. So also does the ebullient Wace, though in his account the disaster occurs in the course of the real retreat of the Norman forces (which, as in the *Carmen* and perhaps the Bayeux Tapestry, follows the feigned flight) and the fosse *(sic)* is that which Harold had caused to be dug before the battle began.[123] Wace's rival, Benoit de Ste-Maure[124] has no Malfosse incident of any kind, either during or after the battle, and nor do the *Carmen*, Gaimar,[125] the *Brevis Relatio*[126] or Baudri de Bourgueil whose early date would have made his testimony especially valuable.[127]

And there, I am afraid, we must leave it. There are thus two versions of the Malfosse incident, A and B, both, it must be confessed, making a somewhat shaky start in one or other of the two most detailed and certainly early accounts of the Battle of Hastings, and I can find no way of choosing between them.[128] Two maddening points remain. One is (and the feeling of frustration will be familiar to many of you) that, as it turns out, J. H. Round said all that I have said, and more, in his diatribes against E. A. Freeman some eighty years ago.[129] The other is that the Malfosse incident, whether or not it took place, whenever it took place, and wherever it took place, quite simply does not matter—that is to say, that as a disaster which overtook the Normans it demonstrably did not effect the issue of the battle. And that, I think, gives me my cue to end this paper, and to do so by returning to the safe ground of what is known and certain. It may conceivably surprise our very welcome French participants at this Conference that almost everything about the Norman Conquest is controversial amongst English-speaking historians, but one thing I do insist upon, which is that the Normans won at Hastings. They won, this paper would suggest, amongst other means by superior military techniques and by superior generalship—and they also gained, I would further suggest, one of the most decisive victories of Western history. But because, though I thus perceive the truth and cling to it, I am at least as unbiassed as William of Poitiers, let me finally end by quoting that splendid epitaph of William of Malmesbury upon the English—'they were few in number but brave in the extreme'.[130]

Les Comtes de Champagne et la 'Normanitas': Sémiologie d'un tombeau

MICHEL BUR

Dans la collégiale de Saint-Etienne de Troyes fondée par le comte Henri le Libéral en 1157, il existait avant la Révolution deux tombeaux de bronze émaillé, élevés à la mémoire du comte Henri et de son fils et second successeur, Thibaud III. Ces monuments sont connus par la description qu'en a donnée en 1704 le chanoine Jean Hugot et, pour celui d'Henri, par une gravure reproduite dans le recueil de A. F. Arnaud intitulé *Voyage archéologique dans le département de l'Aube* (1837, t. 2, pl. 14). Il ne subsiste malheureusement aucune représentation de celui de Thibaud III, plus somptueux et plus chargé de signification idéologique.[1]

Le tombeau d'Henri le Libéral, décédé en 1181, avait la forme d'un sarcophage à couvercle plat. Il était ajouré sur les côtés de dix portiques à travers lesquels on pouvait apercevoir la statue du prince, couché les mains jointes, avec une calotte sur la tête. L'ornementation, commandée par sa veuve Marie de France, fille de Louis VII et d'Aliénor d'Aquitaine, était d'un symbolisme purement religieux.

A Thibaud III, mort en 1201, sa veuve Blanche de Navarre fit élever une sépulture en manière de couche d'apparat avec gisant de grandeur naturelle. Dans les niches ménagées dans le soubassement fut déposée une dizaine de figurines en argent. Tout en témoignant d'une même foi dans l'au-delà, ce second monument se distinguait nettement du précédent par sa riche iconographie toute imprégnée d'intentions politiques et lignagères.

Il ne peut être question dans cet exposé de faire une étude archéologique de ces tombeaux et de les replacer dans l'évolution de l'art funéraire au Moyen Age. Aussi nécessaire que soit une telle étude, elle nous éloignerait de notre sujet et, par conséquent, doit être remise à plus tard. Nous nous contenterons donc simplement d'analyser le programme iconographique du tombeau de Thibaud III au point de vue de la *Normanitas*, c'est-à-dire de la conscience qu'ont eue au XII° siècle les comtes de Champagne de la maison de Blois d'appartenir au monde normand et d'en être à certains égards les véritables héritiers.

I. *Le Tombeau de Thibaud III*

Décédé au moment ou il allait prendre la tête de la quatrième croisade, le jeune comte est représenté au vif les yeux ouverts, les mains jointes sur un bâton de

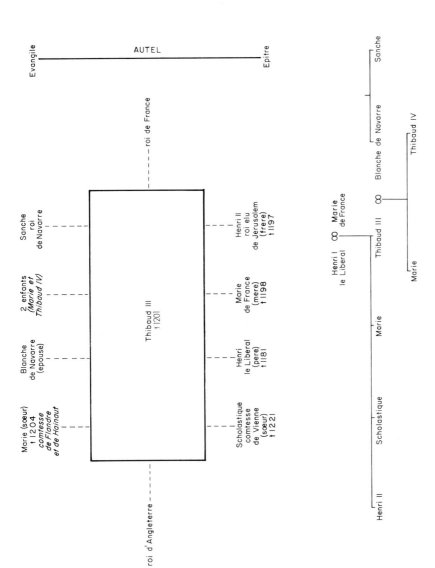

Fig 1. *Diagram of the tomb of Thibaud III at St Etienne de Troyes.*

pélerin. Ses bras sont ornés de bracelets et il porte sur le front 'une espèce de couronne' garnie de pierreries. Les figures qui l'entourent sont identifiées par des inscriptions. En partant du chef et en tournant à droite on rencontre successivement le roi de France, puis du côté de l'Epitre Henri II, roi élu de Jésuralem, frère du défunt (+1197), la comtesse Marie sa mère (+1198), le comte Henri son père (+1181), la comtesse Scholastique de Vienne sa soeur; au pied du gisant, c'est-à-dire à l'opposé du roi de France, le roi d'Angleterre et du côté de l'Evangile, l'autre soeur de Thibaud Marie (+1204), puis Blanche de Navarre son épouse, ses deux enfants et pour finir, symétrique du roi de Jérusalem, le roi Sanche de Navarre.

C'est donc tout le cercle de famille qui se trouve réuni, vivants et morts confondus, autour de la dépouille mortelle de Thibaud III. Une telle représentation—véritable *Memento* dressé dans le choeur de l'église—est unique dans la sculpture funéraire de l'époque. Elle diffère dans son esprit des cortèges de deuillants qui font alors leur apparition sur les tombeaux des puissants. Pour découvrir un modèle ou du moins une source d'inspiration, il faut peut-être regarder du côté de Spire et du monument élevé dans la cathédrale à la gloire des Saliens au lendemain de la mort de l'empereur Henri V, avec la célèbre inscription: *Filius hic, Pater hic, Avus hic, Proavus histic, hic proavi conjux, hic Henrici senioris . . .*[2]

Quoi qu'il en soit du modèle ou des analogies, le tombeau de Thibaud III est d'abord l'expression du sentiment familial tel qu'il est vécu dans la plus haute aristocratie champenoise au début du XIIIe siècle. Pour le jeune comte, la famille se compose essentiellement des ses père et mère, de ses frère et soeurs, de son épouse et de ses enfants: trois générations au milieu desquelles il s'épanouit, connaît son origine et assure sa postérité.

A ce groupe restreint s'ajoute une dernière figure, celle de Sanche roi de Navarre. Il semble qu'il s'agisse non pas de Sanche VI le Sage, beau-père de Thibaud, décédé en 1194, mais de Sanche VII le Fort, son beau-frère, qui régnera sur la Navarre jusqu'en 1234. Deux arguments militent en faveur de cette identification: la place occupée par le personnage en face d'Henri de Jérusalem et l'inscription rédigée au présent. Il était naturel que Blanche dans la situation d'isolement ou elle se trouvait après la mort de son mari, sollicite l'appui moral de son frère et que celui-ci, conformément à la tradition épique qui attribue à l'oncle maternel un rôle prépondérant dans l'éducation des jouvenceaux, vienne lui prêter main forte et protège ses neveux. Ainsi la famille se présente en définitive comme un système buissonnant qui, dans l'instantané du deuil, fige autour du couple touché par la mort, outre les parents et les enfants du défunt, les frères et soeurs des deux côtés.

Mais une famille n'est pas seulement une réunion de contemporains. C'est aussi une succession de générations, un arbre debout avec des racines, bref un lignage ou une lignée. Dans cette perspective il convient de voir dans le roi de France et le roi d'Angleterre qui occupent les deux extrêmités du tombeau, l'un du côté de la comtesse Marie, l'autre du côté d'Henri le Libéral, comme s'ils se partageaient a égalité la dépouille funèbre, avec un surcroît de dignité pour le roi de France placé à la tête, des ancêtres de Thibaud.

De tout temps, les érudits ont assimilé le roi de France à Louis VII (+1180), le grand père maternel de Thibaud, mais leurs efforts ont complètement échoué dans l'identification du roi d'Angleterre. A la différence des autres souverains, celui-ci n'a pas de sceptre et tient sa couronne à la main. Le chanoine Hugot, en 1704, l'appelait Henri, nom que l'historien des comtes de Champagne H. d'Arbois de Jubainville interprète comme étant celui d'Henri II Plantagenêt. Personnellement H. d'Arbois, à la suite de N. Camuzat, penche plutôt pour Richard Coeur de Lion.[3] De simples considérations de filiation invitent à rejeter ces deux noms; des raisons politiques également. Au moment ou Blanche, devenue régente, fait édifier la sépulture de son époux, c'est-à-dire très probablement entre 1204, date de la mort de Marie, comtesse de Flandre et de Hainaut, qui y figure sans ses titres, et 1221, date de la mort de la comtesse Scholastique de Vienne, la Champagne est pratiquement tombée sous la coupe de Philippe Auguste.[4] Jamais ce prince, en guerre contre un vassal félon et excommunié, n'aurait admis que la race des Plantagenêt fut représentée sur le tombeau. Il faut se rendre à l'évidence et chercher le roi d'Angleterre parmi les ascendants paternels de Thibaud.

Avant d'entreprendre cette enquête, il n'est pas inutile de noter à quel point la conscience lignagère des comtes de Champagne est d'essence élitiste et nobiliaire. Parmi les deux personnages statufiés, outre le défunt qui porte le diadème et les bracelets du pouvoir—ces bracelets qu'un jour Rollon, selon la légende, pendit aux branches d'un arbre dans la forêt—, quatre sont des rois, deux des filles de rois. La dernière, Marie de Champagne, aurait pu être qualifiée d'impératrice si elle n'était pas morte au moment ou son mari, Baudoin VI de Hainaut, accédait au trône de Constantinople. Race royale donc et faite pour les trônes, indépendamment de toute règle de dévolution des fiefs et des royaumes et de tout événement, bon ou mauvais, pouvant influer sur son destin.

II. *Anglica Regna Rego Rex Reverendus Ego*

Un inconnu se dissimule encore dans le cercle de famille: le roi d'Angleterre.[5] Il devrait s'agir normalement d'un ancêtre direct d'Henri le Libéral. La généalogie de ce comte n'offre aucune obscurité: Henri était le fils de Thibaud II et de Mathilde de Carinthie. Thibaud II avait pour parents Etienne-Henri de Blois et Adèle d'Angleterre, fille de Guillaume le Conquérant. L'ancêtre recherché serait-il Guillaume? La solution du problème, on le verra plus loin, est un peu plus compliquée.

Avec le mariage d'Adèle d'Angleterre et d'Etienne-Henri, célébré probablement en 1084, la *Normanitas* fait son apparition dans la maison de Blois. Cette union eut des répercussions immédiates sur la géographie politique du bassin Parisien. Elle amena Etienne-Henri a renoncer aux territoires champenois qui lui étaient destinés pour prendre dans l'héritage paternel, conformément aux intérêts de son beau-père désireux d'encercler le domaine capétien, d'une part la Beauce, soit les comtés de Blois, Chartres et

Chateaudun et d'autre part, seconde branche de la tenaille, la Brie avec Meaux et Provins.[6] Parti pour la croisade en 1096, Etienne-Henri mourut en Palestine en 1101. Sa veuve exerça la régence de 1096 à 1107, date de l'adoubement de Thibaud II, mais elle conserva une grande influence sur son fils jusqu'à son entrée au monastère clunisien de Marcigny en 1122. Les contemporains la décrivent comme une femme énergique et fière de sa naissance. Elle conservait dans sa chambre une tapisserie illustrant la conquête de l'Angleterre et dans son entourage se pressaient des clercs venus de son pays d'origine comme ce Guillaume Le Normand qui fut le maître de l'un de ses fils.

De l'époque d'Adèle datent quelques changements significatifs dans le comportement des comtes et dans les institutions de leur principauté. D'abord l'abandon (provisoire il est vrai) du qualificatif de *palatinus* par lequel ils marquaient leur volonté de tenir le premier rang dans le palais du roi de France. En second lieu une accentuation nette de la faveur réservée à Cluny. Etienne-Henri et Adèle confièrent à la grande abbaye bourguignonne, si influente en Normandie, la réforme de Saint-Germain d'Auxerre. L'un de leur fils, Henri, futur évêque de Winchester, fut moine clunisien. Adèle elle même finit ses jours sous le costume de Cluny. En ce qui concerne les institutions, on voit se mettre en place à Meaux, à Provins, à Troyes, villes qu'anime de plus en plus le grand commerce, des vicomtes d'un type nouveau, chargés du contrôle des transactions et de la police des marchés, et dont les attributions évoquent celles des vicomtes normands. Enfin c'est probablement par référence à la chancellerie royale anglo-normande qu'Adèle créa le premier noyau de la chancellerie comtale: *Rogerius clericus regis Anglorum scripsit*, lit-on dans une charte de 1102. Le même Roger en 1107 fait pour la première fois usage du sceau: *Rodgerius cancellarius sigillavit*. Un personnel emprunté à la cour du roi d'Angleterre introduit des habitudes nouvelles dans le milieu blésochampenois sans pouvoir toutefois induire le comte à user du *writ* scellé.

Dans ces conditions, la statuette énigmatique du tombeau représente-t-elle Guillaume le Conquérant? On serait tenté de le croire puisque le souvenir du grand roi resta longtemps vivace dans la maison de Blois. Bousculant l'onomastique de sa belle famille, Adèle fit baptiser son fils aîné Guillaume, réservant au second l'appellation traditionnelle de Thibaud. Celui-ci à son tour reprit le nom prestigieux pour son quatrième fils, le futur archevêque de Reims Guillaume aux Blanches Mains.[7] A la réflexion cependant, il faut renoncer à cette identification car le Conquérant eut des héritiers et les comtes blésochampenois ne pouvaient revendiquer l'exclusivité de son souvenir. Il convient donc de chercher un autre ancêtre qui leur soit plus proche et qui leur appartienne en propre.

Serait-ce Henri Ier Beauclerc, frère d'Adèle, prince magnifique et fascinant, selon Suger, et qui exerça une profonde influence sur ses neveux? Dès sa chevalerie en 1107, Thibaud II lui est tout dévoué. Mettant les liens du sang au-dessus du devoir féodal, il le sert contre le roi de France si bien que celui-ci en exprime un vif mécontentement au concile de Reims de 1119. Grâce à leur oncle maternel, les frères de Thibaud font une brillante carrière dans le

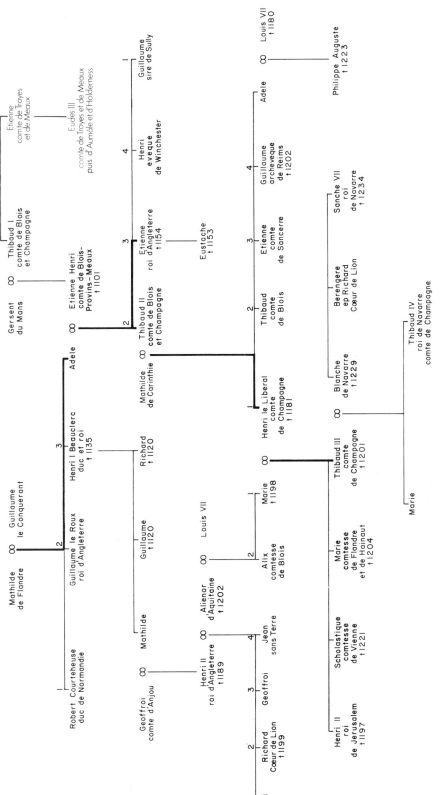

Fig. 2. Family tree of the counts of Blois

royaume anglo-normand, Henri comme évêque de Winchester, Etienne comme sire d'Eye et comte de Mortain. Le nom d'Henri s'impose au fils de Thibaud II, Henri le Libéral (dont le surnom est Richard) et à son petit-fils Henri de Jérusalem. Néanmoins comme il n'existe pas de lien de filiation directe entre ce roi et ses jeunes protégés, comme d'autre part il eut, lui aussi, des héritiers directs (Henri II Plantagenêt ne se réclame-t-il pas constamment, dans les Constitutions de Clarendon comme dans les enquêtes sur le domaine, de son illustre grand père), il faut certainement trouver un autre modèle pour la statuette du tombeau.

Ce modèle, ce roi qui tient sa couronne à la main comme s'il l'avait prise et l'avait rendue, c'est Etienne de Mortain, le successeur d'Henri Beauclerc et le premier membre de la famille de Blois à avoir été investi de la dignité royale.[8] A son égard, les siens ne pouvaient que nourrir des sentiments ambigus. Vrai roi mais faux frère, il était monté sur le trône au mépris des droits de son aîné le comte Thibaud II. De plus il avait été incapable de transmettre la couronne à ses descendants. Si une vieille méfiance à l'égard des Capétiens explique que le nom du roi de France ne soit pas écrit en toute lettre sur le tombeau, un juste ressentiment devait aussi tout naturellement maintenir Etienne dans l'anonymat.

Pour bien comprendre l'importance du personnage, un rappel historique est nécessaire. En 1120 La Blanche-Nef sombrait entraînant au fond de la Manche les fils d'Henri Beauclerc. Désormais, le plus proche héritier du roi est son neveu le comte Thibaud. Cela paraît si évident qu'en Flandre, la même année, dans le *Liber Floridus*, et comme pour appuyer les droits de Thibaud, Lambert de Saint-Omer rappelle la légende du duc des Normands Gerlon, compagnon de Rollon et ancêtre des comtes de Blois.[9] En fait, l'impératrice Mathilde, fille d'Henri Beauclerc, aurait pu transmettre l'héritage à un fils mais elle n'en avait pas. La condition ne fut remplie qu'à la suite de son second mariage et de la naissance d'Henri II Plantagenêt le 23 mars 1133. Jusqu'à cet événement, de 1120 à 1133, Thibaud, qui figure toujours au premier rang des témoins dans les diplômes de son oncle en 1121, 1126-29 et 1131, a pu se croire le légitime héritier du royaume anglo-normand et faire le rêve d'un vaste empire campano-bléso-normanno anglais.[10]

Ce rêve commença à se dissiper en 1133 mais la transition fut très longue car Henri Beauclerc ne s'entendait pas avec son gendre et les barons normands craignaient l'autorité du comte d'Anjou. Quand Henri mourut en 1135, le connétable Hugues Bigod fit savoir que le défunt, sur son lit de mort, avait délié tous ses vassaux de leurs obligations envers sa fille, les laissant libres par conséquent de se rallier à Thibaud. Celui-ci vint à Neufbourg. Les barons l'accueillaient comme leur souverain, quand brusquement arriva la nouvelle qu'Etienne, soutenu par son frère l'évêque de Winchester, avait été proclamé roi par les barons anglais et couronné à Westminster le 22 décembre. Du coup les barons normands abandonnèrent Thibaud.[11]

L'élection bafouait le droit d'aînesse. Peut-être troublé par les revendications des Angevins, le comte n'entreprit rien contre son frère mais ne le soutint pas. Il se désintéressa même complètement de son sort et quand, après la bataille de Lincoln, les barons normands firent de nouveau appel à lui, il refusa de les suivre.

Le souvenir de la couronne manquée n'en demeura pas moins vif dans la maison de Blois. En dépit de ses faiblesses, Etienne illustrait le lignage. Quand il mourut, la rancune s'estompa. Elle se changea même en une obscure vénération, alimentée par la haine des Plantagenêt. Par une curieuse coïncidence, sans que les documents permettent d'établir une relation de cause à effet, trois ans après la mort de son oncle, en 1157, Henri le Libéral décida de transformer la vieille chapelle de son palais de Troyes, consacrée à saint Etienne, en une puissante collégiale, dotée de 9 dignités et de 72 canonicats—soit l'équivalent du chapitre cathédral de Reims, le double de celui de Sens—et d'en faire la sépulture de sa famille. Pour qu'elle soit digne de sa dépouille, il l'enrichit d'abondants revenus et d'un somptueux trésor et, vers 1170, il demanda au pape de l'exempter de la juridiction épiscopale 'comme c'est l'usage pour les chapelles des rois et des princes desservies par les clercs de leur maison'. Cette requête engendra un violent conflit avec l'évêque de Troyes qui soutenu par la majorité du clergé et bien entendu par le roi de France, obtint la révocation du privilège accordé.[12]

Ainsi le roi Etienne finit par usurper sur le tombeau comme dans la vie la place de son frère aîné. Est-ce bien lui d'ailleurs, ou Thibaud II qui tient la couronne à la main comme s'il n'avait pas réussi à s'en coiffer? Peu importe! La statue porte en elle-même sa signification. Aussi puissante et riche qu'elle ait toujours été, la maison de Blois, en filiation patrilinéaire, se trouvait en position d'infériorité par rapport aux femmes qu'elle admettait dans son sein. Adèle d'Angleterre, Marie de France, parce qu'elles étaient filles de roi, brillaient d'un éclat plus vif que leur mari. Les oncles maternels, rois eux aussi, attiraient leurs neveux. Désormais cette infériorité est effacée. Un roi ennoblit le sang des Thibaud. Enracinée dans la *Normanitas*, leur maison s'élève aussi haut que celle des Capétiens ou des Plantagenêt.

III *Les comtes de Champagne et la Normanitas*

Pour les comtes de Champagne, le XIe siècle avait été une période très difficile. Passés maîtres dans l'utilisation du droit féodal, les Capétiens les avaient peu à peu acculés à la soumission. En intervenant à Reims et à Châlons-sur-Marne, ils avaient introduit dans la principauté vassale des germes de décomposition. Enfin en s'appuyant exclusivement sur leurs officiers et leur domaine, ils s'étaient donnés les moyens d'écarter les grands de leur entourage et de prendre des décisions sans eux. L'échec était patent pour les comtes de Champagne qui, au titre de comtes du Palais, prétendaient être les premiers conseillers du souverain.[13]

Le salut leur vint des Normands. Le prestige des maîtres de l'Angleterre et de l'Italie du sud était alors à son zénith. De partout on se tournait vers eux. Une querelle éclate-t-elle entre Thibaut Ier et son neveu Eudes, celui-ci s'enfuit auprès du duc Guillaume qui lui donne sa soeur en mariage et le fait

Map 1: Lands of Champagne, Anjou and Maine, and Normandy

comte d'Aumâle et d'Holderness. Un grand seigneur de la région de Reims, Ebles de Roucy, épouse Sibylle, fille de Robert Guiscard. Il n'est pas jusqu'au souvenir des Vikings qui ne serve d'argument dans un conflit de succession à Bar-sur-Aube vers 1080.

Dans les relations des comtes de Champagne avec la *Normanitas*, trois moments peuvent être distingués. Le premier correspond au mariage d'Etienne-Henri et d'Adèle d'Angleterre. Le comte y puise une nouvelle capacité de résistance au roi de France. Ses fils se sentiront non seulement plus forts mais différents. Ils se voudront normands. Comme il a été dit plus haut, Thibaud II fera toujours prévaloir dans sa politique les liens du sang sur les iiens vassaliques. Hostile aux Capétiens, Henri le Libéral le sera tout autant que son père mais avec les nuances et, pour finir, les faiblesses que lui impose l'insolent triomphe des Plantagenêt.

La seconde période commence vers le milieu du XIIe siècle quand les Angevins s'assurent la possession du royaume anglo-normand. La *Normanitas* cesse alors d'être une réalité pour les Champenois, elle devient une nostalgie. Pour nuire à son trop heureux rival, Henri le Libéral se rapproche une première fois du roi en 1153. Un glissement s'amorce, dont les étapes n'ont jamais été clairement analysées. Il importe d'en dire un mot.[14]

Du mariage de Louis VII et d'Aliénor d'Aquitaine était née en 1145 une première fille qui, en l'absence de garçon, devait hériter de l'Aquitaine. Le 22 mars 1152, Aliénor se sépare de Louis. Le mois suivant, elle épouse Henri II

Plantagenêt. Arguant du fait qu'un vassal ne peut se marier sans l'accord de son seigneur, Louis VII confisque l'Aquitaine et sous prétexte de soutenir les revendications d'Eustache de Boulogne, fils du roi Etienne, sur la Normandie, il envahit le duché. Pour cette guerre, il lui fallait des alliés. Devinant que le comte de Champagne serait heureux de compenser les déboires de sa famille, il lui propose l'Aquitaine et la main de Marie. En 1153, Henri se fiance avec une enfant de huit ans. Là-dessus Henri Plantagenêt repousse l'attaque du roi de France, Eustache meurt, Etienne aussi. En 1154, le comte d'Anjou, duc de Normandie, monte sur le trône d'Angleterre. La même année Aliénor lui donne un fils, héritier de tous les biens et titre de ses parents. C'est l'échec. Frustré dans ses espérances, Henri le Libéral renvoie sa fiancée et rompt avec le roi. Curieusement les fiançailles seront renouées en 1159, mais uniquement dans le but de favoriser un projet d'union entre Adèle de Champagne et Louis VII. Le comte était trop heureux de caser honorablement sa plus jeune soeur, dixième enfant de Thibaut II. Il se prête donc à cette formalité mais ne désarme pas. En 1162, il trahit son beau-frère lors des négociations de Saint-Jean-de-Losne avec Frédéric Barberousse.[15]

Pourtant à la longue, la résistance champenoise faiblit. Quant Marie atteint ses dix-neuf ans (il en a trente sept), Henri l'épouse et son frère Thibaud, cette même année 1164, épouse Alix, soeur de Marie. Cette fois le tournant est pris. Les succès du Plantagenêt ont eu raison de la méfiance atavique du comte de Champagne à l'égard du roi de France. Il accepte de composer. La *Normanitas*, déjà privée de substrat territorial, se vide alors de tout contenu politique. Elle ne subsiste plus qu'à l'état de référence généalogique, comme source d'illustration nobiliaire, mais avec assez de vigueur pour faire obstacle au surgissement de tout autre thème concurrent. Entre 1170 et 1180, le comte de Flandre entreprend d'exploiter à des fins partisanes le *Reditus ad stirpem Caroli*. Il incite le comte de Champagne à se poser en héritier des Carolingiens et par conséquent à reprendre ses distances vis-à-vis des Capétiens. Or la tradition carolingienne est si étrangère au milieu champenois qu'Henri ne voit pas comment l'assumer. Fidèle à ses origines royales normandes, il fait la sourde oreille et c'est finalement le roi qui, par une habile manoeuvre, récupère à son profit le souvenir du grand empereur et la gloire attachée à son nom.[16]

La troisième et dernière période commence en 1181 avec la mort d'Henri le Libéral. Elle est marquée par la minorité d'Henri II, la double régence de Marie de France, l'avènement prématuré de Thibaud III, sa mort, la régence de Blanche de Navarre pour le jeune Thibaud IV le Posthume. La paralysie gagne la Champagne qui tombe au pouvoir du roi. Durant ces années que domine, au point de vue culturel, la personnalité de Marie de France, le climat de la cour de Champagne change complètement. J. Benton a bien montré que Marie, ouverte au courants littéraires nouveaux, était sensible à la courtoisie, qu'elle appréciait les romans de Chrétien de Troyes dont elle commandita le Lancelot.[17] En agissant de la sorte, elle se montrait la digne fille d'Aliénor d'Aquitaine. Cependant, il est permis de se demander si cet engouement pour les romans bretons ne plonge pas ses racines—du moins les plus profondes—

dans l'intérêt que les Champenois portaient traditionnellement au royaume anglo-normand. En d'autres termes, en disparaissant, la *Normanitas* n'a-t-elle pas frayé la voie à la Bretagne bleue? L'enquête sur ce point risque d'être difficile à mener. Il ne peut être question ici que de lancer un fragile jalon. La Bibliothèque Nationale de Paris conserve sous la cote Fr. 794 un superbe manuscrit de cour rédigé vers 1220 par Guiot de Provins et orné par ses soins non seulement d'initiales d'or sur fond pourpre et azur, mais encore de très belles lettrines à rinceaux de feuillage sur fond d'or, dont l'une, tout à fait exceptionnelle, dans la boucle d'un grand P renferme l'image de Marie de France assise sur un trône à coussin vert, vêtue d'une longue robe rouge et d'un manteau bleu et coiffée d'une toque ronde d'étamine nouée par un voile sous le menton.[18] Ce manuscrit dont le contenu a été analysé par M. Roques mêle l'Antiquité à l'histoire de la Bretagne ou plus exactement use de l'Antiquité comme d'un prologue à l'histoire des Bretons.[19] Ignorant superbement la légende épique des Francs, Charlemagne et ses douze pairs, il exalte en des aventures variées le souvenir du roi Arthur et de ses chevaliers. Ainsi se dessine un espace de rêve ou l'imagination se déploie sans risquer de se heurter aux Capétiens qui en sont totalement exclus. En ce complaisant dans cet univers mythique, l'aristocratie champenoise—et elle n'est pas la seule—manifeste son rejet d'une monarchie qui, après la conquête de la Normandie par Philippe Auguste en 1204, fait peser de plus en plus lourdement son pouvoir sur ses vassaux.[20] S'agit-il de dissidence intellectuelle ou, plus simplement, de fuite dans l'imaginaire? La question reste ouverte.

Pour le visiteur qui vers 1220 pénètre dans l'église de Saint-Etienne de Troyes, et contemple le tombeau de Thibaud III, les statuettes des rois de France et d'Angleterre se chargent de signification multiples et contradictoires. Elles évoquent à la fois Louis VII et Henri II Plantagenêt, Philippe-Auguste et Richard Coeur de Lion, Charlemagne et le roi Arthur. Dans leur savante et hiérarchique opposition, elles expriment la volonté des comtes de Champagne de s'appuyer sur les uns pour mieux échapper aux autres.

A cette première lecture s'en substitue bientôt une seconde, toute entière inspirée par la grandeur d'un lignage vraiment royal. Non seulement les comtes de Champagne prennent femme dans les maisons souveraines mais ils ont eux-mêmes porté la couronne. Alors le visiteur identifie Etienne de Blois derrière lequel se profile toute la gloire du royaume anglo-normand.

Enfin il s'arrête à une lecture familiale et conjugale du monument. Entre les portraits des ancêtres, se pressent autour de la couche funèbre ou repose le jeune comte, huit deuillants. Encore trois d'entre eux ne sont-ils là que d'intention puisqu'ils sont déjà morts, le père, la mère, le frère aîné. La veuve est soutenue par son propre frère et par ses deux belles-soeurs, mais pour peu de temps, le premier devant regagner sa lointaine Navarre, les autres, qui son Hainaut, qui son Viennois. Blanche reste seule dans sa détresse avec ses nouveaux-nés. Petite famille en vérité, bien moderne et bien éclatée! Telle est en définition la leçon la plus tragique et la plus vraie que dispense ce tombeau.

The Romanesque Rebuilding of Westminster Abbey

R. D. H. GEM

With a reconstruction by W. T. BALL

The Historical Evidence

The most significant single event for the development of architecture in the reign of King Edward the Confessor was the refoundation of Westminster Abbey. The earliest surviving account of this, contained in the *Vita Aedwardi Regis*, refers to the monastery already existing, and says that Edward decided on the rebuilding because of his piety and his devotion to St Peter, because of the favourable situation of the place near to London and the Thames and, 'principally', because 'he chose to have for himself a place of burial there' (*eligit ibi habere sibi locum sepulchri*).[1] The last mentioned motive indicates a close link between Westminster and the crown, and suggests that the new abbey was likely to embody whatever was thought most fitting in a work of royal patronage.

The rather later account by the monk Sulcard, in his work *De Construccione Westmonasterii*, gives substantially different motives for the refoundation. He says that Edward wanted to go to Rome on pilgrimage, to give thanks for the peace brought by his accession. His magnates, fearing for the stability of the kingdom in his absence, dissuaded him from this, and advised instead that he use the money he would have spent on a pilgrimage to restore some monastery dedicated to St Peter.[2] The *Vita Aedwardi* apparently contradicts Sulcard when it says that the money was provided by a tithe on the king's possessions (. . . *ex decimis omnium redituum suorum*),[3] and makes no mention of any commutation of expenses for a pilgrimage. On the other hand it is strange that the abbey of Westminster should be ignorant of the circumstances of its foundation so short a time after the actual event: particularly when Sulcard does not use his account as a basis for any spurious claims to papal privileges (as do the later compilers of the Westminster charters).

Neither the *Vita Aedwardi* nor Sulcard gives any indication of the date when Edward's patronage or rebuilding of the abbey began, and the only evidence for these is provided by some of the royal writs concerned with Westminster. Like the abbey's charters, the writs have been subject to the activities of forgers, and there is no single early writ of unquestionable authenticity: however, there are seven writs which, insofar as they, as a group, represent

Barry University Library
Miami, FL 33161

authentic documents, were all issued not later than 1051.[4] Of these there are two[5] which possibly may represent original writs issued between Edward's accession and July 1044. Another, spurious, writ[6] claiming to be of a similar date, contains one passage which is possibly authentic and refers to the abbey as under the king's protection (*th' minstre is on minen munde*).[7] But while the validity of these documents remains in question, they cannot be taken to prove conclusively that Westminster was refounded in the 1040s. Furthermore, though Edward's endowment of the abbey may have gained momentum in the '40s, this is not in itself a safe guide to the date when the rebuilding of the church started: there was a monastery standing already, and benefactions to this, as a result of the king's encouragement, may have preceded the rebuilding. However, it may be doubted whether these two facets of the refoundation were very far removed in date; and if the endowment was under way by *c.* 1050 the rebuilding may have been so also.

If the documentry sources are vague on the question of the date of the rebuilding, they do give more information on the nature of the work actually involved. The *Vita Aedwardi* has a long description of the Edwardian church; it says: –

'Ad regis itaque preceptum opus nobiliter ceptum feliciter preparatur, nec impensa siue impendenda pensantur, dummodo deo et beato Petro dignum et acceptum probetur. Principalis arę domus altissimis erecta fornicibus quadrato opere parique commissura circumuoluitur; ambitus autem ipsius edis dupplici lapidum arcu ex utroque latere hinc et inde fortiter solidata operis compage clauditur. Porro crux templi quę medium canentium deo chorum ambiret, et sui gemina hinc et inde sustentatione medię turris celsum apicem fulciret, humili primum et robusta fornice simpliciter surgit, cocleis multipliciter ex arte ascendentibus plurimis tumescit, deinde uero simplici muro usque ad tectum ligneum plumbo diligenter tectum peruenit. Subter uero et supra disposite educuntur domicilia, memoriis apostolorum, martyrum, confessorum, ac uirginum consecranda per sua altaria. Hec autem multiplicitas tam uasti operis tanto spatio ab oriente orditum est ueteris templi, ne scilicet interim inibi commorantes fratres uacarent a seruitio Christi, ut etiam aliqua pars spatiose subiret interiaciendi uestibuli'.[8]

This passage has called forth significantly divergent interpretations; and therefore deserves comment in some detail.

Opus . . . ceptum . . . preparatur. The choice of the word *preparatur* here may be significant: if the writer had wished to denote the completion of the building, the word *consummatur* might have been expected.

Principalis are domus. Principalis here is more likely to qualify *are* than *domus*:[9] there was only one building but several altars. Robinson is most likely right in taking the phrase to refer to the sanctuary: not only, as he points out, because of the contrast with the *domicilia* of the lesser altars;[10] but also because it would be strange to refer to the *whole* church as the house of the *principal* altar.

Altissimis erecta fornicibus. The allusion here remains obscure: *fornix* can mean equally well a *vault* or an *arch*. The same writer apparently uses the word *fornix* below to mean *vault*; but the modern distinction between the two meanings may not have been developed in his mind, and he may have used *fornix* indiscriminately for either. Thus the phrase may refer to high vaults, or to diaphragm arches, or to arches in the walls separating the presbytery from its aisles.

Quadrato opere parique commissura. The fabric was of ashlar work.

Circumuoluitur. This may allude to the apsidal termination of the presbytery.

Ambitus autem ipsius edis. It is not clear why Robinson translated this: 'but the whole church',[11] nor why he should have taken it as 'natural to speak of the nave as *ipsa aedes*'.[12] The conjunction *autem* does not introduce an antithesis to the previous sentence: rather, it indicates that the words following are an expansion of the meaning of the previous sentence; thus *ipsa edis* is the same as the *principalis are domus*. The word *ambitus*, the subject of the whole sentence, Robinson omits altogether: it refers not to an aisle or ambulatory but to the wall forming the periphery of the sanctuary.[13]

Ambitus . . . dupplici lapidum arcu ex utroque latere . . . clauditur. The periphery of the sanctuary had a double arch of stone on either side: whether this refers, on the one hand, to arcades of two bays (thus excluding an ambulatory) or of two stories or, on the other hand, to aisle vaults is uncertain. It is possible that the writer is referring here to the same features as meant by the *altissimi fornices*.

Hinc et inde fortiter solidata operis compage. The feminine gender of *solidata* apparently agrees with *edis* rather than *ambitus*. The contrast of direction in *hinc et inde* may suggest that the phrase refers to transverse arches or vaults in the aisles, abutting the *ambitus*.

Crux templi . . . humili primum et robusta fornice simpligiter surgit. This could refer to the arches of the crossing, but is more likely to refer to vaults carrying tribunes in the transepts.

Crux templi . . . cocleis . . . ascendentibus plurimis tumescit. It is uncertain whether these turrets flanked the tower or the outer angles of the transepts.

Vt etiam aliqua pars spatiose subiret interiaciendi uestibuli. The significance of this clause is of considerable importance and has been much disputed. The new church had been started some distance to the east of the old building so that the monks might continue to use the latter until such time as the former was ready; that is, probably until the presbytery, crossing and eastern bays of the nave were completed. Most writers have held that the *aliqua pars uestibuli* referred to the eastern bays of the nave, but Robinson contended that the *uestibulum* was a porch at the west end of the nave, and that the whole nave was completed by the time that work was in progress on this porch:[14] the evidence is against Robinson's interpretation. First, the description of the building has detailed accounts of the presbytery and transepts, but unless the *uestibulum* were the nave there would be no mention of the latter feature. Secondly, the monks could have moved into the new building when the area of the liturgical quire was complete; this they had not done when the description was written, which implies that work was still in progress on the eastern bays of the nave. Thirdly, the *Vita Aedwardi* says that at the time of the dedication of Wilton Abbey, in September 1065, Westminster was not yet complete;[15] it is at this point that the description of Westminster occurs. Whether the description refers to the building as it was in September 1065 or as it was when the account was written shortly afterwards, it is likely that its unfinished state refers to more than a west porch, for the first dedication is likely to have taken place before the west front of the fabric was reached.

It is now possible to offer a translation of the whole *Vita* passage:

> And so, at the king's command the work, nobly begun, is being prepared successfully; and neither the outlay nor what is to be expended are weighed, so long as it proves worthy and acceptable to God and blessed Peter. The house of the principal altar, raised up with very high arches [*or* vaults], is surrounded with squared work and even jointing; moreover, the periphery of the building itself is enclosed on either side by a double arch of stones, strongly consolidated with a joining together of work from different directions. Further on is the crossing of the temple; which might surround the central quire of those singing to God, and with its twin abutment from different directions might support the lofty apex of the central tower; it rises simply, at first, with a low and strong vault [*or* arch]; grows, multiple in art, with very many ascending spiral stairs; then, indeed, reaches with a plain wall right up to the wooden roof, carefully roofed with lead: indeed, disposed below and above, lead out chapels, fit to be consecrated by means of their altars to the memories of the apostles, martyrs, confessors and virgins. Moreover, this multiplicity of so vast a work is set out so great a space from the East [end] of the old temple that, of course, in the meantime the brethren staying therein might not cease from the service of Christ; and furthermore so that some part of the nave to be placed between might advance.

The second part of the *Vita* appears to have been written in 1067, after the dedication of the church and the burial of Edward. Unfortunately the portion of the text which must have dealt with the dedication is missing,[16] and is preserved only in later compilations. However, it is known that the dedication took place on the 28th of December 1065, in the absence of the king, who was too ill to attend.[17] Edward died a few days later, probably on the 5th of January.[18]

The *Vita* says that Edward directed his grave to be prepared in the Abbey.[19] After his death his body was removed *a domo palatii in aulam dei*; and the following day *coram altare beati Petri apostoli conditur corpus*.[20] These references allude to the royal palace next to the church; and to the site of Edward's tomb in front of the high altar.

The evidence relating to the history of the buildings after Edward's death and after the completion of the *Vita* is rather more fragmentary. The first record that survives from this period is the Bayeux Tapestry which, though strictly pictorial rather than documentary, must be considered at this point (Pl. 1). The tapestry was executed probably in the period 1066 × 1082[21] and the depictions of buildings in it seem to have at least a general representational value. Thus in the case under discussion, the portrayal of Westminster does

1. Westminster Abbey Church as shown on the Bayeux tapestry

accord to some extent with what is known from other sources. Details to be noted are the presbytery of two bays; the crossing tower with flanking turrets, and with secondary turrets (possibly at the ends of the transepts); and the arcaded nave of five bays (with eight bays of windows). The last seems to show clearly shafts rising up the walls over the piers; but this feature also occurs elsewhere in the tapestry in a probably wooden structure at Bosham, and another at the scene of the preparations in Normandy for Duke William's invasion. It has been suggested that the absence of any western towers in the tapestry indicates that these features were not completed by the time of its execution[22] and this may be so. Most of the information derived from the tapestry, however, is merely confirmation of what is known from other sources; and any details which cannot be verified should be treated with reserve.

Although little is known of the history of Westminster in the decade immediately following the Conquest, there may have been some degree of continuity, for Abbot Edwin continued in office until his death, perhaps in 1071.[23] Edwin was succeeded by Geoffrey, whose signature appears first in 1072.[24] The latter had formerly been abbot of Jumièges, but four years after his arrival at Westminster he was deposed by the king and Lanfranc.

In 1076 Vital abbot of Bernay was appointed to Westminster.[26] In a letter written by King William to the abbot of Fécamp sometime after Christmas 1075, he says that he has asked Vital to accept the appointment '*cum enim abbatiam de Bernaco ex minimo multum, ut patet, sublimauerit, intellexi illum dignum esse abbatia Westmonasterio, et utilitate et prudentia*'.[27] It was Abbot Vital to whom Sulcard dedicated his work.

Sulcard's account of King Edward's work at Westminster appears to be derived from the *Vita Aedwardi*;[28] however, the slight changes in emphasis introduced in his first text seem significant. In the first place he does not speak of the old church from the point of view of its (temporary) preservation, but of its destruction: 'there survived up to that time the monastery that we all have seen destroyed, after council had been taken, so that it might rise more noble, as we now see it' ('*perdurabat adhuc idem monasterium quod omnes uidimus habito consilio esse dirutum ut surgeret nobilius, quod nunc uidemus*').[29] That is, Sulcard had seen the old church destroyed so that the new work could advance.

Secondly he says that the work was '*diuersis fultum columnis ac multiplicibus uolutum hinc et inde arcubus*'.[30] Clearly, here he is following the order of the *Vita* in a general way; although it is not certain what he understands the earlier text to mean. *Diuersis fultum columnis* may be parallel to *altissimis erecta fornicibus*, if it is accepted that the second phrase refers to the lateral arcades. *Multiplicibus uolutum hinc et inde arcubus* is a rewriting of *dupplici lapidum arcu ex utroque latere hince et inde . . . . Duplex* is changed to *multiplex* perhaps to suit the extension of the description from the presbytery to the whole church as it then stood.

Leading up to the descrption of the dedication, Sulcard says '*post paucos annos . . . opus usque ad ipsum uestibulum perfectum premonstratur con-secrandum episcopis et cunctis regni proceribus*'.[31] *Vestibulum* is taken straight from the *Vita*, but the two authors do not necessarily understand the same meaning in it. Sulcard could be saying that the church was 'complete right to the entrance itself', without prejudice to the *nave* interpretation of the *Vita*—for he could be thinking of the church as it stood in his own day. Alternatively he also could be using *uestibulum* to refer to the nave.

In summary, there is nothing in Sulcard's account which contradicts the *Vita*. On the other hand, it is apparent that by the time of Abbot Vital (1076 – *c.* 1085) the old church had been demolished, and the new work had advanced considerably, perhaps reaching the west end. This would be entirely consistent with the period of between ten and twenty years which had elapsed since the writing of the *Vita* account.

Apart from the suggestion in the above description, there is direct evidence in Sulcard's work for Vital's building operations; for the monk describes Vital as being the abbot '*de huius beati Petri quod regitis et construitis monasterio*';[32] though he does not amplify this remark. Vital died in 1085, or slightly earlier, and was succeeded by Gilbert Crispin, the early years of whose abbacy termi-nates the period of Westminster history under consideration here. Gilbert probably continued work on the monastic buildings, but there is no documentary evidence covering the relevant period.

A mid-thirteenth-century description of Westminster as it stood on the eve of Henry III's rebuilding is contained in the *Estoire de Seint Aedward le Rei*.[33] This refers to features that are not mentioned elsewhere: thus it says that 'in the middle he raises a tower, and two at the west front' ('*en miliu dresce une tur, e deus en frunt del Occident*'). Also it describes the monastic offices: 'A cloister there he makes, and a chapter house, with a front towards the East vaulted and round . . .; and the refectory and the dormitory, and the offices round about' (*'clostre i fait, chapitre a frund vers Orient vouse et rund, . . . refaitur e le dortur, e les officines en tur'*). The reference to the apsidal chapter house is particularly valuable, as it provides the only surviving evidence for this building.

A final important collection of evidence regarding Westminster in the eleventh century concerns the names of the masons engaged on the work. The first piece of evidence is a writ of King Edward addressed to Abbot Edwin and the sheriff Alfgaet, notifying them that he had given *'Teinfrithe mine circwirhtan th' land aet Sceptertune'*.[34] This must date after Edwin's appointment in 1049.[35] Teinfrith is described as the king's church-wright, which presumably indicates a master mason; he was granted rights in an estate that continued to belong to the abbey (as shown by Domesday Book). Harmer suggested that the name Teinfrith was an eleventh-century or later spelling of Thegnfrith, but pointed out Stenton's objection that this would be an abnormal English name in the eleventh century; there were several continental Germanic names with *Thegan—*, *Tegen—* and *Tegin—*elements, but none compounded with—*frith*.[36]

Another writ of King Edward, but one of perhaps doubtful authenticity, notified Bishop Wulfwig (of Dorchester, appointed 1053) and Earl Leofwine (appointed 1057?) that Leofsi Duddesunu had given some land at Wormley to Westminster:[37] Domesday Book does not confirm this, but it shows one manor in Wormley held of the king by Alwin Dodesone.[38] The spurious *Telligraphus* of William I refers to a *'Leofsinus filius Duddi qui preerat illius ecclesie Westmonasterii cemetarius'*; and the spurious *First Charter* of William I refers to *'Leofsi de Lundonia'*.[39] Although the transactions in land to which these documents refer may be of doubtful authenticity, it is hard to believe that Leofsi Duddesunu is a fictitious character, and it would be reasonable to accept that he was a mason at Westminster. The name appears to be English.

The spurious *First Charter* names as another mason Godwine Greatsyd who gave land to Westminster; his name is referred to also elsewhere,[40] and again there is no reason to doubt his existence. This name also appears to be English.

Teinfrith, Leofsi and Godwine, if they were involved in transactions of land, were clearly men of some status, and must have been senior masons engaged on the works at the abbey. What is particularly noteworthy, in view of what is known of the normanizing character of the building, is that two of them definitely have English names.

Archaeological Evidence for the Church (Fig. 1)

The evidence for the eastern parts of the building is disappointingly sparse. The documentary description, already considered, referred to the presbytery having high arches or vaults and double arches enclosing the periphery on either side; it commented also on the ashlar work: but all this afforded very little certain information. Some elements of the presbytery were found, however, by excavations in 1866 by Scott and in 1910 by Lethaby:[41] these elements were the Reigate stone plinths and bases of certain piers or responds on the north and south sides of the presbytery, and also the foundation of the main apse. The presbytery itself was laid out on a square plan, divided into two bays by a shaft running up the wall on the north and south sides. The shafts were composed of a dosseret and attached half column; the half column had a double scotia base which was returned across the face of the dosseret but not round the ends; the base stood on a plain rectangular block, while under the whole shaft was a shallow plinth with a chamfer on its upper edge.

The supports for the arch leading from the presbytery to the apse made use of similar elements to the intermediate shafts, but were more complicated, as they projected further into the presbytery. The inner two orders were composed of a half column and dosseret, similar to the wall shafts, only broader; outside these was a further rectangular order (on the west side at least) rising directly from a chamfered plinth. These responds logically would seem designed to carry an arch of three orders; of which the outer two probably would have been rectangular and the inner one either rectangular or a soffit roll. Of the apse itself only a small part of the foundation was uncovered, and this was only enough to indicate the general semicircular plan.

The form of the rest of the east end remains quite uncertain on the evidence available: the only fragment surviving is a short piece of chamfered plinth returning eastward from the side of the dosseret in the middle of the north wall of the presbytery; everything else seems to have been destroyed by the foundations of the thirteenth-century presbytery.[42] It is possible that the side walls of the presbytery were solid (with the plinth continuing along the wall) or, alternatively, that they were opened by an arcade of two bays on either side; there is adequate room for such an arcade, although it could not have had a deep east respond (such as is found in some, but not all, buildings of comparable type). The presbytery aisles could have terminated in enclosed or fully rounded apses flanking the main apse, or it is possible that they continued into an ambulatory.[43] Only further excavation can offer any final solution to these problems.

No part of the transepts has been uncovered, although their position seems indicated by the surviving east range of claustral buildings.[44] The documentary description indicated that the transepts had vaulted ground stories with tribunes over, that they had two-storied eastern chapels and that they were wooden roofed; it indicated also that there were spiral stairs for access to the upper parts, and that there was a tower over the crossing.

The quire would have extended from the crossing into the east bays of the nave, which were completed by 1065; but it is uncertain whether the nave was built to a single design which was established by 1065, or whether there was a change in design between the east bays and the west bays which were built later; this is important because the only surviving evidence relates to the west end of the building. The whole nave would have been twelve bays long, with an additional west bay for the towers: excavations in 1930 provided evidence on the south side for the west tower bay and the next four bays to the east.[45]

The sequence revealed at the west end was a complicated one, of which the

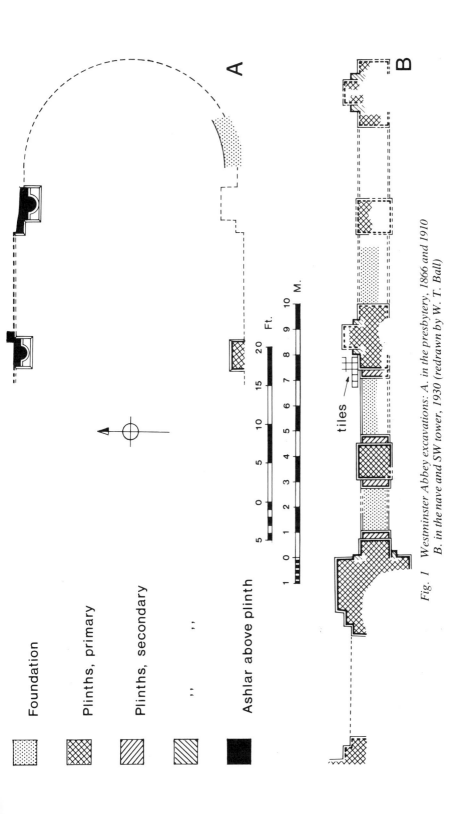

Foundation

Plinths, primary

Plinths, secondary

" "

Ashlar above plinth

A

B

tiles

Ft.

M.

Fig. 1   Westminster Abbey excavations: A. in the presbytery, 1866 and 1910
B. in the nave and SW tower, 1930 (redrawn by W. T. Ball)

interpretation is not simple (Fig. 1B; Pl. 2 and 3). It is clear, however, that the earliest elements in the sequence were a continuous foundation wall and, standing upon it, a series of alternating square and, probably, cruciform plinths of Reigate stone—the parts of the compound plinths towards the aisle were not recovered. The projections towards the nave on the compound plinths were of a similar depth to the plinths of the shafts in the presbytery, though they were somewhat narrower from east to west; it is reasonable to suppose that they were designed for a series of shafts, with half columns and dosserets—albeit, narrower dosserets than in the presbytery—rising up the wall in every second bay. The east and west faces of the same piers had a single deep projection, the full width of the wall; these obviously carried the core of the pier, together with the responds for the arches of the arcades. The design of the responds cannot be settled finally; however, it may be noted that they are of a similar width to the respond of the arch from the presbytery to the apse, which had a single half column against a dosseret. The responds of the arcades then may well have been designed with a simple half column against the core of the pier; although a more complicated form cannot be ruled out. The design towards the aisles is unknown.

The square plinths are greater in width than the responds of the compound piers; this would seem to weigh against a design with square piers as suggested by Clapham. Most likely the square plinths were intended for plain columnar piers. The series of alternating cruciform and square plinths, if anything at the west end of the nave, is likely to represent the first design, established by *c*. 1065.

The complications in interpreting the evidence from the excavation arise in the sequence that followed the initial design. Most problematic are the additional plinths that were added to the east and west faces of the piers; Clapham thought that these were 'hardly, if at all, distinguishable'[46] from the workmanship of the original phase. It is possible either that these plinths were a modification of the first plinths between the laying out of the building and the erection of the superstructure; or that they were added after the building of the superstructure; furthermore it is possible that they were either decorative or structural in purpose. That the plinths were added before the superstructure of the building was erected is unlikely since the existing plinths were large enough to forestall any structural worries at that stage, or to allow a revision of the design upon them. If then, the plinths were added after the superstructure had been built it is difficult to concede that any such major work would have been undertaken for purely aesthetic reasons—that is, adding a further decorative order. It seems more likely, therefore, that they were placed for structural reasons after the church had been built. A structural failure in the building may have been general or local, and it is not known whether the alteration was made throughout the building or only in the two west bays of the south arcade; since, however, those bays are adjacent to a tower it may be reasonable to hypothesize, in the absence of contrary evidence, that the failure was related to the tower and that the strengthening was localized. The added plinths, then,

2. *Excavated pier plinths in the nave, 1930 (R.C.M., Crown Copyright)*

would not be of general relevance to the nature or evolution of the basic Westminster design.

A further feature observed by Clapham was the laying out of continuous plinths between the piers. These plinths either could have carried a continuous wall blocking the arcades—in which case they were clearly structural and not related to the design—or they could have risen no higher than plinth level, forming a decorative feature between the piers. By the time that the third floor level found by Clapham was laid down, the plinths certainly carried no walls, because the floor continued across them.[47]

The most significant alteration to the original plinths undoubtedly was the addition of rectangular elements in the re-entrant angles of the compound piers (on both nave and aisle faces if we may judge by the tower pier). These can be interpreted only in connexion with a provision of supports for vaults both over the aisles and over the nave. However, since the original plinth was cut into to allow for the alterations this operation was clearly posterior to the original construction; it could have happened anytime between the first building and the eventual demolition of the nave.[48]

For the design of any middle story and of the clerestory of the nave there is no evidence.

The excavations provided important evidence for the south-west tower in the form of the plinths of the north-east pier and of the north-west respond against the west wall of the building (Pl. 4). The plinth of the north-east pier had on its east face a respond similar to those of the compound piers of the nave arcade; on the north face was a broad and deeply projecting plinth, while indications of a rather similar plinth existed on the south; on the west the plinth was of two orders, to which the respond against the west wall was similar. Although it would be hazardous to attempt to reconstruct the precise details of the tower piers, the general implications of the evidence are clear. The walls forming the north and east sides of the tower (and, presumably the other two walls) were considerably thicker than the nave walls. More important to note are the indications that the pier at the north-east angle was free standing; the bottom story of the tower thus would have been open both to the aisle and to the nave bay between the towers. Whether the plinth towards the nave carried a shaft continuing up the wall, or the respond of an arch spanning the nave is uncertain.

The Significance of the Design of the Church
The uncertainty over the reconstruction of many of the important details of the church makes it difficult to place the design in relation to contemporary architecure: but what is clear is that its sources are not English. The enormous scale of the building—whether or not the full length was decided upon earlier than 1065—marks it off from anything that is known to have been built in this country before, and places Westminster alongside the greatest contemporary buildings on the continent. The internal length of the building as calculated by Clapham was 322 ft. (98.2 m.), and this he compared in Normandy with Rouen

3. *Excavated pier plinths and secondary floor-level with tiles, 1930 (R.C.M., Crown Copyright)*

Cathedral (about 270 ft.–82.4 m.), La Trinité, Caen (about 259 ft.–79 m.), and Jumièges (about 225 ft.–68.6 m.). St-Etienne, Caen, has lost its east arm, but allowing for this to have been of two bays plus the apse, the main vessel must have been quite similar in length to Rouen. These were some of the largest churches of their date in Normandy and they were quite comfortably exceeded in length (though not in width) by Westminster. Among major churches of towards the middle of the eleventh century in other parts of France one of the largest was Chartres Cathedral which had a main internal length of about 279 ft. (85 m.)—thus not exceeding greatly the Norman buildings. Indeed, it is only in the great Imperial churches of the Rhineland that Westminster is paralleled. Mainz Cathedral had a nave about 233 ft. (71 m.) long, to which must be added both an east sanctuary and a west transept and sanctuary; Speyer Cathedral had an internal length of 325 ft. (109 m.).

It was not only the absolute size of Westminster that set it off from earlier English buildings, but also the fact that the new church was intended to replace entirely the existing earlier church. Previously in England additions had been made to churches which respected the existing historic nucleus of the building. In its disregard of such historical considerations, however, Westminster again shows an affinity with the major Romanesque rebuilding programmes of the Continent.

Turning from general considerations to particular features, it can be seen that what details survive from the east parts of the building seem to relate specifically to Normandy. The division of the presbytery bays by wall shafts composed of half columns against dosserets may be compared with Jumièges[49] (1040–1052) and Bernay (about contemporary with Jumièges?). Double-scotia bases are to be found at Jumièges, Rouen Cathedral, le-Mont-St-Michel and numerous later buildings.

If Westminster were related in plan to the most ambitious contemporary buildings in Normandy it might be suspected that there was an ambulatory surrounding the apse (as at le-Mont-St-Michel, begun 1023; Rouen Cathedral, begun before 1037; Jumièges; St-Wandrille, dedicated 1033?); but the simpler triapsidal form would find a parallel at Bernay.

Transepts with tribunes are again a feature of Norman architecture: they occurred probably at Jumièges[50] and at Bayeux (1046×9–1077), where they extended the full depth of the transepts up to the crossing (the type in which the tribunes are confined to the parts of the transepts projecting beyond the line of the aisles occurs later at St-Etienne in Caen, *c.* 1064–1081). At neither of these Norman buildings do the transept chapels survive, so it is unknown whether they were single or double-storied; but double-storied chapels do occur later in Norman architecture (Caen, St-Etienne; Cerisy-la-Forêt, begun in the 1080s?;[51] Rouen, St-Ouen, begun before 1092).

The comparisons that are possible for the east end of the building are fairly generalized, but when it comes to the nave we can be more specific: the design suggested by the surviving plinths would bear a very close resemblance to the nave of Jumièges (1052–1066) (Pl. 6). In both buildings there would be an

4.   *Excavated pier plinths, NE corner of SW tower, 1930*

5. *Reconstruction view of Westminster Abbey at the end of the 11th century* *(W. T. Ball)*

alternation between columnar and compound piers; in both the compound piers seem to have had rectangular cores[52] with half columns on their east and west faces; in both the columnar piers were set on large plinths which projected north and south beyond the line of the main nave wall; in both there is a division at every second bay by a half column and dosseret rising up the wall.

Alternating systems are by no means common in Normandy (the only other known major example is the church of the abbey of Lyre in the twelfth century),[53] and if the design was favoured in other lost buildings around the middle of the century it was quickly superseded by the revolution exemplified at St-Etienne in Caen.

A brief survey of other eleventh-century systems of alternating supports indeed serves to emphasize both the closeness of Westminster and Jumièges to one another and also the difficulty of placing these two buildings in a precise context. An alternating system was adopted in the nave of the church of St-Hilaire in Poitiers (a dedication took place in 1049, but it is unlikely that any of the present nave is as early as this).[54] The columnar piers were of slender proportions; the composite piers had rectangular cores with half columns on their east and west faces, but there seem to have been no shafts towards the nave. It has been claimed that St-Hilaire is out of place in a Poitevin context and must derive from Normandy;[55] but the absence of a middle story or of any wall shafts, together with the great width of the nave are features that mark it off distinctly from Jumièges.

A building bearing a certain resemblance to St-Hilaire is the cathedral of Jaca in Aragon (*c.*1075×1098 and following).[56] The compound piers have a dosseret and half column on each face, of which those towards the nave continue up the wall as shafts; the columnar piers are quite slender; there is no gallery. The overall plan of the building is very different from Jumièges and it is unlikely that there is any direct connexion.

Closer to Normandy geographically is the group of late-eleventh and twelfth-century churches in le Mans that make use of alternating columnar and composite piers.[57] In the eleventh century they were to be found in the presbyteries of Notre-Dame-de-la-Couture and Notre-Dame-du-Pré, while in the twelfth century they were adopted in the nave of the latter building, following a change of plan (it is possible, however, that they had occurred earlier in the nave of St-Vincent). At le Pré the composite pier at the springing of the apse has a rectangular core with single, applied half columns on its east and west faces to carry the main arcade; towards the main vessel is a half-columnar shaft; towards the aisle is a dosseret and half column. The piers at la Couture differ in that there are twin half columns on the east and west faces, and that the wall shaft has a dosseret behind the half column. The Mancel buildings have intermediate stories with blank arcades pierced by openings to the aisle roof spaces, but there are no true galleries. As a group these buildings are stated in mature Romanesque forms; what is uncertain is whether they derive from early Romanesque buildings in Maine, or Normandy, or elsewhere. The absence of galleries marks a difference from Jumièges, although even a rudimentary

6. *Jumiegès Abbey church, the nave looking W.*

middle storey indicates that they were closer to that milieu than were St-Hilaire or Jaca.

In Italy in the eleventh and twelfth centuries alternating columnar and compound piers were quite common, but many of these were purely decorative in character and did not form part of a consistent, structural bay system. This decorative alternation is to be found, for example, in Tuscany, at S. Miniato al Monte in Florence[58] (following *c.*1070); in Rome, at S. Clemente (dedicated 1128) and S. Maria in Cosmedin (dedicated 1123);[59] in Apulia, at S. Nicola in Bari[60] (begun *c.*1087/9). The origin of such decorative alternating supports in Italy is likely to be a revival of a Byzantine scheme such as was to be found in the fifth-century church of H. Demetrios at Thessalonike.[61] A similar revivalistic current is exemplified by the cathedral of Pisa (begun 1063),[62] which reproduces on the most grandiose scale the sort of cross-transept basilica that was represented by H. Demetrios, and which was designed by a mason with a Greek name, Busketos.

Beside these decorative alternating schemes in Italy there is a number of buildings where alternating supports are used in a more structural bay system; these centre on Lombardy, and are exemplified clearly by the cathedral of Modena[63] (begun in 1099). The intermediate supports at Modena are columns, while the composite piers have on each face a half column attached to a dosseret. Towards the nave the dosserets and half columns continued up the wall as shafts. There were galleries over the aisles, opening to the nave through a double arch over each bay of the arcade below; the clerestory had a single window in each bay. The system of double bays such as existed at Modena was well suited to the building of high vaults, with which experiments seem to have been going on at quite an early date in Lombardy; however, Modena itself was wooden roofed, and there are no indications that such double bays were introduced specifically to cope with the problems of vaulting. Indeed, the Modena system probably evolved from the sort of decorative alternation referred to above; being an adaption to a more 'Romanesque' form of bay construction.

Italy was by no means the only part of Europe that made use of decorative systems of alternation; and there is no need to suppose, therefore, that it was an Italian source that was the starting point for Jumièges. (Although Jumièges and Modena clearly are formally similar developments, it is difficult to be certain whether there is any direct relationship between them, or whether they are simply parallel—Modena can be explained adequately in terms of the development of north Italian Romanesque, while Jumièges is anterior in date to any really comparable Italian building that is known.)

The second main series of decorative alternating supports is to be found in the German Empire. The earliest actually surviving example there is the church of Gernrode in Saxony[64] (begun 959/961) which had a simple alternation in the main arcade between rectangular piers and columns; above the aisle was a gallery, also with a rhythmically arranged arcade. The combination of alternating supports and galleries at Gernrode again may indicate a

Byzantine source; various links between the Ottonian Empire and Byzantium are known, although it is not until 1017—at Paderborn—that there is a specific reference to '*graeci operarii*'.[65]

The great number of buildings with alternating supports in the Empire belongs to the eleventh century (and later); they fall into two main groups: one centred on Saxony, the other on Lower Lorraine. The Saxon buildings, which may be exemplified by St Michael in Hildesheim (1010–1033), Hildesheim Cathedral (dedicated 1061) and Gandersheim (1063–1094), are characterized by a dactyllic rhythm in the alternation; that is, with two columns placed between every rectangular pier. These alternating supports do not form part of a structural bay system, and the buildings in which they occur have no galleries. Alternating supports are not an innovation of the eleventh century in Saxony, for not only is there the tenth-century precedent of such buildings as Gernrode, but also the cathedral of Hildesheim built between 852 and 872 seems to have had a system with three columns between rectangular piers.

In Lower Lorraine also it has been suggested that alternating supports occurred in the late Carolingian church of Werden (dedicated 875), but this is unproven. The eleventh-century series may be exemplified by the churches of Echternach (1016–1031), Zyfflich (first quarter of the eleventh century). Susteren[66] (probably mid-eleventh century) and Lobbes[67] (of uncertain date—it has been claimed as Carolingian but is more likely eleventh century). These had a simple alternation of rectangular and columnar supports, with relieving arches connecting the rectangular piers—above the arcade proper—and forming a double-bay system; however, there were no wall shafts between the bays, and no galleries. Probably to be connected with this group was the great church of St Bavo in Ghent (dedicated 1067).

The one building in Lower Lorraine that does combine an alternation of supports with a structural bay system and galleries is the church of Soignies;[68] the date of this, however, is uncertain, and it may well represent an incursion of influence from the Anglo-Norman school in the late eleventh or early twelfth century.

It is clear that alternating supports were widespread in Europe in the eleventh century, but they had a history going back to the tenth and even ninth century, and it is possible, therefore, that by the later date there was no longer any direct connexion between different regional groups. The earliest examples seem to have been conceived in largely decorative terms, and this form continued in some areas into the eleventh and twelfth centuries. Elsewhere, however, what had started as a decorative motif was taken up to form an important element in a more architectonic bay system. One of the most far-reaching and earliest examples of this Romanesque transformation appears to be the nave of Jumièges: but what is the real nature of the relationship between Jumièges and Westminster?

At Westminster the design of the eastern bays of the nave was established before 1065, and was probably identical or closely similar to that of the western bays which can in part be reconstructed. The nave design, moreover, may have been worked out in its main elements from the date of the opening of the works at Westminster—a date that the documentary evidence would allow to be put around 1050. At Jumièges, on the other hand, the nave design is not continuous with that of the eastern parts of the building, but represents a change in design. This change came not earlier than 1052, the *terminus post quem* for the construction of the nave. On this evidence, therefore, it is not possible to state with any certainty whether the design of Jumièges or Westminster actually had chronological priority.

On more general considerations, however, it is possible to suggest an hypothesis that gives Westminster priority. It is certainly tempting to assign the plan for rebuilding to the period before 1052 when King Edward was most heavily influenced by Norman ecclesiastics—and particularly by Robert Champart who had left the abbacy of Jumièges to become bishop of London (in 1044) then archbishop of Canterbury (in 1051). Robert himself had started the great rebuilding of Jumièges in 1040 and continued to support the project financially when he moved to England. When he returned to Jumièges in 1052 the new church *'avoit ni nef ni vitraux'*, and it was only then that the construction of the nave was undertaken[69]—to the revised design. What more natural than to suppose that the change reflected Robert's involvement in the Westminster project, and his desire to apply to Jumièges the fruit of this experience?

To reverse this supposed chronological relationship between Westminster and Jumièges actually involves difficulties. If the design of Jumièges were established first, around 1052, then its influence could have appeared at Westminster only after that date; and for this it is not easy to supply a convincing historical context. Moreover, if the nave of Westminster derived from Jumièges, then there must be supposed a separate and prior Norman influence on the east end (for in this Westminster does not follow Jumièges): but it is Jumièges, not Westminster, that actually displays in its fabric evidence for two distinct phases of design.

To claim such a priority for Westminster is intended in no way as implying that it is an 'Insular' building. What, on the contrary, is absolutely clear is that there was no possible preparation in earlier English architecture for such a highly sophisticated Romanesque building. Normandy, on the other hand, could well be seen as providing the preparation; and I have discussed already the Norman parallels for particular features of both the east end and the nave.

Nevertheless it remains true that although the preparation for Westminster may have taken place in Normandy, there is no complete prototype for it. Moreover, we have seen that in its acquaintance with various systems of alternating compound and columnar piers there is a suggestion of a wider experience of European architectural currents. In this light Westminster must itself be seen as the point of synthesis—as the moment of architectural creation. Nor should it be overlooked that a contribution to this creation was the patronage that financed it: the resources of the English crown. It is this last factor more than any other that may explain why Westminster happened in England, not in Normandy.

We are left, however, with one paradox. We might suppose that the master mason with overall responsibility for the design was a Norman: but of the important masons actually known to have been employed on the project, two have unmistakably English names, while the origin of a third remains uncertain.

Before finally leaving the consideration of the church itself, some comment must be made on the design of the west end. The date of completion of this work is uncertain, but if the building carried on after 1065 without serious delay and the west end was reached by the '80s, the design would be one of the earliest known in which twin west towers were fully integrated with the nave and aisles—contemporary with St-Etienne in Caen and probably Christchurch in Canterbury. Here again, then, Westminster would have been in the forefront of the development of Anglo-Norman Romanesque.

The Monastic Offices (Pl. 5)

Unlike the church itself, there are considerable portions of the original monastic offices still surviving at Westminster.[70] These buildings must have become necessary when the monks moved into the new church in 1065, and their construction probably started about that date and continued for some twenty or thirty years.

South of the thirteenth-century chapter house there survive nine bays of the undercroft of the east claustral range. In the seven northern bays most of the original openings have been replaced, but the internal arrangements are well preserved. Down the middle of the range runs a row of columnar piers, which have plain rectangular responds of two orders. The piers had a simple echinus and base, with respectively a rectangular impost block and plinth. The undercroft is covered by quadripartite groin vaults with ashlar transverse arches and east and west wall arches. The eighth bay of the range is a passageway through to the later infirmary cloister; it has simple arches of two orders at either end, and is covered by a barrel vault. The ninth bay is an enclosed, barrel-vaulted chamber. Externally there are indications that the walls, where they were free-standing, had a series of buttresses, inter-connected by blank arches at ground-story level.

Over the undercroft ran the monks' dormitory (Pls. 7, 8). This has been modified considerably over the centuries but some evidence has survived for its original windows; these had plain internal faces (except for a cavetto chamfer on the arris of the embrasure) but externally the openings were framed by an outer order carried on colonnettes. The capitals of the colonnettes had broad leaves at the angles, and T-shaped brackets beneath the imposts.[71]

South of the dormitory range, and adjoining it at right angles was the reredorter. At ground level this was divided into three parallel compartments: the two lateral ones contained the drains; the central one is much broader and is

7.   *Internal face of windows and doorway in W wall of dormitory*

8. *External face of window in E wall of dormitory*

9.   North wall of the refectory

10.   Exterior west wall of refectory, stone and tile chequer work

barrel vaulted. Part of the north wall of the upper story survived until the nineteenth century (when it was demolished); photographs show it to have had a series of windows or internal niches of a single arched order.[72] The part of the east wall now visible in the infirmary cloister is decorated externally with a band of *opus reticulatum* which is notable because the facing is of alternate bands of stone and glazed tile.

Little remains of the range which bounded the south side of the cloister, but what there is suggests that the construction is secondary to the dormitory; while the decoration would also be consistent with a slightly later date. Between the west wall of the dormitory and the east wall of the refectory runs a barrel-vaulted passageway, giving access between the two buildings to the cloister. The construction of this vault interferes with the buttressing system of the dormitory wall and indicates that it was planned after the latter.

The refectory appears to have had no undercroft, and its floor is at a slightly higher level than the cloister passageway or than the dormitory undercroft. The surviving north wall (Pl. 9) had an internal dado of a simple blank arcade carried on colonnettes with cushion capitals.[73] Externally the north-west corner of the range (now visible above Cheyneygates) displays a rich decoration of *opus reticulatum* executed in glazed red tiles, tufa and freestone (Pl. 10). This decoration presumably extended over the whole gable wall, and perhaps over other parts of the building. South of the refectory, and detached from it stood the kitchen.[74]

For the west range of claustral buildings there is no surviving evidence earlier than the thirteenth century. It has been suggested, however, that already in the eleventh century the abbot's chamber with the outer parlour below it was situated in the west range at its junction with the south range:[75] this was certainly its position later, while the main part of the range itself was occupied by the cellarer.

Of the cloister itself, part of a walk on the west side preceding that now existing was discovered in 1909.[76] This foundation may have belonged to the elaborate twelfth-century cloister of which fragments survive, but at the same time it may have preserved the line of a simpler earlier cloister. Abbot Vital, and his twelfth-century successors, were buried in the south walk of the cloister.[77]

Unfortunately too little has survived or has been excavated of early claustral arrangements in Normandy to make comparisons with Westminster significant. However, the surviving Westminster buildings fill an important gap in relation to the church, in that they allow the techniques of construction and not just the general form of the abbey buildings as a whole to be compared with other sources.

In the first place it is important to note, thus, that the capitals of the dormitory windows bear some resemblance (allowing for the difference in scale) to the nave arcade capitals at Jumièges—and also to the capitals in St John's chapel in the Tower of London (under construction *c.* 1077 × 1087).[78] Also comparable with Jumièges, and with St-Etienne in Caen and Christchurch in Canterbury, is the form of buttressing with blank arches thrown across from bay to bay. The dormitory undercroft vaults formed with ashlar transverse arches and wall arches may be compared with the nave gallery vaults at Jumièges; while Bilson drew attention to similarities between the Westminster vaults and those in the crypt of Winchester Cathedral (begun 1079), suggesting that the former seemed a little the earlier.[79]

The above comparisons would as well allow a date for the dormitory range at Westminster in the 1070s as they would allow it a few years earlier. Quite distinct from all the great Anglo-Norman building projects undertaken from the '70s onwards, however, is the character of the masonry itself. The latter buildings employ fairly small and regular blocks of ashlar with thick mortar joints between; a technique characteristic of Calvados and other areas of France in the latter part of the eleventh-century. The Westminster dormitory, on the other hand, is built with large blocks of ashlar, fairly close jointed; and this suggests a date before the other system became standard.

A significant feature that appears in the dormitory range and becomes more pronounced in the reredorter and refectory is the occurrence of decorative patterns in the laying of the masonry. In the former range the arched openings and the vaulting arches are built with an alternation of freestone and tufa voussoirs. To this technique is added in the later ranges the decorative treatment of the wall surfaces themselves with *opus reticulatum* in freestone, tufa and glazed tile. The simple banding of arches is of widespread occurrence in Romanesque architecture, while the use of *opus reticulatum* seems to have enjoyed a particular fashion in England in the late eleventh century (e.g.: Chepstow Castle, 1067×1071; Chichester Cathedral, begun *c.*1091 or earlier; Milborne Port church, *c.*1090; Westminster Hall, under construction 1097). However, the use of glazed tiles in this context at Westminster is without parallel.[80] Recent work has demonstrated that decorative glazed tiles on floors and on vertical surfaces were used in England in the latter half of the tenth century and in the eleventh, and it may be that Westminster was influenced by this tradition. It may also be significant in this context that the Bayeux Tapestry depicts some buildings with a decorative lozenge pattern on the walls (e.g. the palaces of Westminster and Rouen)—significant particularly if, as is likely, the Tapestry is an English production. Such rich decoration may suggest that, whereas Romanesque Westminster in its purely architectural inspiration derived from Normandy, in its ornamentation it may have adapted itself more to English taste: if so, it was already a pointer to the direction in which Anglo-Norman architecture was to develop subsequently.

Acknowledgements

We are most grateful to the following for their advice and practical assistance, without which our work would have been impoverished or impossible: Mr Peter Foster, Surveyor of the Fabric of Westminster Abbey; Mr Drummond, Clerk of Works at Westminster School; Miss Cecily Clerk; Mr Brian Davison; Mr Richard Halsey.

Chichester Cathedral: when was the Romanesque church begun?

R. D. H. GEM

It is the generally accepted view that the Romanesque cathedral church of Chichester was founded and built by Bishop Ralph Luffa who was elected to the see in 1090 or 1091. Willis queried the view but did not challenge it seriously, stating that 'perhaps the foundations of the church were prepared by Stigand; but as this is a question which can never be certainly answered, and after all only affects the date of the building very slightly, I shall leave it, and similar uncertainties, to writers whose taste inclines them to such discussions'.[1] In the light of the master's warning it might be deemed pedantry to take up the issue now: however, what is in question is a matter of as much as ten or fifteen years in the date of the building, and architectural studies have advanced considerably in the century since Willis so that such a difference is important. Either Chichester is an extremely conservative building of the 1090s and following, standing well outside the mainstream of development and scarcely meriting the architectural historian's attention; or else it is a rare surviving representative of an earlier generation of buildings, most of whose major monuments have disappeared (e.g. Christ Church and St Augustine's, Canterbury).

Stigand, one of the royal clerks, was appointed to the South Saxon bishopric following the deposition of Bishop AEthelric at the Council of Windsor presided over by the papal legate, Ermenfrid, in 1070.[2] The see of the diocese at this time was fixed at Selsey, where it had been established by St Wilfrid in the seventh century,[3] but at the Council of London in 1075 Stigand was given permission to remove it to Chichester.[4] William of Malmesbury says that at Chichester there 'had been in former times both a minster of St Peter and a convent of nuns',[5] and the minster is probably to be identified with that to the priests of which King Eadwig may have made a grant in 956.[6] That it was in St Peter's Minster that the see was first established is suggested by the fact that the nave of the later cathedral church (itself dedicated to the Holy Trinity) served as the parish church of St Peter until the late fifteenth century.[7] The Canons of Chichester are recorded in Domesday Book as holding in common 16 hides which had never paid geld and were worth 8 pounds:[8] this presumably was the endowment of the old minster. At the same time the only land in the city (which was itself held by Earl Roger) recorded as held (in demesne) by the Bishop was six haws appurtenant to his manor of Selsey.[9] Bishop Stigand died in 1087 and in his place was appointed a royal clerk, Godfrey, who was ordained in 1088 but died the same year.[10] It was not then until 1090 or 1091 that William Rufus appointed his friend and chaplain, Ralph Luffa, to the see.[11] The latter held it for over thirty years until his death in 1123.

The earliest date recorded that refers to work on a new cathedral church is that in the *Annales de Wintonia* s.a. 1108: *hoc anno Radulfus Cicestrensem fecit dedicari ecclesiam.*[12] This gives no indication, however, either of when the work was begun, or of how much may have been completed by 1108. On the other hand, a dedication usually may be taken as implying that the main liturgical area of the building was ready for use: that is, the east arm containing the presbytery, the crossing and easternmost nave bays containing the choir, and the flanking transepts. Only six years after the dedication, in 1114, there was a disastrous fire and *exarsit ecclesia S. Trinitatis Cicestrie et pene tota civitas.*[13] Florence of Worcester also records s.a. 1114: *civitas Cicestrie cum principali monasterio, per culpam incuriae . . . flammis absumpta est;*[14] and then s.a. 1117 (an entry which has been interpreted also as referring to Chichester): *secundum regis Henrici praeceptum, apud Cirenceastre novum opus est inceptum.*[15] What has been taken as the critical source for dating the work of the church is William of Malmesbury's reference to the fire (presumably of 1114) and its sequel. He relates how Bishop Ralph refused to pay taxes to Henry I: *dictitans pauperem esse episcopatum, ecclesiam incendio absumptam, non debere tributis expilari sed oblationibus augeri.*[16] Ralph apparently prevailed, for subsequently, William says: *ecclesiam suam, quam a novo fecerat, cum fortuitus ignis . . . pessumdedisset, liberalitate potissimum regis, brevi refecit.*[17] It was Godwin at the beginning of the seventeenth century who first took this passage to mean that Bishop Ralph 'built his Cathedrall Church from the ground':[18] but I suggest that this interpretation places the wrong emphasis on William's words. The passage in question is describing the achievements of Bishop Ralph's episcopate: strange then that he should choose to comment principally on his repair of the building after the 1114 fire, and to pass over his foundation of it in a relative clause. And if the reference really is to the foundation of the church, why does he not use the standard wording *a fundamentis* rather than *a novo*? My own view is that William is commenting here only on the newness of the building consumed in the 1114 fire (doubtless he was aware that Ralph had been responsible for work before 1114, and he may even have had in mind the 1108 dedication); but that he is stating the church actually to have been founded by Bishop Ralph I remain unconvinced.

If we reject the foundation interpretation of William of Malmesbury, we are left with no documentary date for the opening of the new cathedral works (the only firm points of reference remain the dedication in 1108, and the repairs following the fire in 1114). But before examining the hypothesis of an early commencement against the actual fabric, it is worth looking at some of the historical analogies to the situation at Chichester. In 1075 the removal of two other sees besides Selsey was decreed: Sherborne to (Old) Salisbury, and Lichfield to Chester.[19] At the former of these a new cathedral church was begun consequent upon the move and before 1078;[20] at Chester there is no evidence for a new church, but *c.*1087 the see was moved again to Coventry Abbey[21] (and subsequently returned to Lichfield). At about the same time other sees also were moved.[22] Dorchester was transferred to Lincoln where, although there was an existing minster church of St Mary,[23] a new cathedral was begun and was far enough advanced by 1092 for a dedication to be planned.[24] The see of Elmham was moved as a temporary measure to Thetford, apparently into an existing church,[25] and then again in 1095 to Norwich where a new cathedral was begun almost immediately.[26] From these cases it appears that where sees were removed to what became permanent sites (Old Salisbury, Lincoln, Norwich) new cathedral churches were begun very quickly. Only where the move was tentative (Chester, Thetford) is there no evidence for building being undertaken. These comparisons would at least suggest a possible early start to Chichester; though, of course, they by no means prove it.

It is not the intention of this note to examine in detail the surviving Romanesque fabric of Chichester, but only to state briefly some of the salient facts that weigh for or against the hypothesis that the building may have been begun before 1090. A first general consideration is that the overall plan of the structure is extremely irregular,[27] suggesting that it was not all laid out at one time. This could be explained as indicating that the work proceeded in a rather intermittent way, though consistently from east to west; or it could indicate that parts of the structure have been redesigned or rebuilt after their first erection. A second general consideration is that, although there may be minor changes detectable in the masonry, there is no very marked break in technique such as occurred at Winchester following 1107 when the masons changed from thick to thin mortar joints between the ashlar. This suggests a continuity in the works, but does not in itself help to date the fabric. If the building was only partly up by 1108, the works may have been open still in 1114 when the fire occurred; the repairs may then have carried on without a break.

The very character of the masonry, at least in some parts of the building, is one of the factors suggesting an early commencement. Thus in the north transept where some of the original pointing is trapped behind a later twelfth-century wall painting, it can be seen to have been the broad ribbon pointing characteristic of work of the '70s and '80s at Canterbury and Winchester cathedrals, and is certainly more difficult to parallel following *c.*1100. In the east bays of the nave also the original masonry detailing (where unrestored after the fire of 1187) has a primitive character that is suggestive again of an early date. There is nothing, indeed, in the masonry technique, nor in the actual design of the transepts and easterly nave bays that would point to a date later than the '70s or '80s, and the whole would fit comfortably into the milieu of e.g. St Augustine's, Canterbury (*c.*1073–1087 and following) or Rochester Cathedral (*c.*1077–1083 and following).

What apparently weighs most against an early date for the building as a whole is the design of the eastern arm. The elaboration of the plan of this—with three straight bays leading up to the apse and ambulatory[28]—and the form of the sculptured capitals, would be out of context before the later years of the eleventh-century and early years of the twelfth century. It is these parts of the building, indeed, that have made most commentators happy to accept a post-1090 starting date. But the question needs to be asked whether the present east arm (the work prior to the alterations following 1187) is the earliest part of the church, and whether even it could be a rebuilding. Only archaeological excavation could answer the question of whether there was an earlier east arm which the present one replaces. But a significant analogy may be made with Christ Church, Canterbury, where the church begun shortly after 1070 had a short, solid-walled(?), presbytery of two bays terminating in an apse échelon scheme, and where, following c.1096, this was replaced by a much more elaborate east arm with aisles and ambulatory. Canterbury could have provided an impetus for a remodelling of the east of Chichester: though the relationship of any such work either to the dedication of 1108 or the repairs following 1114 I would hesitate to conjecture upon further without more concrete evidence.

The coming of the Cluniacs

BRIAN GOLDING

The settlement of a small band of monks from Cluny at Lewes in 1077 by earl William I de Warenne is one of the most famous episodes in English monastic history.[1] All the circumstantial details of this story are to be found in the foundation chronicle which forms part of the forged (probably in the early fourteenth century) foundation-charter of Lewes.[2] Nevertheless this account probably preserves a reliable tradition. The chronicle tells how William and Gundreda his wife were journeying to Rome, staying en route in French and Burgundian monasteries. Unable to cross from Burgundy into Italy because of the war between Henry IV and Gregory VII, they stayed at Cluny. Here they were so impressed with the community's piety and charity that their love for it surpassed that for any other monastery that they had visited. While there they were received into confraternity, and resolved that they would found a Cluniac priory on their return to England. This was in accordance with a much earlier decision they had taken on the advice of Lanfranc to found a monastery on their English estates. On returning to Lewes (whose Rape William controlled) they sent to abbot Hugh to ask him to send a few monks to whom they would give the church of St Pancras (an ancient wooden structure that William had rebuilt in stone lying below Lewes hill) and enough land to maintain 12 monks. At first Hugh refused the request, claiming that England was too far away and lay overseas. Clearly he believed that it would be difficult for the mother-house to maintain close contact with, and control over, such a distant daughter. At length Hugh relented: permission was obtained from William I to bring the monks to England, and Hugh sent Lanzo, who became the first prior, and three others to form the nucleus of the new community. The priory was not yet, however, securely established. Shortly afterwards Lanzo returned to Cluny, where he remained for a year. William de Warenne thought of transferring his foundation to Marmoutier. Fortunately a meeting was arranged in Normandy between the king, earl and abbot, and Lanzo returned to rule the new house, where he soon acquired a considerable reputation for his piety.[3]

In 1066 there were no Cluniac priories in Normandy: that is, there were no communities owing direct allegiance to Cluny. At the same time the influence of Cluny on Norman monasticism was very strong.[4] In 1001 William of Volpiano, who had been sent in 978 from Cluny to reform the community of St Bénigne, Dijon, moved to Fécamp which he also reformed according to

Cluniac principles. From there a number of other Norman monasteries were restored on similar lines. Bernay was founded *c.*1026 by Judith, wife of duke Richard II, and William of Volpiano became its abbot as well as abbot of Fécamp. Reform of Jumièges, St Wandrille, Mont St Michel and St Ouen followed. They in turn brought more communities under Cluniac influence, with the result that about three-quarters of all Norman monasteries in 1066 were in some way inspired by the Cluniac example.[5] Only Bec, Lessay and St Etienne stood outside Cluny's ideology. The ties with Cluny were personal, not institutional, but they were none the less real. Orderic Vitalis aptly demonstrates the introduction of Cluniac spirituality to his own monastery of St Evroul. Abbot Thierry of St Evroul learned monastic customs from William of Volpiano and from William's pupil, Thierry of Jumièges. The latter had come from Jumièges to St Evroul. Thierry of St Evroul's successor, Robert of Grandmesnil, had visited Cluny itself as a novice and had spent some time there. Orderic tells us that in his time the monks still preserved the customs of the Cluniac reformers and taught them to the novices.[6]

By 1066, therefore, the inspiration of Cluny in Normandy was strong, and it is not surprising that Cluniac influence was brought to the Anglo-Norman kingdom also. It is hard to assess how close were the ties between Cluny and William I. He asked for and obtained rights of confraternity with Cluny, in return for which he and his wife sent rich vestments to the Burgundian house.[7] His role in the establishment of Lewes has already been noticed.[8] He is also known to have asked abbot Hugh of Cluny to send him some monks from Cluny to aid him in his reform of the English church. Hugh refused. William was insistent and offered to pay Cluny 100 marks *per annum* for each monk sent. Not surprisingly Hugh regarded such an offer as simoniacal and refused again. Initially the king is said to have been furious with Hugh's reply but later to have accepted it.[9] Nevertheless he is not known to have made any grants in favour of the English Cluniac houses founded during his reign though he did issue general and particular confirmations in favour of Warenne grants to Lewes and also confirmed a grant by Roger, earl of Shrewsbury, to the French Cluniac house of Marcigny-sur-Loire.[10]

However lukewarm William's own support of Cluny was, the response of the Anglo-Norman magnates in favour of Cluny was considerable. Between 1077 and 1154 some 30 Cluniac houses or cells were founded in England.[11] They ranged in size from Lewes (with an assessed income of £920 in 1535) or Bermondsey (£464 in 1535) to small cells that were entirely subject to a mother-house.[12] The precise constitutional position of Cluniac foundations varied from house to house. All owed allegiance and an annual money payment to the founding community but beyond that ties could vary enormously.[13] Dom David Knowles suggested that only about 12 foundations were 'fully organised monasteries'.[14] The number of independent priories varies according to the criteria of independence adopted, but it is probable that the independent priories founded before 1154 comprised Barnstable, Bermondsey, Bromholm, Castle Acre, Daventry, Dudley,

Lenton, Lewes, Monk Bretton, Montacute, Much Wenlock, Northampton, Pontefract and Thetford. Other houses were more or less dependant upon these larger establishments. Though the larger Cluniac houses were by no means poor, their income did not put them in the same league as many of the old-established Benedictine, or even some of the Cistercian, abbeys. In 1535 only ten houses of the Cluniac congregation had an income of more than £200.[15]

Nevertheless, many Cluniac priories were prestigious foundations and their founders were in the front rank of the Anglo-Norman nobility. Thus William I de Warenne founded Lewes; William, count of Mortain, Montacute; Roger of Montgomery, earl of Shrewsbury, Much Wenlock; Robert de Lacy, Ponte-fract; Roger Bigod, earl of Norfolk, Thetford; William Peverel, lord of the Peak barony, Lenton; Simon of St Liz, earl of Northampton, Northampton; and Johel of Totnes, Barnstable. Of course these lords were also benefactors or founders of other monasteries. Roger of Montgomery founded the Benedictine abbey of Shrewsbury and the priory of St Nicholas, Arundel, as a dependancy of St Martin, Sées. He also made grants in favour of St Etienne (Caen), St Evroul and Cluny itself.[16] Such eclectic piety could be paralleled in almost every other case. The grants of the earls of Warenne and Mortain and of the Lacy family will be considered in more detail in the second part of this paper.[17]

There is, however, some evidence to suggest that in many cases the closest links were felt with the benefactors' Cluniac foundations. It is true that com-paratively few of the founders are known to have been buried at their Cluniac houses. The Warennes were buried at Lewes, and it is probable that Simon of St Liz would have been buried at Northampton had he not died while on a journey to the Holy Land. As a result he was buried at La Charité-sur-Loire, the mother-house of Northampton and the place whence that house's first monks had come.[18] William, count of Mortain, after his long imprisonment by Henry I, finally took the habit and was buried at the Cluniac priory of Bermondsey, not as his foundation of Montacute.[19] Roger, earl of Montgomery was buried at his other foundation of Shrewsbury, which was of course close to the *caput* of his honour.[20] Clearly when one family supported many different communities it could be hard to determine the place of burial, and the fact that such burial could bring prestige to the monastery could occasion dispute. The clearest example of this is the case of Roger Bigod. Orderic Vitalis was under the impression that Roger had been buried at Thetford. He goes so far as to give the epitaph inscribed upon Roger's tomb.[21] If there was such a tomb it must have been prepared before Roger's death, for both a fifteenth-century Thetford chronicle and a charter of Henry I (to be dated before 1108) make it clear that Roger was buried at Norwich. The chronicle tells how he unfortu-nately died at an episcopal manor, not far from Norwich, where the bishop happened to be staying. In defiance of Roger's wish to be buried at Thetford the body was taken to the cathedral, and there interred in a position of honour. The prior and four monks of Thetford immediately went to the cathedral to demand the body, but it was too late. The bishop refused to yield. The charter describes the sequel. The monks brought a case against the bishop, claiming that Roger had given the body of himself, his wife and sons to Thetford. The bishop produced parishioners as witnesses, who claimed that the earl had given his body 'with those of his barons' to Norwich cathedral before monks came to Thetford. At this the monks gave in, admitted the injustice of their claim, and begged for pardon.[22]

The evidence from burials that the founders of Cluniac houses thought more highly of these than they did of other communities with which they were associated is, therefore, far from conclusive. At the same time there are other indications that the Cluniac foundations were highly regarded. Though their founders did make grants to other houses both in Normandy and England, they were nearly always more generous to the Cluniacs.[23] Moreover, there is clear evidence that in many cases the priory was founded at the *caput* of an honour and in close (sometimes too close) proximity to the baronial castle. Some years ago Professor Matthew cited a number of examples demonstrating the close geographical proximity of many Anglo-Norman alien priories to founders' castles or *capita*. He suggested that communities were established in these places in order to provide for the spiritual needs of the baronial castle and household, and that the monks performed a parochial function there.[24] Such ties were perhaps even closer in the case of the Cluniac houses. St Pancras, Lewes, was sited at the foot of the hill on which stood the Warenne castle; St John's, Pontefract, lay at the *caput* of the Lacy's Yorkshire estates and close to their castle.[25] Robert de Lacy, the founder of the priory, stipulated that the castle chapel of St Clement should be granted to none but the Cluniacs, and his successor Hugh de Laval referred in his confirmation charter to the monks of St John's 'in my castle'.[26] The close connection between the priory and the Lacys' secular lordship here was reinforced by Hugh's grant of the castle chapel of Clitheroe, the centre of the Lancashire estates of the Lacys, together with all the tithes of Clitheroe castle.[27] The nucleus of Johel de Totnes' foundation at Barnstaple was the chapel of St Mary Magdalene outside his castle, which served as the headquarters for Johel's north Devon estates. Since this chapel was not the parish church of Barnstaple (which was also granted to the new foundation) it is likely that it was the castle-chapel.[28] Montacute, founded by William of Mortain at the end of the eleventh century, was actually endowed with William's castle there and, according to Leland, the castle was partly demolished in order to provide stone for the conventual buildings.[29] St Andrew's, Northampton, lay close to the castle which the priory's founder, Simon of St Liz had built, and the priory at Castle Acre was initially situated within the castle itself.[30] Then, because the site was not surprisingly too constricted, William II de Warenne moved the monks to another site at the other end of the town. Hugh de Leicester originally founded a Cluniac house by his castle of Preston Capes, but a few years later gained permission from his lord, Simon de St Liz, to move the house to Daventry since the monks were suffering from a shortage of water at Preston and also from the proximity of the castle *(propter castelli propinquitatem).*[31]

The constitutional ties that bound house to house have already been touched on.[32] In England there were two main Cluniac 'families' or groups. The first and earliest was that owing allegiance to La Charité-sur-Loire (itself the eldest daughter-house of Cluny). With the exception of Lewes and Lewes' daughter-house of Castle Acre, the first five English Cluniac houses, Wenlock, Bermondsey, Daventry, Pontefract and Northampton, were all daughters of La Charité. Abbot Hugh of Cluny's reluctance to found English houses has already been mentioned, and this may well be the reason why only Lewes was founded from Cluny until Montacute (*c*.1100). The second main affiliation was that of Lewes and her daughter-houses, of which the most important were Castle Acre (1089) and Thetford (1104). In addition to these, a small group of houses under the control of St Martin des Champs was founded in the south-west: these were Barnstaple, St. Clears, and St. James, Exeter. Montacute also possessed four small houses all founded in the first half of the twelfth century, and none wholly independent of the mother-house.[33]

These ties of religious and constitutional structures were reflected in, and in part created by, ties either of kin or lordship that connected the founders of Cluniac houses. Castle Acre priory was founded by William II de Warenne, the son of the founder of Lewes who had himself wished to found a Cluniac community upon his Norfolk estates.[34] William of Mortain was also responsible for the foundation of the small house of St Cyriacus as a cell of Montacute.[35] Montacute's cell of Holme was founded by Robert, son of Alfred of Lincoln.[36] Both Alfred and Robert were major tenants of the Mortains and had already granted lands to Montacute in Dorset.[37] Another of the Mortain tenants, Winibald of Balloon (or Caerleon) was responsible for the foundation of Montacute's Welsh cell of Malpas.[38] It is probably no coincidence that Hugh de Leicester, the founder of Daventry (*c*. 1090) was not only sheriff of Northamptonshire but also the seneschal of Maud, sister of Simon I de St Liz, the founder of Northampton priory (1084).[39] Simon I himself gave his consent to the transfer of Hugh's foundation from Preston to Daventry, and Maud granted the church of Daventry, five carucates, a mill and woodland there to the new community.[40] Monk Bretton was founded *c*.1153-4 as a daughter-house of Pontefract by Adam fitz Sweyn.[41] The fitz Sweyn family was the wealthiest family of Anglo-Saxon thegnly descent to survive as honorial barons in the Pontefract honour, and in 1166 the family held eight fees of the Lacys, the largest holding of any tenant. Both Adam's father, Sweyn, and grandfather, Ailric, had already proved generous benefactors of Pontefract.[42]

Just as daughter-houses were sometimes founded by feudal tenants, so too the charters and cartularies of the Anglo-Norman Cluniac houses demonstrate that individual priories were almost exclusively dependant upon the vassals of their founders for their benefactions. This is very clearly seen in the case of Montacute. Henry II's confirmation charters in favour of the house reveal the generosity of William of Mortain's tenants and household.[43] Bretel of St Clare, who was one of Robert of Mortain's most important Domesday tenants holding estates in Somerset, Dorset and Devon, gave the hide of land he held of the

Mortain barony in Montacute itself.[44] Richard son of Drogo granted half a hide in Montacute (representing half of his father's holding there) together with the manor of Thorn, held by his father in 1086 at an assessed value of £1.[45] In association with Osbert his chaplain, Richard also granted the church of Yarlington to the priory, and two of Richard's own knights, Robert and William, also granted half a hide.[46] Thus, in this instance, links between the priory and the barony reached to the level of a tenant's own household and vassals. William of Mortain's butler, Alured, gave extremely generously. In 1086 Alured *pincerna* was one of the most important of the Mortain tenants in the south-west, his lands being concentrated in Cornwall and Somerset.[47] He was a witness to William's foundation charter and to Henry I's confirmation charter to Montacute.[48] He granted lands, churches and demesne tithes in Somerset, Dorset, Devon and Cornwall.[49] Ranulf 'the chancellor' gave his share of the manor of Thorn Coffyn and tithes of several Somerset and Dorset estates.[50] He can be identified with Ralph the priest who held a manor valued at £1 12s. at Thorn Coffyn in 1086.[51] Geoffrey the count's chaplain granted the church of Brimpton to Montacute, and other notable tenants who gave generously to their lord's foundation include Geoffrey *de Lestra* and Alfred and Robert of Lincoln.[52]

Similar support for Pontefract came from the tenants of the Lacy honour. The grants of Ailric and his son Sweyn have already been mentioned; William Foliot granted one carucate of land in Pontefract 'before the castle' when Robert de Lacy founded the priory. He also witnessed the foundation charter.[53] In 1166 the Foliot fee of five knights (two in Yorkshire and three in Lincolnshire) was the largest holding of the Lacys' Norman tenants, and the fact that he was the principal addressee of a charter of Henry I confirming a grant by Robert I de Lacy to Nostell priory, suggests that he was the foremost Lacy vassal when Robert's estates were forfeit to the crown.[54] The family of Friston does not appear to have been enfeoffed until the time of Hugh de Laval, but by 1166 held five fees of Pontefract.[55] Robert de Friston granted a mill in Friston to Pontefract in the second quarter of the twelfth-century, and his son William II gave two bovates and three acres there.[56] Close ties could exist between the priory and the founding family's vassals, as they could between the community and the founders. In the mid-twelfth century Henry de Lacy was involved in the sale by a tenant, Ralph de Chevercourt and his sister Beatrix, of the vill of Barnsley. The monks agreed to appoint a monk for the grantors' mother and one for each of the grantors. They also agreed to receive Ralph as a monk when he wished to leave the world. For this grant the monks paid Beatrix 10 marks, Ralph, 3 marks, a monk's tunic (*pellicea monachorum*) which was perhaps an earnest of their promise to receive him, and a pair of boots every year. Jordan, Ralph's son, received a palfrey, and another son, Richard, 3 marks.[57]

So far I have considered the establishment of the English Cluniac houses by the Anglo-Norman nobility and examined the web of relationships, constitutional, personal and tenurial, that bound community to community and community to founders and benefactors. In the second part of this paper I wish to consider in more detail how generous the founders were to their Cluniac foundations and how closely linked to them they were. Ties between founders and priories can be examined in a number of different ways, and the relative generosity of the early benefactors can be examined from two perspectives, that of the founder and that of the priory. How much land, and of what quality, was granted to the priories from the total demesne or subinfeudated holdings of the benefactors? How great a proportion of the total *spiritualia* and *temporalia* of the houses derived from the grants of the founders or their families? I shall consider in detail the endowment history of four priories: Lewes, Pontefract, Montacute and Bermondsey. The first three of these communities were founded by three of the greatest Anglo-Norman families, the last by an obscure English merchant, Ailwin Child.

William de Warenne's foundation charter conveyed to Lewes his demesne in Falmer, land in Swanborough (close to Lewes) a further carucate in an unnamed vill and the church of St Pancras with its appurtenances.[58] Later charters reveal that he also gave lands elsewhere in Sussex and in Cambridgeshire and Norfolk. Of these the manors of Carlton (Cambridgeshire), Walton and Heacham (Norfolk) were the most significant.[59] Grants of churches included those of Clayton, Rottingdean (Sussex), St Olave's, Southwark and High Roding (Essex).[60] Little more was added to the priory's estates in the vills where William granted lands.[61] In the *Valor Ecclesiasticus* the priory's lands in the six vills of Falmer, Swanborough, Withdean, Carlton, Walton and Heacham were valued at £227 18s. 8d. To this sum should be added the £6 derived from pasture and meadow in Ditchling granted by William, and probably most of the assessed value of lands in Southover and Kingston, that is, lands lying outside the priory gates, an amount of £21 4s. 6d. The total assessed value of the Lewes *temporalia* was nearly £600. Thus, even if some allowance is made for the later grants made in these vills, it is clear that the founder's endowment represented something of the order of 33 per cent of the total income from lands at the Dissolution.[62] How generous was William to Lewes within the context of his total Domesday holdings? In 1086 the value of William's Sussex estates was assessed at a little over £500. Of this some £232 was derived from demesne manors and income from the town of Lewes.[63] Domesday records only the Swanborough and Falmer holdings of the priory. Together these were valued at £23.[64] Even if the other lands granted later in Sussex by William I are added to this figure, it is clear that William did not beggar himself by generosity. Moreover, the estate of Falmer had belonged to Wilton abbey in the time of the Confessor, and it seems likely that this had been merely confiscated by William to grant to Lewes. This manor was valued at £20 and was the largest of Lewes' holdings at this time.[65] Lewes' manor of Carlton was valued at £8. The total value of William's Cambridgeshire holdings was £51 5s. of which £22 was derived from demesne manors.[66] The Norfolk manors of Walton and Heacham (both of which had formed part of the fee of Frederick, William's brother-in-law) were valued at £17 10s. and £18 respectively, and were amongst the most valuable of William's Norfolk estates.[67] Finally, how generous was William to other communities? In Normandy he probably granted the service of lands in Calvados to Holy Trinity, Rouen.[68] It was certainly his intention to found a daughter-house of Lewes at Castle Acre. Prior Lanzo of Lewes promised to send monks from Lewes to the new foundation, and William endowed it with two carucates of land and the parish church.[69] It was, however, left to William II to complete the priory's establishment. To the Cluniacs William was known as a benefactor; to the monks of Ely he was a despoiler. William played an important role in the expedition against Hereward (in which his brother-in-law Frederick was killed) and the *Liber Eliensis* records a moral story that on the night that William died miserably (of wounds received at Pevensey), the abbot dreamed that he heard the earl cry out 'Lord, have mercy! Lord, have mercy!' as he was carried off by demons. William had usurped several vills belonging to the abbey. A few days later William's widow arrived and offered 100 shillings for her husband's soul, but no monk dared take such tainted money.[70]

It is clear, therefore, that although William's generosity to Lewes was not outstanding, he was far more generous to Lewes than to other monasteries. Moreover, the economic fortunes of Lewes throughout the medieval period were clearly based upon the grants of the founder. Both William II and William III de Warenne continued to concentrate their grants on Lewes and Castle Acre, though many of these grants consisted of churches or tithes, a fact that did not go unnoticed by either William II or the religious who were present at the dedication of the priory church *c.*1095. In his grant made then, William specifically referred to the churches and tithes 'which I could not myself keep in my own hand or have at my disposal'.[71] The Warennes made very few grants to other houses, and the most important of these was William II's foundation of Holy Sepulchre priory, Thetford. This was endowed with land granted to William by Stephen (of whom William had been a rather half-hearted supporter) perhaps with the express intention that the priory be founded with these lands. The reason for the foundation is clear: William took the cross on Palm Sunday, 1145/6, and he explicitly referred to his fellow-crusaders when he asked in the foundation charter that his brother *palmiferes* protect his grant.[72]

A final indication that the early Warennes regarded Lewes as 'their' priory *par excellence* is provided by the fact that all the Warennes and their successors as earls of Surrey from William I to earl Richard I (died 1375/6) were buried in the chapter-house or church of the priory, with the exception of William III who died on crusade in Laodicea in 1147/8, and his successor William de Blois who died and was buried at Toulouse during the 1159 campaign.[73]

Robert I de Lacy founded Pontefract towards the end of the eleventh century. The exact date and veracity of the foundation charter has been the subject of considerable debate, but even if it is not wholly genuine the account it gives of the foundation probably reflects a genuine tradition. It states that Robert, on the advice of Thomas I, archbishop of York, and other religious men, founded a house subject to La Charité, whose prior Wilencus sent brethren to settle in the new foundation. It was granted the site of the priory, land in Pontefract, the custody of the hospital of St Nicholas where the brethren had first dwelt, four churches and land in seven Yorkshire vills.[74] With the exception of Dodworth, which lay some 20 miles to the southwest of Pontefract on the edge of the Pennines, all these lands and churches lay close to Pontefract, none being more than five miles away. The initial endowment was therefore compact and within easy reach both of the abbey and of its lord. The endowment was also comparatively modest. The total recorded value of Ilbert de Lacy's estates in 1086 was £251 7s. 6d. Some 40 per cent of this was derived from demesne estates, most of which lay in Yorkshire where the demesne manors were valued at £90 11s. 8d.[75] Only one estate granted to Pontefract, that of Ledston, was still held in demesne in 1086. Then it formed part of the large manorial complex of Kippax valued at £16.[76] Though Ledston was one of the largest members of this soke, it is unlikely that it accounted for more than half of the total value of the estate. Thus Robert when he founded Pontefract a few years after the compilation of Domesday probably alienated no more than 5–8 per cent of his demesne land. All other lands granted to the priory had already been granted to tenants. It has been suggested that the Lacys were cautious in their grants both to their knights and religious houses, and that the latter were granted 'almost entirely' churches and tithes of little value to lay men.[77] Certainly Robert's generosity appears limited if his grants are compared with the size of his territories, but it is clear that his grants were by no means negligible if compared with the total holdings of the priory. In 1535 about 50 per cent of the priory's income from *temporalia* came from lands granted by Robert.[78] Moreover his grants to other communities were on an even smaller scale. Though he may have been responsible for the foundation of Augustinian Nostell, his grants there were very modest indeed, and his foundation of St Nicholas' hospital, Pontefract, was later granted by him to the Cluniacs, and served as the monks' temporary home.[79]

After the banishment of Robert I (*c.*1114) and his replacement by Hugh de Laval, both Pontefract and Nostell continued to be supported. Such grants may well have been politically essential, certainly they stressed continuity between the old and new lord of Pontefract. Nevertheless Hugh's grants to Pontefract consisted of little except churches.[80] His successor, the intruder William Maltravers, apparently saw little need to support the Lacy foundations. He granted one bovate to Pontefract and gave one mark *per annum* from the rents of his assarts, in return for the monks' surrender of the church of Whalley granted by Hugh de Laval.[81] It is, however, interesting to note that, when mortally wounded in 1135, it was to Pontefract that he was taken, where he received the habit and died three days later.[82] The return of legitimacy after Maltravers' death did not result in more grants. Ilbert II does not appear to have made any grants in Pontefract's favour, and his brother, though he made generous grants to a number of monasteries, gave little to Pontefract. By the mid-twelfth century the spiritual 'centre of gravity' had shifted from Cluny to Cîteaux, and it is not surprising to find that Henry's grants were directed to

Cistercian houses, notably Kirkstall which he founded in 1147.[83]

No Cluniac house owed more to the generosity of its founder than Montacute. Montacute (known as Bishopston until the Norman settlement) was a centre of some religious and military importance. According to the late-twelfth century account of the foundation of Waltham abbey, a wonder-working cross was found here *c*.1035 by Tofig the sheriff, on a hilltop on his Bishopston estate. The cross was moved to a new religious foundation on Tofig's Essex estate of Waltham, while the place where the cross had been found was granted to the local monastery of Athelney. Following the Conquest, however, the estate quickly passed into the hands of Robert of Mortain, who granted Athelney the manor of Purse Caundle (Dorset) in exchange for Bishopston. In 1086 the latter was assessed at twice the value of the former; it is clear that here as elsewhere Robert's behaviour to Anglo-Saxon monasteries was more than a little highhanded.[84] On the hill he acquired Robert threw up a castle which became the *caput* of his honour.[85] Sometime between 1086 and the founding of the priory the count of Mortain also established a small borough at Montacute.[86]

The priory was founded *c*.1100 by William, count of Mortain, Robert's son. He endowed it with the parish church, the borough and market, the castle and castle chapel, his demesne orchards and vineyard, the manor and its mill and the local fair on Hamdon hill. He also granted the manors and churches of Tintinhull, Creech St Michael, East Chinnock, Closworth and West Mudford, besides other lands and churches in Somerset, Dorset, Devon and Cornwall.[87] This was a generous endowment by any standards. In 1086 Robert of Mortain was the most important lay tenant-in-chief in Somerset. He then held eight manors in demesne, and retained a demesne interest in two more. They represented a little over 20 per cent of the total assessed income of his estate, and it is clear that he had, like most other tenants-in-chief, retained the most productive manors in his own hand and granted out the less valuable.[88] The two most valuable demesne manors, Tintinhull (£16) and East Chinnock (£12), both passed to Montacute, as did Closworth (£7) and Montacute itself, where half the estate (valued at £6) was held in demesne.[89] The only manor granted to Montacute that was not held in demesne in 1086, West Mudford, was valued at £4, while in 1086 the manor of Creech was still held by the king.[90] Thus over 30 per cent of the Mortain demesne manors in Somerset was alienated to Montacute at its foundation. From the point of view of the priory's total landholdings, William's generosity is yet more clearly seen. In 1291 nearly 90 per cent of Montacute's total income from *temporalia* came from manors granted by William.[91] By 1535 the proportion had fallen, but it was still the case that over 70 per cent of the priory's income came from this source.[92] Neither the grants of William nor his father to other monasteries were on anything like the same scale. Bec, Marmoutier and Grestain all received small grants of either manors or churches in England, but it is clear that William's generosity was focussed on Montacute.[93] Perhaps its most interesting and strange aspect is the fact that he not only granted away a considerable proportion of his Somerset demesne, but also alienated the *caput* of his Somerset estates together with his castle. It is almost as if he was dismantling his interests in the county, and is a feature that needs further elucidation.

The three priories so far considered all depended, to a greater or lesser extent, upon the generosity of their founder or his family for a large proportion of their grants. The case of Bermondsey is different. Its foundation and early endowment history is complex and confusing. The Annals of Bermondsey, compiled in the mid-fifteenth century, though based on reliable sources, are themselves of uncertain value. As Rose Graham wrote, 'no statement in the Annals about Bermondsey can be accepted without reserve, unless it can be proved from another source'.[94] According to them Ailwin Child, a wealthy (and otherwise unknown) English citizen of London, granted rents in London to La Charité-sur-Loire in 1082. He is also said to have inspired many lords both temporal and spiritual to give presents, churches and manors to the priory.[95] The Annals also correctly quote the Domesday (which they mistakenly date 1083) entry that there was a 'new and beautiful church' at Bermondsey.[96] They go on, however, to state that four named monks from La Charité did not come to Bermondsey until 1089, a statement corroborated by the Lewes annals.[97] It was in this year, too, that William Rufus is said to have granted the monks his manor of Bermondsey, a large estate valued at £15 in 1086.[98] It is not impossible that Ailwin did grant rents to La Charité, but unlikely that the 'new church' of Domesday was the priory church, since that surely could not have been maintained by rent income alone and without resident monks. Rufus' charter can be dated between 1093 and 1097, and it also confirmed grants made by others, including Robert Bloet, William's chancellor, and Winibald of Ballon, the founder of Malpas.[99] Certainly Rufus was closely connected with the new foundation, even if he cannot be regarded as the founder. Professor Brooke has suggested that William sold the manor to Ailwin 'for a handsome sum' in order that Ailwin might then endow the priory, or that his grant was a thank-offering for English support during the great rebellion of 1088.[100]

The Anglo-Norman monarchy continued to support Bermondsey after Rufus' death, both Henry and Stephen endowing the community with manors and churches in Surrey, Kent and elsewhere.[101] Moreover it was from Bermondsey that the first monks for Stephen's foundation at Faversham were drawn.[102] Other grants were obtained from a large number of benefactors. Since there was no founding family on whom the convent could rely, the priory received grants from any available source; as a result its holdings were much more widely scattered than those of other English Cluniacs. Even in the case of Bermondsey nearly half of its temporal income in 1535 was derived from the lands it held in Bermondsey itself, that is, the manor granted by Rufus.[103] Here, too, the community depended upon its earliest grants for much of its income and the scale of the first generation of grants largely determined the wealth and status of the house until its dissolution.

The Cluniac phenomenon was shortlived. By 1154 most English Cluniac houses had been founded and all the important priories were in existence. So, too, were the two Cluniac nunneries, Arthington and Delapré (Northampton), founded by Peter de Arthington and Simon de St Liz II respectively.[104] By the mid-twelfth century some chroniclers and satirists were beginning to criticise the Cluniacs. Though William of Malmesbury strongly approved of them, as did Walter Map to a less marked degree, the Cluniacs were reproached by Nigel Wireker and especially by Gerald of Wales.[105] The unfortunate use by Gerald of *Cluniacensis* as a synonym for *niger monachus* makes it difficult to determine whether his strictures were intended to apply to all Benedictines or were reserved for Cluniacs.[106] It may be no coincidence that Peter de Leia, bishop of St David's and one of Gerald's most hated *bêtes noires*, had been prior of the Cluniac priory of Wenlock; certainly in 1198 Gerald, in a letter to the archbishop of Canterbury, declared his willingness to accept any man as bishop of St David's so long as he was not a black monk.[107] The black monks were lax in morals and in the observance of the Rule, they were infected by gluttony and avarice. In a famous passage in the *Itinerarium Cambriae* Gerald states that if a flourishing estate is given to the Cluniacs, if they are well endowed and have large revenues, their avarice and gluttony is such that all their resources will be squandered and their lands and the inhabitants beggared.[108] Even allowing for Gerald's bias there can be little doubt that the Cluniacs were declining in popularity. In another famous passage Gerald explains the foundation by Ranulf de Glanville of the Augustinian house of Butley. Ranulf first looked at the Cluniacs but they were too fond of their stomach *(illos tandem ventri prout videbatur nimis addictos)*, then to the Cistercians who were too ambitious and avaricious but finally he found true religion amongst the Augustinians.[109] This story, however apocryphal, does illustrate a change in religious patronage during the twelfth century, since Renaulf's kinsman William had been a benefactor of the Cluniacs and had founded Bromholm priory in 1113.[110]

In less than ninety years the Cluniacs had established themselves as an important, if not outstanding, presence in the English monastic landscape. How should the Cluniac dynamic be explained? In part their growth and expansion was inevitable. As demonstrated at the commencement of this paper, Norman monasteries were already heavily indoctrinated with Cluniac ideas.[111] There is not time to discuss here the influence of Cluny upon the Anglo-Norman episcopate. It suffices to mention the use made by Lanfranc of Cluniac customs in drawing up his Constitutions, and his friendship with William de Warenne.[112] Anselm was a friend of abbot Hugh and stayed at Cluny.[113] Herbert Losinga was involved in the foundation of Thetford, established in the buildings of the former cathedral.[114] Archbishop Thurstan took the habit, died and was buried at Pontefract.[115] Above all Henry of Blois had been brought up at Cluny, had become its prior and had maintained close relations with Peter the Venerable. He had also proved a generous benefactor to the mother-house.[116]

The role of the monarchy was more ambiguous; close support of Cluny did not really come until the reigns of Henry I and Stephen. Though both kings founded monasteries, Reading and Faversham, which were Cluniac in all but formal affiliation, they may well have followed rather than set the trend.[117] Certainly Peter the Venerable explicitly stated that Henry of Blois was the motivating force behind the generosity of Stephen to Cluny.[118] Perhaps the most important reason for the popularity of Cluny in the first generations after the Conquest can be found in the attitude of the Anglo-Norman nobility towards monastic endowments. As is well known, the new nobility did not look with favour upon the old-established Anglo-Saxon Benedictine houses, which were rightly regarded as centres of ideological resistance, if nothing more, to the new order. The magnates wishing to insure their souls had two alternatives: they could grant English lands to Norman monasteries with which they were already associated, or they could found new monasteries on English soil. A Cluniac foundation gave them the best of both worlds. There was no 'English dimension' to Cluny; Cluniac monasticism was therefore sound, both politically and spiritually. At the same time a Cluniac foundation offered something more than did support of a Norman monastery. For magnates intending to settle permanently in England it was hardly fitting or convenient to maintain close links with Norman communities for ever. Cluny offered a unique chance to build French, if not Norman, monasticism on English soil.

The buildings of Battle Abbey: a preliminary survey

J. N. HARE

Nowhere was the impact of the Norman Conquest greater than on the site of the battle that had given William his new kingdom. The conflict had been fought on wasteland, but here the Conqueror was to found an abbey that was to become one of the great monasteries of medieval England. Comparative figures of monastic wealth should be treated with caution, but they still point to the scale of the community's financial resources. Already by the time of Domesday Book, only fourteen abbeys possessed a gross income greater than that of Battle.[1] In 1535, there were more who seem to have exceeded her income, but she still possessed a net revenue of £880.[2] Outside this wealthy community, a new town developed to serve the needs both of the abbey itself and of the growing population of the area around.[3] Although the monastic buildings have suffered heavily since the dissolution of the abbey in 1538, enough survive to remind us of the wealth and power of the abbot and monks.

While substantial portions of the monastic buildings have survived, much has disappeared and archaeological excavations have not hitherto been extensive. In the nineteenth century the eastern crypts of the church were uncovered and trenches were dug on the site of one of the ranges that lay to the east of the dormitory range.[4] Between 1929 and 1934 limited excavations were carried out by Sir Harold Brakspear in the claustral area and on the eastern part of the church. These enabled him to complete a plan of the central part of the abbey. He also made a detailed study of the abbot's house during its restoration after extensive fire-damage.[5] A new phase in the archaeological study of the site began with the acquisition of the monument by the Department of the Environment in 1976. Since then, they have financed a three-year programme of archaeological excavations (1978–80) on areas to the north and east of the surviving dormitory range.[6] The final publication of these excavations will follow, but some preliminary conclusions have been incorporated into this brief sketch of the development of the monastic buildings. It is important to stress the preliminary character of this survey for much work is still required: on the excavated material, on the buildings themselves, and on the documentary sources.

The peculiar circumstances of the origin of the abbey were to influence profoundly its subsequent history and its buildings. William had founded the

BATTLE ABBEY · EAST SUSSEX

GROUND PLAN OF KNOWN BUILDING
STANDING AT DISSOLUTION 1538

50 M
150 FT

= WALL STANDING OR TRACED

RW

N

1 CHURCH
2 CLOISTER
3 CHAPTER HOUSE
4 PARLOUR
5 EAST RANGE, DORMITORY ABOVE
6 REREDORTER
7 REFECTORY
8 KITCHEN (8. CELLAR)
9 WEST RANGE, ABBOTS HOUSE ABOVE
10 ABBOTS HALL
11 CELLARERS RANGE, GUESTS(?) ABOVE
12 GATEHOUSE & LODGES

monastery as a thank-offering for his victory, or as a penitential offering—a response to the heavy penances imposed on his followers for their part in the death and plunder of the Norman Conquest.[7] He seems to have taken an especial interest in his new foundation, endowing it generously and establishing its tradition of independence from external authorities.[8] The abbey thus acquired a tradition of royal protection and an association with the victory that had established the new Anglo-Norman inheritance.[9] These traditions were to be vital elements in allowing Battle to wage its struggle for immunity from external ecclesiastical control, particularly from that of the bishop of Chichester. But by the early thirteenth-century this especial royal protection had ceased, and the abbots had to compromise with the bishops of Chichester. By contrast, the circumstances of its foundation and the topography of the battlefield were to influence the monastic buildings until the dissolution.

William had decided that the new abbey was to be built on the battlefield itself, and with its altar on the site where Harold's standard had fallen.[10] He thus chose a site that was in many ways unsuitable for a great abbey. It was restricted by the road to the north, fell gradually to the east and west, and very sharply and quickly to the south. Although the restricted nature of the site has been partially concealed by later alterations, it is still easily apparent why the first monks should have decided to move elsewhere having 'decided that it seemed hardly suitable for so outstanding a building'.[11] William, however, would not countenance such a move and thus left considerable problems for successive monastic architects. Their attempts have reduced but not concealed the strength of Harold's position and the site's unsuitability for a large monastic community. On top of the hill there has been very little change in the ground level since the early days of the monastery; there the foundations of the Norman east end, which were below the floor level of the later church, were found only a few inches below the present turf-line.[12] But elsewhere, there has been a considerable build-up of material, both in the monastic and post-monastic periods. The monks extended the site by building large earthen or clay platforms and by constructing extensive undercrofts. When a much longer eastern arm was added to the church, one end was built on a series of crypts. When the dormitory was rebuilt on a much larger scale, it had to be constructed on a series of progressively higher undercrofts in order to maintain the level of the dormitory floor. Here the falling ground level culminates in a drop of nine feet between the two most southerly undercrofts and in the impressive height of the most southerly one (Pl. 1). East of the dormitory, a building platform was established at the top of the slope, and at the bottom the reredorter range was erected on the hillside and the ground was then levelled inside it and to the north. Further build-up behind this range occurred both during the monastic period and afterwards. The result is that the present slope bears little relation to the much steeper one up which the Norman cavalry would have had to charge. Elsewhere, a range of cellarage was required in order to provide a level platform for a new and larger kitchen. Finally the topography of the outer court was to be transformed after the dissolution when Sir Anthony Browne, the new

1.   *The southern undercroft of the dormitory range, looking north*

owner, levelled and extended the courtyard. Hitherto the surviving undercroft of the cellarer's range and the adjacent buildings had been above ground having been built on the hillside itself. Sir Anthony now built up the ground to produce a large level courtyard, and in so doing buried the windows on the north side of the range and those belonging to the covered passage-way that ran north from the cellarer's range.

Little survives of the Norman buildings of Battle Abbey, for most of them were destroyed in the thirteenth century, when the monastic buildings were rebuilt on a much grander scale. Later, further destruction took place in the aftermath of the dissolution of the monastery. Of the monastic church, a fragment of its west end still survives where it adjoined the abbot's house and where therefore it could function as a buttress to the house after the dissolution (Pl. 2). The rest of the church was then destroyed although the base of the south aisle wall and its foundations were uncovered in 1813 when a path was cut through the site of the nave.[13] The plan of the eastern arm of the Norman church was established in Brakspear's excavations of 1929–30. From his small-scale trenches, he was able to produce a conjectural plan, that has recently received confirmation from work on the site of part of the south transept. The remains of the eastern part of the Norman church have been heavily disturbed by the construction of a new and longer eastern arm as well as by the destruction at the time of the dissolution and by subsequent root disturbance. But despite these problems the evidence suggests that it was apsidal, and possessed an ambulatory around the apse, from which radiated a series of three chapels. The easternmost of these was excavated and this showed that its walls were strengthened by a series of pilaster buttresses. Both transepts had single apsidal chapels.[14] This arrangement of the eastern arm is confirmed by the seal of abbot Odo (1175–1200), which portrays the church from the north with the roof-line ascending in a series of steps: the low roofs of the chapels, the higher aisle roof and then the high main roof of the choir. The seal also suggests the regular use of pilaster buttresses.[15] Both the nave wall and the walls of the transept chapel possessed an internal chamfered plinth. The church walls were constructed with wide rubble footings, but the walls themselves seem to have been thin and of fine ashlar construction. There was a wide cross arch between each bay of the aisle, and the latter was vaulted.

These few sad remnants of the church can, nevertheless, still hint at the building's importance. It was one of the earliest major Norman churches in England. The monastery was in existence by 1070 or 1071[16] and the eastern arm of the church was probably in use in 1076 when Abbot Gausbert was blessed before the altar of St Martin, the monastery's patron saint, at Battle.[17] The design of the church was thus a product of the early 1070's, which probably makes Battle the first church in England to incorporate the combination of an eastern apse, ambulatory and radiating chapels. Such a combination was to be common in the great Norman churches that were subsequently built in England, as at St Augustine's at Canterbury, Bury St Edmunds, or Gloucester, but it was not common in Normandy where the great churches usually terminated

2. *The surviving fragment of the west end of the Norman church, viewed from the north-east*

in three parallel apses. Its use at Battle may reflect the influences of the monks of Marmoutier who were brought over to establish the new abbey and who came from a part of France where this design was common.[18] The early date of the abbey church is also relevant when considering its size. With its length of 225 feet, it may have seemed small by comparison to such churches as St Augustine's, Canterbury (349 ft.), Norwich Cathedral (440 ft.) or Winchester Cathedral (533 ft.),[19] but they were not started during the first decade after the Conquest. The beginning of the new cathedral at Winchester in 1079, seems to usher in a new and much larger scale of church building. But what may have appeared to be modest in the 1080s or 1090s may not have appeared so in the 1070s, and perhaps the chronicler was right to describe the abbey church as 'in those days thought an outstanding building'.[20] The building of the church seems to have run into various delays but it was eventually consecrated in 1094.[21] Thereafter, the only alterations recorded by the chronicler concerned the leading of the roof and the enrichment of the interior.[22]

Even less is known about the Norman conventual buildings than about those of the abbey church. The monk's buildings were constructed by abbot Gausbert (1076–1095) and were evidently small and simple. The chronicler in describing them stated that 'he constructed in them nothing ostentatious, as is the way of many, nothing marvellous, but being at home in spirit only with humble things, he sought the humble'.[23] The writer, in the later twelfth century, seems to have made virtue out of necessity, for its buildings evidently compared unfavourably with those of other monasteries. It was not therefore surprising, that in the following century the monks should decide to rebuild their abbey on a new and much grander scale.

One building which survived until the dissolution, albeit in a much altered form, was the chapter house. It was destroyed after the dissolution but has now been excavated (Pl. 3). The chapter house was built against the south wall of the south transept and on the other side it abutted an earlier version of the dormitory range. It was a large apsidal building, with the apse strengthened externally by a series of wall buttresses. As in the church, these pilasters rose from the foundations and not from any containing plinth. The early form of the building and its plan would suggest that this was the building in which abbot Henry was buried in 1102. His was one of two documented burials in the chapter house,[24] although altogether six have been found there.

Outside the claustral area, however, fragments of Norman building may still be seen standing above ground. Most of the abbey's precinct wall still survives, although not all of it dates from this period. The chronicle records that the enclosure wall was first completed by abbot Ralph (1107–1124) who also enlarged the courtyard (presumably the outer court) and surrounded it with new buildings.[25] Of the Norman buildings in the outer courtyard, there still remains a tower, or possibly entrance tower, incorporated into the later gatehouse range, and fragments of a building lying east of the later 'Court House'.

Such are the scanty remains of the first century of Battle Abbey, but even less

The chapter house excavations from the east

survives of the only major rebuilding recorded by the chronicle. It records that abbot Walter de Luci (1139–1171) pulled down the humble earlier cloister walks and replaced them by cloisters built with columns and pavements of polished marble.[26] Later remodelling or subsequent destruction has removed the evidence, although some of the recently excavated capitals and architectural fragments may well have come from de Luci's cloisters. In addition to rebuilding the cloisters, this abbot had arranged before his death for the construction of a new *lavatorium* or wash place, which was to be built to the same design as the cloisters. This would seem to have been one of the separate free-standing buildings such as were found in several monasteries at this time, particularly in south-east England. Battle Abbey's own daughter-house of St Nicholas, Exeter, also had such a building, the capitals of which would seem to bear a close resemblance to some found recently at Battle.[27]

It was the thirteenth century, however, that was to see the great transformation of the abbey and the construction of most of the surviving buildings. The nature of our evidence now changes, for although we no longer have the chronicle, we do at least have much of the buildings. During this century, most of the buildings around the cloister were rebuilt, and on a much larger and grander scale: first the abbot's range and the monk's dormitory, then the refectory and the kitchen, while at some time the chapter house was remodelled and the church was extended. Such a grandiose rebuilding reflected several developments in the history of the abbey. For some time, the existing buildings had seemed inadequate, and the chronicle had contrasted their humble buildings with those of other monasteries. But Battle was now in a much better position to do something about this long-standing grievance. The colonization of the Weald and the reorganization of her estate administration enabled Battle to benefit, perhaps more than most landlords, from the high rents and increased rentals of the period.[28] In addition, its revenue was now more secure. In 1211 the abbey had acquired control of its land during a vacancy and effective control of the appointment of the new abbot, while in 1235 a compromise with the bishop of Chichester removed a legal conflict that must have been a financial strain.[29] But such developments helped both to strengthen the abbey's financial resources and to turn its back on a wider world. It may be significant that after 1215, and by contrast to the previous century and a half, the abbots seem to have been local men, many of whom had already served as monastic officials. It was to be one of these—either abbot Richard (1215–1235), previously the almoner, or more probably abbot Ralph of Coventry (1235–61), formerly the cellarer—who was to begin the great rebuilding programme.

The new abbot's hall and the new dormitory seem so similar in style that it seems most useful to see them as part of a continuous building programme. They both use, for example, simple round-headed doorways in buildings which are otherwise characteristically Early English in style. The architectural evidence would suggest that they were constructed at some time during the second quarter of the thirteenth century. The abbot's or west range has already been the subject of a detailed examination.[30] On the ground floor it comprised an open porch and a series of vaulted rooms serving as an outer parlour and for other accommodation. The main rooms, however, were on the first floor. Here was the main hall with at one end a chamber with chapel above it, and at the other end, at right angles to the hall, was a large chamber with adjacent small chapel. There were also some rooms that have since disappeared. Despite the disguise of subsequent medieval and post-medieval alterations, we still have here a remarkably complete example of an abbot's house of this date.

But perhaps the most impressive remains of the abbey are to be found in the contemporary new dormitory, or eastern, range. Even today, it provides a fitting reminder of the abbey's wealth and pretensions, and of its ability to overcome the problems posed by its founder's choice of site (Pl. 4). The range has lost its roof and its north end, but otherwise it survives almost intact. The dormitory itself was, as was usual, on the first floor and was raised on a series of four undercrofts, whose identifications are doubtful but are traditionally referred to as: the parlour, the warming house, an unidentified room and the novices' room. They were clearly rooms of importance, as is reflected in the fine carved heads of the corbels in the warming house or in the simple grandeur of the novices' quarters (Pl. 1). The height of the latter room was a product of the steeply falling hill side on which it was built and of the need to keep a level floor for the dormitory which ran the whole length of the range. The height of

4. *The dormitory range from the south-east, with remains of the adjacent reredorter range*

the room seems to have produced a change of design. The marks of a vaulting shaft on its eastern wall suggest that originally it may have been designed with a smaller bay size and with the vault therefore being carried on two lines of columns; like the other rooms of the range, but unlike the single line of columns that was eventually built. But the room has undergone many subsequent alterations and still poses many problems: not the least of which is its use. It possessed a fireplace, a stairway to the reredorter block, and its main entrance would seem to have been from the west. The great long dormitory which ran the length of the range, had two entrances: the main entrance from a stairway to the cloisters, and a small entrance with a spiral staircase on its eastern side. It was lit by a series of lancet windows, both along its side walls and at its south gable end (Pl. 5). The windows were glazed except below the transoms where there were shutters. Traces of its decoration survived until the nineteenth century: a geometric pattern of plain floor tiles and the wall plastered and painted with 'masonry joints'.[31] At the north end of the room, the rise of the hillside was such that had the dormitory floor been level, there would have been inadequate space for the parlour below. But although only one shaft survives of the windows above the parlour, it is much shorter and starts well above the level of those of the other dormitory windows. This would suggest that here the floor was stepped up above the general level, in order to create the

5.   *The dormitory from the north*

necessary space below. East of the parlour, and running at right angles to the dormitory range, was a small vaulted room with benched seating; it was probably a porch.

The construction of this new dormitory range was accompanied by that of a new reredorter range. Although most of the latter had subsequently been destroyed, evidence for it survived on the wall of the dormitory range and in the arches and piers that remained from its southern wall. Now excavations have revealed further substantial remains (Pl. 6). The building ran eastwards from the south end of the dormitory, so that the monks would have access to the latrines from their own accommodation. Because of the latter's height, the reredorter also had to be a very tall building. On its ground floor was a tall vaulted room, with a hooded stone fireplace, and with windows, which were probably glazed, and doors along its northern side. The function of this room is not known, although it would seem to have been a room of importance. Behind the room, and on the outside of the monastery lay the main drain. On the first floor would have been a large room along one side of which would have been a line of latrines that would have emptied into the drain below. In addition, and at an intermediate level were two small additional latrines one of which had access from outside the building to the north and the other which was entered by a staircase from the novices' quarters. The drain itself, which ran the length of the building, was stone lined, but had a solid wall on only one side. On the outside there were a series of great open stone arches, presumably in order to economize on the use of stone.[32] The flow in the drain would be maintained by timber shuttering at the base of the openings of the arches. Some of the slots for timbers to hold such shuttering in place may still be seen. The reredorter block had been built on a steeply sloping hillside so that considerable levelling was required, both inside and outside the building.

Later in the thirteenth century, a new building programme was begun when a new frater, or refectory, was built. At the same time, the adjacent parts of the cloisters were rebuilt. Most of this work was destroyed at sometime after the dissolution, but the plan of the building has been established and some important fragments still survive above ground. Its west end still survives, albeit in a damaged form with its interior panelling, the fragmentary jambs of its west window and the jamb of one of its side windows. We also possess the rear panelling of two bays of the cloister, where it still remains in the wall of the abbot's house and which includes provision for the construction of a stone vault (Pl. 7). But enough survives to point to the very high quality of the work, and also to its similarity to the work in the new east end at Bayham Abbey (Sussex), built in about the 1260s.[33] Together with the refectory we should also consider the new kitchen. This survived until 1685 when it was pulled down and its materials sold.[34] Its plan, however, was established by Brakspear's excavations. Its only surviving architectural details are in its cellar, and this is inaccessible at present, but a new kitchen was evidently being planned in 1279 when timber was being cut for it.[35] The plan would suggest it was a large square building consisting of a central kitchen area and hearths, surrounded by four

6.   *The reredorter excavations from the west. The reredorter drain is on the right*

7. *The view across the site of the cloisters, showing the west end of the refectory and the rear panelling of the west cloister walk.*

other lower ranges. On the lower, southern side a cellar had to be built in order to create a level platform for the building.

It was probably also in the later thirteenth century that the church received its great new eastern arm. Although this was razed to the ground at the dissolution, three crypts at its east end were uncovered in 1817, when they were believed to belong to the Conqueror's church, and parts of the choir were uncovered by Brakspear.[36] The seven-bay extension was 152 feet in length and must have been a much needed lengthening to what had hitherto been a small church. It would seem to have had a *chevet* of five radiating chapels, although two of these have not yet been tested for, and the deep buttresses would suggest that the walls supported a stone vault. Unfortunately, we possess no documentary evidence and little architectural evidence for the dating of this new work. The latter is, moreover, ambiguous and has suggested both thirteenth- and early fourteenth-century dates. In the light of this uncertainty we should perhaps turn to the very distinctive ground plan, which would suggest a derivation from Henry III's rebuilding of Westminster Abbey, the eastern arm of which was built between 1246 and 1259.[37] For Battle stands as an isolated example of a chevet in south-east England, and there is nothing in the history of the abbey at this period to suggest any likelihood of continental contacts, such as could have led her to derive the plan directly from France. Westminster would seem the most likely source of Battle's unusual plan, and this in turn would suggest that it was begun in the later thirteenth century, when

Henry's great new church was still at the centre of architectural attention.[38]

The remodelling of the chapter house should probably also be ascribed to the thirteenth century, and particularly to its latter half. It seems improbable that such an important building would have been left unaltered at a time when so much else was being rebuilt on such a grander scale, and the limited evidence available would seem to tally with such a dating. The almost complete destruction of this building at the dissolution and afterwards, has, however, left us with a very incomplete picture of these alterations. A broad stone bench and a higher narrower offset, such as could have provided the base for wall arcading, were added around the inside of the building. The building would thus have acquired features that were normal in chapter houses of this period. We know very little about what happened above this level. Window glass of a very high quality and of later thirteenth century date was, however, installed, and this suggests the liklihood that the Norman windows themselves may have been replaced as part of a major modernization of the building at this period.[39]

Such were the buildings that can certainly or probably be ascribed to the period of the great rebuilding in the thirteenth century. But there are others for which no date can be provided. This particularly applies to a group of buildings which lay to the east of the chapter house and dormitory, but are now hidden below the ground in an area still largely untouched by excavations. To the north-east of the chapter house lay a building whose function is unclear. It post-dates the former building and a series of stone-lined drains, some of which it blocked, and it was probably not part of the monastic church. A sacristy might provide a possible identification. To the east of the parlour lay a complex that probably included the infirmary buildings. The first building was a large free-standing one, which lay askew the main axis of the monastery and for which space was made by creating a large artificial platform. Its size and position would suggest that this might have been an infirmary hall. The character of its footings does not suggest that it belonged to one of the later stages of monastic building, and it may have been destroyed before the dissolution in order to make way for another major range that lay to the east. The latter has completely disappeared except where a small section of walling just protrudes through the grass, but it was trenched in the nineteenth century when it was erroneously believed to have been the chapter house. It would have appeared to be a two-storey building and with at least three chambers on the ground floor, two of which were each 70 feet in length. At least one room possessed a fireplace, the base of which may still be seen. We possess a nineteenth-century plan of this range,[40] but it is not clear how accurate this is. It suggests, however, that it would have been difficult, although not impossible, for this and the partially excavated 'infirmary' building to have existed together, and that the former may have been partly built on the site of the latter. To the south of the former range, and probably associated with it, was a small vaulted room, which was subsequently destroyed or hidden by the construction of the ice house. This is evidently an area of considerable potential interest. There was one other building in the church area which is known from fifteenth- and sixteenth-century documents but not from excavation, and this was the monastic bell tower.[41]

This rapid rebuilding of the abbey was not, however, confined to the claustral area. To the monks of the thirteenth century, the outer court and its buildings must also have seemed inadequate. In order to overcome the restricted nature of the hill top, new buildings were erected on the hillside to the south. The 'cellarer's range' was later incorporated in Sir Anthony Browne's new range and part of it still survives as a series of vaulted undercrofts. It had an upper storey, and the undercrofts were originally above ground on both sides. The latter consisted both of store rooms and, at the east end, of a group of rooms of a more domestic or office character, with fireplaces, windows on both sides and a passageway leading to the monastery. To the north, another vaulted room was recorded in the nineteenth century.[42] Further west along the hillside were another two ranges. One of these incorporated a large blocked doorway, such as would have been suitable for carts, and was probably a barn.

The most dominating feature of the outer courtyard did not appear, however, until the fourteenth century, when the great gatehouse was built (Pl. 8). A licence to crenellate was granted in 1338 and it was probably built soon afterwards.[43] When completed it must have dominated town and courtyard alike. But although it survives so completely, the rest of the monastic court has been transformed out of recognition since the dissolution.

The main gatehouse viewed from the outer courtyard.

Such were the main monastic buildings at the end of the great rebuilding. In many ways its plan was typical of the great Benedictine houses. But its remains still remind us that such normality could only be achieved at great expense, as the demands of this wealthy community so far outstripped the restricted site that their founder had given them. What is remarkable is that in about a century—and most was done in much less than this—a virtually complete new monastery had been built and on such a grand and opulent scale. It is not a century that has left a chronicle or an image of Battle as an exemplar of the monastic ideal,[44] but it evidently produced administrators of note and in its buildings has left us much to admire.

It was not surprising that after this period of hectic activity, the later Middle Ages should appear as a period of quietude in which the pace of building was much slower. The monks now had buildings which were generally large enough. The latter would now generally be modified rather than rebuilt. In the abbot's house, and at the same time as the new gatehouse was being built, new accommodation was built over the earlier porch. In the dormitory, the addition of a small new window later in the century, points to a subdivision of this great room. But we are faced with two main problems in assessing the extent of building operations in this period: alterations, both major and minor ones, could have disappeared without trace, particularly since so many of the buildings survive in only a fragmentary state; and some of the buildings that we have already discussed cannot be accurately dated and may belong here. Despite these difficulties, it is clear that building continued. In the fifteenth-century, Battle, like so many other abbeys, decided to extend the abbot's accommodation. The old first floor hall was replaced by an adjacent larger and grander ground floor one. It has lost its original roof and window tracery, but still remains an impressive reminder of the continued building activity of the English monasteries in their last century, or more, of existence. Together with the hall, a new kitchen was built between the hall and the earlier main kitchen, and which would have served the abbot's household. The fifteenth century was also to see the construction of a new west cloister walk, which was under way in 1421.[45]

It was the dissolution of the abbey in 1538 that was to inaugurate the next stage in the history of the monastic buildings. The political power of the abbot in East Sussex was to be inherited by the new owner, Sir Anthony Browne, and the monastic site was transformed to fit in with his needs. His intention was to make Battle the centre of his new power, and this was symbolized in his building works at the abbey and in the erection of a magnificent tomb in the parish church there. At the abbey, the monastic church was razed to the ground, but other buildings continued in use. The old outer and inner courts now reversed their roles. It was to be the outer court that was to provide the main residence, both in the remodelled abbot's house and in the great new range which he built above the cellarer's undercrofts. Finally the gap between the hilltop and the latter range was filled in, thus burying the ground floor undercrofts. By contrast the claustral area, which had for so long been the centre of the monastery, now took over the functions of the old outer court providing the service and storage areas for the new lord. The reredorter and dormitory blocks survived but with other uses, the latter acting as a barn in the following century. New buildings were constructed but with low stone, tile and mortar footings for what would have been timber structures: so different in character from the monastic buildings. In the course of this transformation layers full of monastic debris were deposited outside the reredorter. It was a debris which included large quantities of metal work, worked bone, pot and glass, and which when studied should shed much light on the monastic world at the dissolution. The history of the site and of its buildings was not yet over, and it is a story that is of sufficient interest to justify a paper to itself. But we have already travelled far in time, though not in place, from the Anglo-Norman world. The dissolution provides an appropriate end. Some of the monastic buildings would live on, but William the Conqueror's great monastic legacy had been finally destroyed.

William fitz Osbern and the endowment of his abbey of Lyre

S. F. HOCKEY, O.S.B.

The abbey of Lyre in the diocese of Evreux does not rank with Jumièges and Saint-Wandrille, for it had only been founded in 1046.[1] If it has left little imprint on the general history of French monasticism, its name is constantly coming before the notice of researchers into English royal and episcopal records. A monk of Lyre in about 1739, transcribing some of the abbey archives into a big register, concluded his work with a declaration of the temporalities of Lyre made in 1684 and renewed in 1692:

> 'Formerly the abbey possessed in England 3 or 4 priories, 48 churches with their advowsons, 11 chapels, 40 seigneurial demesne tithes, the tithe on 3 forests, two manors and in three or four places a carucate of land. And the abbots of Lyre were canons of Hereford.'[2]

What is interesting about this extensive endowment is that almost all of it dates from the earliest years after the Conquest, well before the compilation of the Domesday record. William fitz Osbern needs no presentation here. He and his wife Adelise had founded two monasteries, Lyre *c.*1046 in the diocese of Evreux and Cormeilles *c.*1060 in that of Lisieux. William intended to be buried at Lyre, where his wife was buried in the year of the Conquest; in the event, after fitz Osbern was killed at Cassel in Flanders in 1071, his body was brought back to Cormeilles. What is undoubtedly the primitive endowment of Lyre can be conveniently recovered from the confirmation charter of Henry II: 16 churches with tithes, mills and rents, all in the diocese of Evreux.[3] Then, at the Conquest, some twenty years after the foundation, Lyre was to share in fitz Osbern's newly won possessions, for Lyre, like almost all the Norman abbeys, was insufficiently endowed. They seem to have accepted gratefully grants in England without much consideration of how they were to exploit these distant sources of revenue.[4]

Since fitz Osbern was dead by 1071, these English benefactions to Lyre must count among the earliest from the Norman knights to the Norman abbeys. Lyre held the highest number of churches recorded in Domesday and appears there also as the greatest recipient of ecclesiastical tithes.[5] More interesting is the fact that the geographical distribution of these churches follows the career of their donor and marks out the spheres of his activity, first in the Isle of Wight and then in the Welsh marches, where he penetrated as far as the principality of Gwent. To plot out a map of the places named in Herefordshire, Worcestershire, Monmouthshire and part of Gloucestershire would probably show the boundaries of his palatine power; his earldom dated from 1067. Rather than encumber this paper with place-names, we have appended them all in their modern form as a sort of gazetteer, where we feel sure that the very listing of so many scattered benefactions will be more impressive than any description of them.

William, fitz Osbern was killed in Flanders, as we have said, in 1071 and his body brought back for solemn burial at Cormeilles. His brother Osbern was to succeed Leofric as bishop of Exeter in 1073, ordained by Lanfranc. Of William's children, William de Breteuil succeeded to the Norman lands; though he died in the monastic habit at Bec in 1102, he was buried at Lyre.[6] Roger, the second son, Roger fitz William, became lord of the Isle of Wight and earl of Hereford. Against the wishes of William the Conqueror, the daughter Emma in 1075 married the ill-fated Ralph de Gael, earl of Norfolk, around whom opposition to the Conqueror was very soon to gather. We have three moving letters from Lanfranc, begging Roger to desist from open rebellion.[7] In the event the rising of 1175 was soon crushed; Ralph escaped from Norwich to Brittany; Roger forfeited all his lands and spent long years in prison.[8] The lordship of the Isle of Wight was next granted to Richard de Redvers, from Reviers (Calvados) in the Cotentin peninsula. He confirmed to the abbey of Lyre all that fitz Osbern had granted to it, without himself substantially adding to it, though many of the lords who had come with him to the Island from the Cotentin were to become benefactors of Lyre. As for the Welsh marches, there also the possessions of Lyre remained intact when the earldom was suppressed.

After the time of fitz Osbern there seem to have been only two significant benefactors of Lyre in Herefordshire. In the Hereford Domesday we find a tenant, Hugh Asinus (Asne, Lasne, Lane) holding 39½ hides by grant of the Conqueror; in the hundred of Radlow he held also as many as nineteen manors, with one more in the hundred of Sulcet. Among the Radlow manors appear the names of Hope, i.e. Fownhope, and Credenhill: these appear later among the Lyre records. More important is the marginal note to an unlocated hide: *Acla monacorum de Lira*.[9] It was here at Aclea, Lyre Ocle, Livers Ocle that the monks were later to set up a priory. From the royal licence this donation to the monks can be dated to 1 December 1100.[10] In the rental of the Lyre properties the entries for Hope and Credenhill are preceded by the rubric *H. Asinus*, to distinguish them from the donations of earl William.[11] As a distinguished benefactor his name appears in the obit-roll of the monks of Lyre on 22 October.[12]

The endowment of Lyre was to extend into two more counties through the benefactions of Robert le Bossu, earl of Leicester, count of Meulan, who inherited his father's lands in 1118. By his marriage to Amice, a granddaughter of William fitz Osbern, daughter of Emma and Ralph de Gael, he received as her dowry the fitz Osbern lordship of Breteuil. Amice had earlier been contracted to marry Richard, king Henry's son, who was lost in the *White Ship* in 1120. In 1121 she married Robert le Bossu, on whom king Stephen was to confer the borough of Hereford, though not the earldom. No doubt it was in consequence of becoming lord of Breteuil, that he added to the endowment of Lyre some churches in the soke of Hinckley in Leicestershire, with a pension from the church of Nuneaton (Warw.), and in Dorset three more churches with land near Wareham, at Shapwick and Kingston Lacy, as well as other churches in Normandy. This benefaction to Lyre is, however, insignificant among his total bounty, for he was the founder of N. D. du Désert in 1125, destined to be united to Lyre in 1233, and, in England, of St Mary du Pré in Leicester for the Augustinians, Garendon for the Cistercians, a Benedictine priory at Luffield and a nunnery for Fontévrault at Nuneaton, where Amice became a nun in her widowhood.[13]

After this, in England, Lyre was to receive no more benefactions of any importance. The abbey now held churches and tithes with some land in ten counties and in six dioceses: Winchester, Worcester, Hereford, Lincoln, Salisbury and Llandaff. It was an endowment which had cost the donors but little. Occasionally we find fitz Osbern disposing of his tenants' land, for example at Marcle, Feckenham, Bushley and Eldersfield. In Berkshire it was as an ordinary tenant-in-chief that he held land and was to grant to Lyre the churches of Shinfield, Swallowfield and Basildon. And here we must not lose sight of the fact that fitz Osbern had also founded Cormeilles and was also increasing the endowment of that abbey, even if less spectacularly. All the archives of that monastery were lost in a fire in the thirteenth century and details of its English property, even of its line of abbots, have to be recovered through the priory at Newent (Gloucs.).[15]

It is now time to enquire how the abbey in Normandy collected the revenue from these fragmented and scattered sources: churches, land, pensions. All the churches paid pensions which remained fixed; these could be as high as £26 or as little as half a mark. Their origin is certainly to be sought in the foundation of churches by local lords to serve their estates. In this way the churches were considered as a form of property, which the lord could control and from which he was entitled to a form of rent, for the church was 'in his gift'. Similarly, tithes could be granted away or sold. *Spiritualia* and *temporalia* were thus much confused, but at this very period the canon lawyers were already busy transforming the ancient proprietary system by introducing the notion of advowson, which implied duties towards the churches. The abbey and convent of Lyre were to be patrons with regard to their English churches, thus holding a very considerable amount of patronage. By these 'presentative advowsons', Lyre presented its nominee for its church to the bishop, who then proceeded to institute him, ordering his archdeacon to induct him to the benefice and its temporalities. This right to nominate was acknowledged by the payment of the pension in return. In the cartulary of Carisbrooke we find Lyre acceding to the requests of notabilities, using its right of patronage in favour of a clerk of Savaric de Mauleon to the church of Niton, a chaplain of Philip de Aubenay to

Swallowfield, Philip de Lucy, a kinsman of bishop Godfrey de Lucy, to New-church, a nephew of Peter des Roches also to Newchurch.[16] From the diocese of Evreux, presentations were occasionally made to English churches. In 1267 Godfrey de Clermont, a canon of Lyons, had been granted the church of Fownhope (Heref.) by papal provision. In the presence of Godfrey, the bishop of Hereford ordered him to resign the church to Lyre and to accept a pension of 20 marks from the monks. His place is stated to have been taken by Pierre le Mancel, monk of Lyre. Is this a case of a monk doing parish work?[17] Even as late as 1336 a priest from the diocese of Evreux, Michael de Gastina, was presented to Whippingham and later to Wareham.[18] The abbot was technically the rector; the parishes were staffed by his vicars, whose sufficient maintenance it was the duty of the bishop to approve and to renew. In England it was the procurator who acted for the abbot. He is stated to have had a residence in Castle Street, Hereford.[19] Complicated as all this may seem, it was nothing in comparison to the question of tithes.

The tithes which Robert le Bossu mentioned in his well-known letter to pope Alexander III in 1168/81, must be the same tithes in Dorset which he after-wards gave to Lyre. The earl tells the pope how his father had first given them to the monks of Préaux, but, because they found them troublesome to collect, they exchanged them for an estate at Spettisbury.[20] After himself enjoying the revenue from these tithes for some years, the earl had scruples about retaining them and finally presented them to Lyre. Although Lyre must have already gained a certain experience of tithes after more than a century of ownership in England, the monks accepted them.

Tithes had been divided by custom into greater and lesser, to ensure that something would be retained for the priest, although clearly the greater tithes (corn, hay, wood) could in certain regions be of less value than the smaller tithes (wool in particular). A tenth of agricultural income was in any case valuable, but it had to be collected and collection was difficult on distant properties. Some twenty-five years ago R. Lennard used the references to the Lyre properties of Herefordshire and Worcestershire as given in Domesday, to demonstrate that the grant of tithes *cum rustico* or *cum homine* indicated a man to collect the tithe.[21] This is expressly stated in the cartulary of Carisbrooke: *unum hominem quietum et liberum cum terra qui decimam custodiat*, while the *et unum hominem* appears eight times in the section for Hereford and Worcester.[22] Even if agricultural produce is wealth, it is bulky, while it can be stored and preserved only for a limited time against damp, vermin or thieves. Lyre was in Normandy and not near the coast; money is the only really mobile form of wealth. It is often asked how were these eggs and vegetables and cheeses disposed of. By chance there is in a Winchester register for 1333 a licence for Lyre to sell tithes to suitable persons.[23] Such licences were perhaps customary, almost automatic, and hence not normally thought worth entering into a bishop's register. 'Suitable persons' may well mean just not in the public market, or to men who would pay a proper price. There was, however, a natural and urgent tendency to accept a money payment in lieu of tithes; this involved less odium than going into the field to check the surrender of the tenth sheaf. But in any such bargaining over a commutation the monks stood in the weaker position. The tithes of the land between the Usk and the Wye, the ancient kingdom of Gwent, were already divided equally between Lyre and Cormeilles; Lyre farmed out its share permanently for a half of this half.[24] But even at the time of the loss of the alien priories, Lyre was still collecting some tithes in kind.[25]

Following the usual solution for the problem, Lyre set up priories to safe-guard its properties, appointing a procurator to act for the abbot in England. When Baldwin de Redvers I confirmed to Hildearius of Lyre all the abbey's Isle of Wight possessions, he allowed him to send monks for a foundation should he wish.[26] This charter is to be dated 1142–1147, hence Carisbrooke was probably set up soon after that time. Then followed the other priories, Lyres Ocle (Heref.) and Llangua (Monm.) which cared for the fitz Osbern endowment, Hinckley (Leics.) and Wareham (Dorset) the Leicester endowment. They were not intended to be true foundations, but were manned from the mother-house: at the most 5 monks at Carisbrooke, 2 or even 1 at the other priories, so much so that one often reads that there is no evidence for a priory, though Llangua held 480 acres of land.[27] The inventories in time of war also indicate the smallness of the personnel in these establishments. But even if the priories were small and mere collecting stations, the procurator is found in activity, though only rarely discovered by name. He was frequently changed, at times was prior of Carisbrooke. One procurator, Richard de Aldereya, left Hinckley to become a Dominican.[28] Administrative work, collection of revenue, supervision of churches, maintenance of chancels and perhaps particularly the settlement of disputes kept him a busy man, even in time of peace. By contrast, Cormeilles could concentrate everything around the priory of Newent.

It will be useful at this stage to consider what the mother-house in Normandy reckoned to receive from England, in spite of the trouble and expense of collecting. From the royal exchequer both Cormeilles and Lyre received annu-ally £12 at Hereford and £9-5s. at Southampton; they shared equally the tithes of Gwent. In the rental already mentioned, which is to be dated mid-thirteenth century rather than twelfth century as in the Bibliothèque Nationale catalogue, Lyre stated that its revenue from England was £180 22s. 2d., i.e. £181 2s. 2d., which is an appreciable sum in medieval money, whether gross or net. From this rental a few sum-totals can be extracted:

fo.168r—from the dioceses of Hereford, Worcester and Llandaff £60 0s. 2d.

fo.168v—from the Island, excluding tithes £15.

fo.169r—from land at Freshwater £1 6s. 8d.

> —*Summa extra Insula*, i.e. collected at Carisbrooke, but deriving from Hants. and Berks. £16.

fo.169v—from Hinckley 20 marks, i.e. £13 6s. 8d.

fo.170r—total procuration in Hereford £60+£19 10s. 6d., in all 118 marks 4s. 2d.

> —revenue of Lyre in England: £181 2s. 2d.

One might note immediately that Sheen charterhouse, the successor to Carisbrooke, was able later to farm out that priory for £133 6s. 8d.[29] The *Taxacio Nicholai IV* carefully distinguishes temporalities from the spiritualities of Lyre according to their diocese, detailing the pensions. On a rough calculation, granted that the figures are unreliable or incomplete, for they rarely coincide with those of the rental, the spiritual revenue constitutes 80 per cent of the whole income of Lyre in England. The cost of maintaining the priories was deducted from the revenue available to produce the 'apport'. Difficulties in transferring the funds begin after 1204 and increase with the war with France from 1242–3.[30]

The costs of litigation in defence of all this dispersed endowment must have been very high. There does not seem ever to have been a head-on collision with any of the different diocesans with whom Lyre must have had to negotiate questions of patronage. When Thomas de Cantilupe of Hereford was in conflict with archbishop John Peckham, he retired to Lyre abbey in 1279, remaining there for close on two years. But the bishops of Hereford were canons of Evreux, just as the abbots of Lyre were canons of Hereford.[31] The cathedral of Hereford did, however, have a dispute with Lyre over tithes and churches. When in 1269 the abbot of Lyre granted to bishop John le Breton the advowson of the church of Shinfield with the chapel of Swallowfield (Berks.) and the pension of 3 marks due from them, the bishop handed over this grant and pension to the dean and chapter of his cathedral. The bishop of Salisbury, Herbert le Poor, had then approved a pension of 40s. on Shinfield as due to the abbey. By 1286, however, the procurator was disputing with the dean and chapter over the tithes of Lyre Ocle and the pension on Shinfield, since this pension had not been paid to the dean and chapter for over 15 years, following on some exchange over tithes. The bishop of Hereford, Richard Swinfield, arbitrated: the procurator was to retain the tithes in question, paying 40s. from their *camera* in Hereford at Michaelmas, without waiting for the pension from Shinfield to arrive and deducting expenses. The damages due to the dean and chapter for the arrears were assessed at 35 marks. Later Adam de Orleton secured a lease of the tithes of these places for £20 annually to Lyre; when he became bishop of Worcester, he was able by papal dispensation to retain them, for they had been granted only for the time he held the see of Hereford.[32]

It was with religious houses that most of the complications arose over the rights of the abbey in England. In 1132 Baldwin de Redvers gave the land of Arreton (I. Wight) to his own foundation of Quarr abbey, thus causing an awkward monastic situation since the tithes of this place had already been granted to Lyre by fitz Osbern. Hildearius, abbot of Lyre (1142–47), came to England and settled that the Savigniac monks of Quarr should keep these tithes and pay annually 40s. to Carisbrooke.[33] On the same visit to England the abbot of Lyre agreed that Tewkesbury abbey should keep the tithes of Forthampton (Gloucs.), Bushley (Worcs.) and Queenhill (Worcs.) in exchange for a pension of 2½ marks. As so often, this was later to be revised.[34] With Tintern a dispute over the tithes of Tidenham (Gloucs.) was settled by the grant of ½ acre of land instead of the tithe of a meadow.[35] Similarly with Bordesley abbey a claim to the tithe on three crofts in Tenbury (Worcs.) and Feckenham (Heref.) was settled by a composition.[36] A dispute with the monks of Saint-Florent in their priory at Monmouth over the tithes of Mitchel Troy was settled by a pension of 8s., but this pension was perpetually in arrears.[37] There was already strife with the canons of Wimborne in 1184; they had agreed before judges-delegate to grant a pension of 8 marks for retaining the tithes of Shapwick and Kingston (Dorset), but continued the bickering to the extent that at one time the dean was owing 240 marks to the prior of Wareham. There are two papal bulls on this question.[38] Compositions settled other disputes with the abbot of Saint-Vincent du Mans over the church of Grosmont (Monm.) in 1190, with the prior of Abergavenny and the prior of Little Malvern in 1236 over the church of Hanley Castle (Worcs.), farmed to them for 16 marks.[39] A duel was even fought over the right to the advowson of Tenbury (Worcs.) church and its 9 acres of glebe, when the rights of Lyre were upheld.[40] In 1346, before judges-delegate, Lyre was obliged to renounce its claims to tithes of mills, woods and quarries in favour of the priories of Nuneaton (Warw.) and to accept 3s. 4d. payable at Hinckley.[41] But this is only a selection from the trials and troubles of the procurator of Lyre. If it has been tedious, it will well illustrate the situation of a foreign monk in charge of upholding a Norman abbey in its rights. How much simpler to have been given a few manors, if possible adjoining!

For one moment more, let us look under a glass at just one village. Shorwell (I. Wight) was a daughter-church of the church of Carisbrooke itself and so adjoining. The patronage of the church was long disputed, notably in 1205 with Walter de Insula. It also sought to show its independence by trying to secure its own cemetery, and grasped this privilege in 1430 as soon as Lyre was no longer in control. It had a boundary dispute with the prior of Carisbrooke in 1321 over the tithes of Wolverton and Atherfield. In 1335 its vicar, Peter de Upton, was claiming the valuable lesser tithes, mainly of lambs and wool, from the manor of the abbess of Lacock, when the prior agreed to pay annually 6s. 8d. to the vicar in order to keep these tithes.[42] Nearby a difficult problem was set when sheep were being pastured in Carisbrooke parish and folded for the night in the parish of Shalfleet. How should the tithe be shared? The papal judges-delegate decided that ⅔ of the tithe should go to the parish where the sheep had pastured.[43] The long tussle between Isabella de Fortibus, the last of the Redvers, and the prior at the priory, with the little valley between them, is well documented. Even so, how much of the argument over rights, the efforts to gather in the arrears of pensions from disgruntled men and the presentation of olive branches and douceurs has remained unrecorded!

After the transfer of the 'apport' became first difficult and then impossible, as relations between England and France deteriorated, Lyre had to take its share in the tribulations of the alien priories. But the abbey did not abandon its English endowment without a struggle and some attempts at salvage. Already in 1271 Lyre had sold to Adam de Stratton for 80 marks all its interests in Bramley (Hants.), which had been farmed out for 106s.[44] In 1315 it recovered the appropriation of Godshill (I. Wight) church and had been acquitted of the accusation of paying £200 to the bishop's nephew in order to secure his consent.[45] In 1405 it allowed Quarr abbey to appropriate the church of Arreton (I. Wight).[46] In the next year Beaulieu abbey sought to appropriate the valuable church of Newchurch, the parish of which stretched from the north to the south coast of the Isle of Wight. Through the clever offices of a lieutenant of the Tower of London a pension of £50, payable in France, was purchased in exchange for an estate at Soberton (Hants.).[47] An earlier plan of Sir John Cheyne to purchase land from Lyre seems to have fallen through.[48]

In 1414 Henry V founded his Carthusian priory at Sheen and in the following April used all the property of Lyre in England, except Hinckley priory, towards its endowment. The king had first offered this to the Celestines, who had refused to accept. The properties of Lyre indeed formed the most valuable part of the income of Sheen. Hinckley was granted to another Carthusian house, to Mountgrace in Yorkshire, hence it was the Carthusians who inherited at the expense of Lyre. Other foreign abbeys whose English priories had also been given to the Carthusians—Jumièges (Hayling Island, Hants.), St Peter's, Ghent (Lewisham) and Evroul (Ware)—collectively appealed to the Council of Constance in 1421 for redress.[49] But Constance had its own urgent business, while the tide kept flowing fast against the interests of the French monasteries. Still, the abbots must have felt they had some chance, for they declared to the Council that the English king had promised the Carthusians a rent of £400 from his domains in the event of their not receiving the property from the priories.[50] Other abbots, meeting probably in Rouen at much the same time, drew up proposals for a direct appeal to Henry V for the recovery of their English properties. In this document it was stated that a monk of Lyre had given the encouraging information that a new parliament was going to look into the question of the priories: the monk hoped that 'something would be done about our revenues'. Simon of Lyre was among the eight abbots who prepared this circular letter.[51] The monk of Lyre who claimed to be thus well informed is hardly likely to have been Odo des Ormes, the last prior of Carisbrooke, who had been granted special permission to stay on in England;[52] perhaps it was Robert de Valeto, accused by Odo of claiming to be procurator of Lyre; or perhaps Richard Bausseyn, the monk of Lyre to whom Sheen granted a pension of £12.[53] But there was no way out of the impasse. The archives of the priories were transferred to Sheen; we have the cartulary in which Sheen just listed the deeds.

Lyre abbey survived this financial crisis, though it had fortunately not been sudden. At the Revolution its interesting set of buildings were demolished and the stone sold.[54] Nothing now remains of William fitz Osbern's abbey at Lyre, nor at Cormeilles where his body lies, but in England a host of churches and place-names continue to recall to the historian his benefactions from his English domains.

GAZETTEER FOR THE PROPERTIES OF LYRE
Churches or chapels in italics; t. for tithes
In NORMANDY (Eure)
Auvergny; Bosc-Hughes; Bordigny, 60 sol. land, t.; *Breteuil*, t.; Chambray, 1 cust. ten.; *Champ-Dominel; Corneuil; Glos-la-Ferrière*, t.; *Gouttières*; Gualon; *La Barre*; Laigle, 1 cust. ten.; *La Neuve Lyre*, (¼), mills; *La Vieille Lyre*, 2 mills, land; *Les Bottereaux*, salt; Loraille; Marnières; *Morainville; Noyen-en-Ouche; Pacy-sur-Eure*; Pîtres, t.; Pont-Audemer, 1 burg.; Pont-St-Pierre, t.; Rubremont; Trisay, mill.
In Rouen 3 ch. in Pont-St-Pierre; market stalls.

26 places; 16 churches

Priory of CARISBROOKE (Isle of Wight)
Afton, t.; Appuldurcombe; Apse, t., 1 virg.; *Arreton*, t.; Atherfield, 5 solid.; Billingham, t.; Bowcombe, t., 1 virg.; Bramley (Hants), t.; Brook, t., 1 virg.; Cadland (New Forest), 1 virg.; *Carisbrooke*, t., pens. 50s.; *Chale*, ½ ch., t.; Chessell, ⅔t.; Chillerton, t.; Chilton, 12½ac.; Compton, t., 1 virg.; *Freshwater*, t., 1 virg.; *Godshill*; Heasley, t.; Knighton, t.; Luccombe, t.; *Newchurch; Newport*; Ningwood, t.; *Niton*, t.; *Northwood*; Nunwell, t.; Osborne, t.; St Lawrence, t.; Shalcombe, t.; Shalfleet, ⅔t.; Sheat, 8½ac.; Shide, t.; *Shorwell; Southampton*, ch. of St John, pens., 2 burg.; Stenbury, t., 1 virg.; Wellow, t.; *Whippingham*; Wike, t.; Winchester, 2 burg.; Wolverton, t.; Wootton, 1 virg.; Wroxall, t., 1 virg.; Yaverland, t.
In Berkshire: *Ashampton*, t.; *Basildon*, 1 virg.; Nether Avon, rents, 1 virg.; *Shinfield; Stratford Tony*, pens.; *Swallowfield*.

50 places; 17 churches

Priory of LIVERS OCLE (Heref.)
Acley (Livers Ocle), rents, 1 hide; Alvington (Gloucs.), t.; *Bridstow* (St Brigid); Bushley (Worcs.), t., 1 virg.; *Chedworth* (Gloucs.), 2 virg.; Credenhill, t.; *Dewsall* (Fonte David), t., 80ac.; Dinedor, t.; Duntisbourne Leer (Gloucs.), 2 hides; *Eardisland*, rents; Eldersfield (Worcs.), t., 1 virg.; Ewyas Harold, t.; *Falley; Feckenham* (Worcs.), t., 1 virg.; 'Fickenappletree' (Worcs.), t.; Forthampton (Gloucs.), t., ½ virg.; *Fownhope*, rents; Gloucester, pens, 2 burg.; *Hanley Castle* (Worcs.), rents; Hardwick (Gloucs.), 1 virg.; Hereford, pens.; Hinton, 1 virg.; King's Caple, t.; Kinlet (Salop.), t., ½ virg.; *Leadon*, ½ virg.; *Linton-by-Ross*, t., rents, 1 virg.; Lugwardine, t., 1 virg.; Malvern (Worcs.), t. of forest; *Much Marcle*, rents, 1 hide; Nass (Gloucs.), t., ½ virg.; Pauntley (Gloucs.), 1 virg.; *Poulton* (Gloucs.), t.; Queenhill (Worcs.), t., ½ virg.; St Briavels (Gloucs.), 1 ten.; *Sapperton* (Gloucs.), t.; Stanford Bishop, t., 1 virg.; *Strangford*; Studley (Warw.), t.; Sutton, 1 virg.; *Tenbury* (Worcs.); Thornbury, t., 1 virg.; *Tidenham* (Gloucs.), rents; Walton (Gloucs.), t.; Westhide or Westwood; *Wilton*, t.; Worcester, pens.

46 places; 16 churches

Priory of LLANGUA (Monm.)
(½t. with Cormeilles)
Abergavenny, rents; Grosmont, t. of forest; Llangua, manor, 4 caruc.; Llantony, t.; Michel Troy, ½t.; Newport, ½t.; Raglan, ½t.; *Striguil* (i.e. Chepstow), ½ ch., t. of toll; Wentwood Forest, ½t.

9 places; 1 church

Priory of HINCKLEY (Leics.)
Attleborough (Warw.), t.; *Dadlington*, rents, 1 virg.; *Fenny Drayton; Higham on the Hill; Hinckley*, t.; Leicester, 1 cust. ten.; *Lindley; Nuneaton* (Warw.), t.; *Sibstone*; Stoke Golding, rents; Studley (Warw.), rents; *Upton; Wallesburgh*; Wigston Magna, rents; *Witherley*.

13 places; 10 churches

Priory of WAREHAM (Dorset)
Blandford, 3 virg.; *East Stoke*; Egliston; *Gussage*, 100 solid.; Kingston, t.; *Knowle; Newburgh*;

Ringwood; Shapwick, t.; Steeple; *Stratford St Mary*; Tyneham; *Wareham*, 3 ch., 1 hide; Whiteway, land; *Winfrifth.*

15 places; 11 churches

Possession in England: 133 places; 55 churches

The Gesta Normannorum Ducum: *a history without an end*

ELISABETH M. C. VAN HOUTS

During the eleventh and twelfth centuries the *Gesta Normannorum Ducum (GND)* were the most widely diffused history of the Norman dukes and therefore of Normandy. In retrospect we can say that Dudo of Saint-Quentin stands at the beginning of a historiographical tradition in Normandy. Dudo was the first historian to write a history of the Norman dukes. During the first decades of the eleventh century he wrote his history now known as *De Moribus et Actis primorum Normannie Ducum*.[1] About sixty years later he was followed by another historian, William of Jumièges, with whom the process of continuing and interpolating the history of the Norman dukes started. Basing himself mainly on Dudo's work, William wrote the history now known as the *Gesta Normannorum Ducum* in about 1070–1 in the monastery of Jumièges.[2] His history went through several versions and adaptations, but was finally reworked by Robert of Torigny in the first half of the twelfth century.[3] During the eleventh and twelfth centuries the history of the Norman dukes circulated in at least forty copies, representing a wide variety of versions. From the medieval library catalogues and the surviving manuscripts we know that the *GND* were spread in England from Durham to Reading and on the Continent from Fécamp to Angers. In Normandy the *GND* were read in the monasteries of Jumièges, Saint-Wandrille, Bec, Fécamp, Lyre, Mont-Saint-Michel and undoubtedly in many others.[4] Just one look at the checklist of *GND* manuscripts (Appendix II) illustrates that not only in the eleventh and twelfth centuries but also later this history was widely read in England and France.[5]

Today I should like to discuss the history of the Norman dukes as represented by the *Gesta Normannorum Ducum*, beginning with Dudo of Saint-Quentin and ending with Robert of Torigny. First I will call your attention to the main versions of the *GND*, where and when they were probably written (see Appendix I). Secondly I will offer an explanation of the different aims of each of the authors who wrote a version of the *GND*. Emphasis will be laid on the redaction of Robert of Torigny.

Dudo of Saint-Quentin wrote his history in the period 996 to 1015 by order of Duke Richard II (d. 1026) who renewed the commission of his father Duke Richard I (d. 996).[6] The dedicatory letter is addressed to Bishop Adalbero of Laon (977–1031).[7] Apart from this letter the work consists of four books, each devoted to the history of one duke, and many poems.[8] First Dudo describes the *mores et actus* of Hastingus the first real leader of the Vikings in France. Then follow accounts of Rollo, the first duke of Normandy, his son William Longsword (931–42), and finally his grandson Richard I (942–96).

At the moment we know of twelve manuscripts of this text, which are mainly from the eleventh and twelfth centuries. In the manuscripts Dudo's work is mostly entitled *Historia Normannorum*. Like the *GND* of William of Jumièges this work was known more by its title than by its author. This is a problem for us because if we find a reference to the *Historia Normannorum*, the *Gesta Normannorum* or the *Gesta Normannorum Ducum* we do not know whether the work of Dudo or of William is meant. In the Middle Ages, too, people were sometimes confused. In some manuscripts the work of William of Jumièges was attributed entirely or partly to Dudo.[9] This uncertainty in the Middle Ages is one of the reasons for treating Dudo's work as the starting point in a discussion of the different versions of the *GND*.

Dudo composed his history of the Norman dukes modelled as a *Gesta* history. By *Gesta* history I mean to say: a history about a line of succession of individual persons, who follow one another by hereditary or other means. In such a history emphasis is laid on the function of the person more than on the person himself. Here lies the main difference between this type of historiography and biography. Until the publication of Dudo's work at the beginning of the eleventh century there only existed *Gesta* histories about popes (the famous *Liber Pontificalis*), bishops and abbots, as far as I know. But this is not the place to digress on the *Gesta* genre. Enough to say that Dudo was probably the first medieval historian to use this genre for a history of a series of secular princes and this form of history continued to be the most popular form for describing the deeds of the Norman dukes during the next hundred years.[10]

In 1070–1 the monk William of Jumièges dedicated his *GND* to William King of England and Duke of Normandy. He abbreviated the work of Dudo and continued it up to the moment of England's pacification. Jean Marx published the most recent edition of William's work in 1914. He distinguished six redactions, A to F.[11] Neither the E nor the F redaction could possibly be the original one because of later interpolations and continuations. None of the other redactions A, B, C, or D could be the original one because of a reference to Robert son of William the Conqueror as reigning duke. According to Marx such a reference could not have been included during the lifetime of William the Conqueror. King William died in 1087 so this date constituted a *terminus post quem*. Marx concluded therefore that the original text of William of Jumièges has not been preserved. Another problematic passage refers again to Robert as reigning duke and can be found in the long epilogue at the end of the *GND*. A and B have a short epilogue which lacks the reference to Robert. C, however, has the long epilogue. D breaks off in chapter xvi of Book VII; it is therefore unknown whether D contained the long or the short epilogue. Marx concluded that, because of its short epilogue the A redaction must be nearest to the original text of William of Jumièges, followed by B, C and D.

Both Professor Engels in 1973[12] and Professor Davis in a recently published article[13] denied that A and B could be close to the original text because of an interpolation in both, concerning the life and death of Nicholas, son of Duke Richard III, who died as abbot of Saint-Ouen in Rouen.[14] This interpolation gives a *terminus post quem*, namely 1092, the year Nicholas died, for the A and the B redaction. An elimination of these two, leaves only the C redaction to be considered. Davis proposes to accept C, despite the two references to Robert as reigning duke, as the original text of William of Jumièges written during the lifetime of William the Conqueror. The King of England had made his son Robert Duke of Normandy to act more or less as regent during the king's absence. Independently from Professor Davis I came to the same conclusion and I agree with him that C represents the original text. The D redaction is difficult to fit into the manuscript tradition and text development because all manuscripts of this redaction are incomplete. For the moment I can say that D is closer to C than to A or B.

My conclusions so far are that the original version of William of Jumièges' *Gesta* is represented by C and possibly D, written in about 1070–1. A and B must have been written after 1092 because of the reference to Nicholas who died in 1092. I shall show the significance of this series of observations in due course.

Let us now return to the *GND* to see how the text was formed and where the main alterations were made by several interpolators and continuators. The original work of William of Jumièges, as represented by redaction C, begins with a dedicatory letter to William the Conqueror. The author states that he has abbreviated Dudo's work, but that he has not taken over Dudo's stories about the origins of Rollo, his prophetical dream and other exploits at the time Rollo was still a pagan. He considers these stories to be flattery, neither honest nor useful.[15] In the first book William aims to tell the history of the first Vikings in France. In the following three books he describes the history of Rollo, William Longsword and Richard I, basing himself mainly on Dudo but also adding from other sources, such as the *Miracula sancti Benedicti*, the *Historia Francorum Senonensis* and the *Vita sancti Aichadri*.[16] In William's abbreviation, Dudo's work has been reduced by approximately two-thirds. From Book V onwards William offers his own story of the Norman dukes based on what he himself heard and saw and also based on the *Historia Francorum Senonensis* and probably on some charters too.[17] Books V, VI and VII concern Richard II (996–1026), the brothers Richard III (1026–1027/8) and Robert I (1027/8–1035), and finally William the Conqueror. The author concludes with the long epilogue in which he eulogizes King William and his son Robert Duke of Normandy.

The next phase in the development of the *GND* occurred some time after 1092 when the previously mentioned Nicholas passage was added; and, probably at the same time, the long epilogue was shortened by the omission of the reference to Robert as reigning duke. 1096 makes a possible *terminus post quem*, because in that year Robert left Normandy for the Holy Land and sold the duchy to his brother William Rufus.[18] Both the A and B redactions derive from this phase in the development of the text.

The A redaction can be characterized by the fact that it contains only Books V, VI, VII and the short epilogue. In two of the three manuscripts of this version, William's *Gesta* follows the complete work of Dudo.[19] So instead of William's abbreviation someone thought it more suitable to copy the entire work of Dudo.

The B redaction contains the dedicatory letter to William the Conqueror, Books I to VII and the short epilogue, followed by a small tract entitled *De Obitu Willelmi (DOW)*. The *DOW* describes the final illness of King William, the deathbed scene, the division of his inheritance, and it offers a portrait of the king. Professor Engels, who edited this text, showed that it is modelled mainly on the Life of Louis the Pious by the so-called 'Astronomer' and on Einhard's *Vita Karoli Magni*. Apart from the *DOW* we find in the B redaction four anecdotal stories concerning the dukes Richard II and Robert I.[20] Although we can trace these four anecdotes in several other chronicles, such as the *Roman de Rou* of Wace, the *Chronicle* of Ranulf Higden, the *Kirkstall Chronicle*, the *Cantatorium sancti Huberti* and in the manuscripts containing an abbreviation of the B redaction; yet we have not found any trace of the *DOW* as represented in this version.[21] Some of these stories can be dated to the eleventh century, but the B redaction as a whole must be dated in the first decades of the twelfth century.[22]

The next group of interpolations was added by the author of the E redaction, who is commonly identified as Orderic Vitalis. In another place I have argued that the date of this version must be later than 1113; this view I still hold to be correct, although it is impossible to deny that the author must have worked from a period before 1109.[23] It is very probable that E is based on D, and definitely not on C as Marx concluded. Both D and E have the same rubrics, the same error dating the big Viking raid on the Scheldt to 806 instead of 876,[24] and the same small addition naming *Frisia* as the place where Bier Ironside, a helper of Hastingus, died.[25] But because D has survived mutilated it will be difficult to give a more definite answer to the question on which redaction E was based.[26]

The E redaction contains the dedicatory letter, Books I to VII and the long epilogue. The interpolations in Book II come from Dudo and the *Historia Francorum Senonensis*.[27] In Book VI there is also a Nicholas passage at the same place as in A and B although that in E was written independently from that in A and B.[28] In Book VI and especially in Book VII we find many interpolations concerning the monastery of Saint-Evroult, some important Norman families like the Bellêmes and the Montgomeries, and the Normans in Southern Italy.[29] So on the whole we can conclude that the main change in E is interpolation more than continuation.

The last redaction, which I shall discuss, F, is that written by Robert of Torigny in about 1139.[30] Robert of Torigny was monk at Bec from 1128 to 1154, when he was elected abbot of the monastery of Mont-Saint-Michel. Because of the fact that the autograph is still preserved (it is ms Leiden UB BPL 20), we can follow step by step the way in which Robert worked. He ordered a scribe to copy a manuscript of the E redaction and to leave blank spaces for his own interpolations and additions. Unfortunately as a result of the loss of the first two quires the manuscript is not complete and misses most of the first four books.[31] From the very beginning, however, numerous copies were made from the original, so we can fairly easily reconstruct the missing four books.

F consists of the dedicatory letter and the seven main books, but no epilogue because an eighth book has been added, devoted to Henry I. At the end of the work we find the so-called *Additamenta*, six anecdotal stories on the first dukes of Normandy, Rollo, Richard I and Richard II. The interpolations and additions are these: in Book II Robert reinstates Dudo's stories about Rollo which William of Jumièges had left out.[32] Consequently Robert was forced to omit from the dedicatory letter the sentence in which William of Jumièges manifested doubt about the veracity of these stories. Apart from some smaller interpolations in Books III, IV and V Robert adds in Book VI the history of the foundation of the abbey at Bec[33] and he speaks of the foundation of other monasteries in Book VII.[34] At the end of Book VII he discusses Robert Guiscard, basing himself mainly on the *Gesta Roberti Wiscardi* written by William of Apulia between 1095 and 1099.[35] In the last chapter of Book VII he describes the illness and death of William the Conqueror.[36] I will return later to the contents of Book VIII devoted to Henry I.

So far I have offered you a somewhat elaborate outline of the textual development in the *GND* from Dudo to Robert of Torigny. We need this information for the next part of my paper where I want to point out the aims of the Norman historians in writing their version of the *GND*.

Dudo's purpose in writing his history of the Norman dukes has often been seen as apologetic.[37] Dudo wanted to legitimise the arrival and, more importantly, the settlement of the Vikings in Normandy. He was ordered to write his history by Duke Richard I and the commission was renewed by his son Richard II.[38] Dudo's *Gesta* can be listed alongside other examples of histories written to legitimise rather young 'nations', for instance the *Historia Saxonum* of Widukind of Corvey and the *Historia Francorum* written by Pseudo-Fredegar. According to Grundmann these works belong to the genre of *Origo gentis* histories. The authors of this type of history do have a common purpose, for they write history with a strong flavour of legend based on a vigorous oral tradition of heroic songs and sagas.[39] Dudo says that he based his history on information given to him by Ralph of Ivry, the brother of Duke Richard I.[40] His other sources are rather difficult to trace as Barbara Vopelius has shown in her thesis on Dudo. Dudo hardly ever quotes his sources word by word.[41] We do know that Dudo was engaged in the preparation of charters at the ducal court. He therefore must have had knowledge about their contents, but so far we can see he very rarely used them as a source for his history.[42]

Why Dudo chose this particular form of a *Gesta* history to write his history of the Norman dukes is an unsolved riddle for me.[43] But it is undeniable that history written precisely in this form exercised a strong appeal to his continuators for more than one century.

His continuator William of Jumièges was less concerned to legitimise the Viking settlement in France and the birth of the Norman duchy. At his time less than a decade after the Norman Conquest, there was another settlement to defend. He wrote in order to legitimise the decision of William the Conqueror to claim the English throne by force. Professor Davis and Professor Jäschke have pointed out that both Dudo and William of Jumièges paid attention to the relations between England and Normandy throughout their histories.[44] Jäschke studied in particular the passages in William's work concerning the 'English Question'. He concludes that William composed his *GND* in a tradition of panegyric historical writing in order to legitimise the way William Duke of Normandy became King of England: a status the Norman dukes had long been eager to gain to judge from their competitive relationship with the English kings from the moment of their settlement in France to 1066.

Unfortunately we do not know whether King William entrusted William of Jumièges with the task of writing history, as Duke Richard II had entrusted Dudo with that task. On 1 July 1067 King William, accompanied by many prelates and magnates, attended the dedication ceremony of the new abbey church at Jumièges.[45] It is tempting to suppose that William of Jumièges then decided to write his history of those Norman dukes who in the end became kings of England.

William continued Dudo's work and adopted the same form of *Gesta* history. He did not take over the many poems Dudo inserted in his history. Each duke got his own book and this structure made it easy for continuations to be added. William wrote less about more dukes than Dudo, and so the *Gesta* form is easier to distinguish in his work than it is in Dudo's. We see a clear pattern in each book: first a portrait of the new duke, followed by his struggle for power either against his own lord the French king or, as lord, against his principal vassals; his marriage and his children, his ecclesiastical foundations; and finally just before his death we see each duke proposing his eldest son as successor and ordering his magnates to accept him as his lawful heir.

These are the topics we meet over and over again in every book, and roughly speaking, we may even say that exactly these topics are the most interpolated ones. A few examples will demonstrate this.

In the A, B and E redaction a Nicholas passage has been added to clarify an unusual succession. In 1028 Robert I inherited the ducal title from his brother Richard III. Richard had a son called Nicholas who could not succeed his father because he was given as an oblate to the monastery of Fécamp. The original version of the *GND*, the C redaction, does not say anything about Nicholas, probably because William of Jumièges wrote not long after the events and did not think it relevant to mention. Whereas later generations needed an explanation of the fact that Robert I succeeded his brother although his nephew Nicholas was still alive.

In the B redaction anecdotal stories are added to emphasize the good and generous character of Dukes Richard II and Robert I. The same interpolator follows the *GND* with the *DOW* giving a proper end to Book VII, namely the death of William the Conqueror. Besides this, he includes an elaborate portrait of William and, more importantly he recounts the unusual division of the inheritance.

In the E redaction we mostly find stories about the difficulties William the Conqueror had as duke with those vassals who did not want to accept his lordship during his minority. This is the kind of interpolation we find in the redactions A, B and E. They do not substantially alter the main theme of attempting to legitimise the Norman Conquest. We have to wait for Robert of Torigny, the author of the F redaction, who adds another aspect to the legitimisation theme in Norman historiography.

The most remarkable parts of Robert's redaction can be found in Book II and Book VIII. As we have seen, Robert brought back in Book II all the information on Rollo which Dudo had given, but which had been omitted by William of Jumièges. Robert obviously did not share William's doubt about Dudo's account of the exploits of the pagan Rollo. Robert seems to prefer the pagan hero as represented by Dudo to the Christian duke as portrayed by William of Jumièges. For obvious reasons Robert had to omit the sceptical sentence formulated by William in his dedicatory letter expressing his doubt on some of Dudo's stories.[46]

Robert's purpose however in writing his version of the *GND* can be identified mainly from Book VIII devoted to Henry I. Although this king is the central person around whom this book was written, the first chapters describe his brothers Robert Curthose and William Rufus. Robert of Torigny wrote about them because he did not want to disrupt the *ordo historiae*.[47] After Henry's succession to William Rufus as King of England, the new king's marriage with Matilda of Scotland is described; they have two children William and Matilda, the later empress.[48] Then follows the struggle between Henry I and his brother Robert, who on his return from the Holy Land claimed the English throne as eldest son of the Conqueror. After the battle of Tinchebrai in 1106 Henry was Duke of Normandy as well as King of England, but there still existed a pretender in the background, William Clito, son of Robert Curthose. Robert of Torigny therefore devoted some chapters to Clito and to his involvement in the affairs of Flanders. Because of the loss of two folios at this point in the autograph manuscript of Robert of Torigny, three entire chapters are missing. They cannot be reconstructed since the two missing folios were lost before the first copies were made.[49] Robert portrays Henry as an excellent king who punished false-moneyers and who was together with his daughter Matilda a great benefactor of the monastery of Bec.[50] He also describes Henry's monastic foundations as well as his work in castle-building.[51] Henry died at the end of the year 1135 after an attempt to secure the succession by the designation of Matilda as his lawful heir. The story of Henry alternates with chapters concerning the genealogy of some Norman families.

The impression develops that Book VIII ended originally with the death and epitaph of Henry I, since the text ends there like all other books of the *GND* with the formula '. . . *per omnia secula seculorum amen*'. The book however continues with eight more chapters describing the relationship between the royal and ducal house on the one hand and some Anglo-Norman families on the other; it ends rather abruptly with some chronological notes on the abbots of Bec as well as on the French and German kings in 1137. The autograph manuscript has one half blank folio after these notes, but it then resumes on the verso side of this folio (fol. 31v) with the so-called *Additamenta*.[52] Presumably Robert of Torigny intended to continue his work for otherwise he would surely have ended the *GND* in a more suitable way.

I shall now discuss the reason why Robert of Torigny wrote his redaction of the *GND* and why he did not finish it.

It is important to bear in mind that Robert wrote in around 1139, about four years after the death of Henry I, a benefactor of Bec and father of Empress Matilda, an even more important benefactor of Robert's monastery. During the so-called Anarchy after Henry's death, Robert decidedly chose the side of Matilda and her husband Geoffrey of Anjou in their struggle against Stephen of Blois. Until now Robert's position in this struggle has mostly been deduced from his *Chronicon* a continuation of the *World Chronicle* of Sigebert of Gembloux.[53] It is however interesting to see how Robert used his version of the *GND* as propaganda material supporting Matilda as legitimate heiress against Stephen of Blois.

In the book devoted to Henry I Robert of Torigny pays much attention to the problems concerning Henry's succession. After securing the Anglo-Norman *regnum* for himself Henry had to be cautious, for there still remained possible claimants to the throne: his nephew William Clito as well as the sons of his sister Adela, Theobald and Stephen of Blois. When Henry's son William died in the disaster of the White Ship in 1120 the problem of succession became acute. Henry had lost his only legitimate male successor, and though he remarried in the hope of a new legitimate heir, he was obliged to acknowledge his daughter Matilda as lawful heir. This had been made possible because of the death of Matilda's first husband, Emperor Henry V of Germany in 1125. Reluctantly Matilda returned to Normandy to join her father there. As her father's successor as well as a benefactor of Bec, Matilda receives much attention in Book VIII. Because of her first marriage to a German Emperor, Robert calls her empress Matilda—as do most twelfth-century historians—even after her second marriage to Geoffrey of Anjou. Writing about this marriage Robert apologizes for the fact that Empress Matilda married only a French count. He stresses the fact that the counts of Anjou descended from the French royal line; but the story is fictitious.[54] So he tries to convince his readers that it was not a *mésalliance* after all.

Robert strongly defends their children Henry, Geoffrey and William as legitimate heirs of the English *principatus*: '. . . not only because of King Henry their grandfather but also because of the second queen Matilda their grandmother. This couple (i.e. Henry and his wife Matilda) is, although both in a different way, closely connected in consanguinity to the old English kings as is shown in the book containing the Life of this queen'.[55] The book mentioned here must be the *Vita sanctae Margaretae*, the Life of Saint Margaret of Scotland. Margaret was the mother of Queen Matilda II and grandmother of Empress Matilda; she descended directly from the Anglo-Saxon royal house, which is described in her *Vita*. In the quotation I gave, Robert of Torigny wrongly states that it is the Life of Matilda II instead of the Life of her mother Margaret. He was probably confused because the long version of the Life of Saint Margaret begins with an apostrophe to Matilda II to whom the book was dedicated.[56]

So Robert of Torigny sets himself up as defender of Matilda's case in the struggle for power following the death of Henry I. He collects every piece of evidence he can find to support Matilda's claims to the throne. Since the Life of Saint Margaret contains reliable proof of Margaret's, and thus Matilda's, descent from the Anglo-Saxon kings, he explicitly states that he may add this Life to the *GND*.[57] There is however no manuscript evidence that the *Vita sanctae Margaretae* was ever actually added to the *Gesta*.

Another piece of evidence for Robert's concern with Matilda's succession and that of her children can be found in his attention paid to the Angevin connexion. We have heard how Robert defends the marriage of Matilda, a king's daughter and by marriage an empress, with a French count who could only claim some royal dignity far back in the past. Robert considered it his task to draw Geoffrey out of his background and give him the attention he earned, not least in order to make him a more equal partner to his royal wife.

A letter is known written by Robert of Torigny when prior of Bec to Gervase, prior of Saint-Céneri, after the death of Geoffrey of Anjou in 1151. The manuscript containing this letter is now lost. We have however a transcript made by Luc d'Achéry in the seventeenth century.[58] As far as I know this letter has up to now only received attention in the context of the discussion of Robert's authorship of the F redaction of the *GND*.[59] But it is directly relevant to this analysis. Robert asked Gervase to write a history of Normandy from the death of Henry King of England and Duke of Normandy to the death of Geoffrey Duke of Normandy and Count of Anjou, that is from 1135 till 1151. He continues: '. . . If you are going to write this work I want you to do it in this order. First you sum up, briefly as if you are recapitulating, the names, genealogy, and succession of the counts of Anjou from Ingelgerius to Geoffrey, how many years each of them has reigned as count and what deeds they have performed either in worldly or in spiritual affairs which are worthy to memorize in annals . . .'.[60] He further asked Gervase to do the same for the counts of Maine, because Geoffrey's mother was a daughter of the count of Maine. Robert would have done this work himself if only he had the time, the opportunity and the chronicles relating to these two counties. He adds that he himself had already written the history of Henry King of England and Duke of Normandy and that he had added it to the *GND*. Finishing his letter Robert writes: '. . . Because of the passage of time I want the work I ask you to write to be added to this work (namely the *GND*), so that we transmit, by our writing, the things which happened in our time in our province to the knowledge of those in the future'.[61]

There is a problem of interpretation posed by Robert's question to Gervase. Is he asking Gervase to write a history of the counts of Anjou and Maine with, as an epilogue, a biography of Geoffrey? Or does he mean a history of Geoffrey as Duke of Normandy with a short history of the counts of Anjou and Maine as a prologue? I prefer the second interpretation because it gives us a perfect reason why Robert would like to add a history of Geoffrey as Duke of Normandy to the *Gesta Normannorum Ducum*.[62] We do not have evidence that this history was ever written by Gervase of Saint-Céneri, a priory of Saint-Evroult.[63] The only known biography of Geoffrey was composed by John of Marmoutier as part of the *Gesta Consulum Andegavorum* written in the second half of the twelfth century.[64] Neither do we have evidence that such a history was ever added to the *GND*.

We may conclude that Robert of Torigny never really finished his redaction of the *GND*. The abrupt ending of Book VIII and both his references to the Life of Saint Margaret and the history of Geoffrey of Anjou prove the contrary. It is obvious however that Robert added a third aspect to the legitimisation tradition within Norman historiography. He defended the legitimate inheritance of the Anglo-Norman throne by the children of Empress Matilda and Geoffrey of Anjou. Their strongest claims to the throne were based on their mother's descent from both William the Conqueror and the Anglo-Saxon kings. Another claim, less strong but no less legitimate, came from their father who became Duke of Normandy because of his marriage with Matilda, after the death of Henry I.

From the beginning of the eleventh century the *GND* were the official history written to legitimise the reigning ducal, later royal, family; first in Normandy, then after 1066 in England and still later in the middle of the twelfth century also in Anjou. The *Gesta Normannorum Ducum* proved to be a useful form of historiography to be continued and adapted at any place at any moment but with only one purpose: legitimisation of the reigning prince. The *Gesta Normannorum Ducum* proved to be an endless history in the Middle Ages as well as an unfinished history today.[65]

Appendix I The Gesta Normannorum Ducum

	Dudo of Saint-Quentin 996–1015	William of Jumièges C (D?) 1070–1	A after 1092	B after 1092	Orderic Vitalis E after 1113	Robert of Torigny F c.1139
Epistola (dedication to)	Adalbero of Laon	William the Conqueror	Epistola and first four books = Dudo of St Quentin	W the C	W the C	W the C
Book I	Hastingus	Vikings in France		V in France	V in France	V in France
Book II	Rollo	Rollo		Rollo	Rollo	Rollo (+Dudo)
Book III	William Longsword	William Longsword		William L	William L	William L
Book IV	Richard I	Richard I		Richard I	Richard I	Richard I
Book V	—	Richard II	Richard II	Richard II	Richard II	Richard II
Book VI	—	Richard III	Richard III	Richard III	Richard III	Richard III
		Robert I	Robert I (interp. 1092)	Robert I (interp. 1092)	Robert I	Robert I
Book VII		William the Conqueror (to 1070–2)	William C (to 1070–2)	William C (to 1070–2)	William C (to 1070–2)	William C (to 1087)
					(interp. 1113)	(later interp.)
Epilogue		long	short	short	long	—
DOW		—	—	DOW	—	—
Book VIII		—	—	—	—	Henry I († 1135) (to 1137)
Additamenta	—	—	—	—	—	Rollo, Richard I, Richard II

Appendix II Checklist of the Manuscripts of the Gesta Normannorum Ducum

Dudo of Saint-Quentin

Antwerp Plan. Mor. 196	12th c	France
Berlin DSB Phillipps 1854	11th c	Fécamp
Bern Stadtbibl. 390	11/12th c	?
Cambridge Corpus Christi Col. 276	11/12th c	Canterbury, St Aug.
Douai BM 880	12th c	France?
Leiden UB Vossius lat. F 47	16th c	France
London BL Cotton Claudius A xii	11/12th c	?
London BL Cotton Nero D viii	12th c	England
London BL Harley 3742	after 1445	Oxford, All Souls C.
Oxford Bodl. Lib. coll. R. James	17th c	England
Paris BN Nouv. Acq. lat. 1031	12th c	Saint-Wandrille
Rouen BM Y 11 (1173)	11th c	Jumièges

William of Jumièges

A

London BL Cotton Nero D viii	12th c	England
London BL Harley 3742	after 1445	Oxford, All Souls C.
Rouen BM Y 11 (1173)	12th c	Jumièges

B

London BL Harley 491	12th c	Durham
?Oxford Bodl. Lib. Rawl. G. 62	13th c	Waltham
Oxford Bodl. Lib. Magd. Col. 73	12th c	England

C

London BL Arundel 41	13th c	France?
Oxford Bodl. Lib. Bodley 517	11/12th c	Normandy (Lyre?)
Paris BN lat. 15047	12/13th c	Paris, Saint-Victor

D

Cambridge Trin. Col. O. 1.17	14th c	Whalley
Liège UB 369C	c.1130	Durham?
Paris BN lat. 2769	12th c	France
Paris BN lat. 6046	13/14th c	England?
Würzburg UB M Ch F 140	16th c	Würzburg

E

Copenhagen KB Thott 1333	13th c	?
London BL Additional 39646	12th c	Braine-sur-Vesle
London BL Cotton Nero A xi	12/13th c	?
Paris BN lat. 4861	1220–1226	St Taurin Evreux
Paris BN lat. 6001	17th c	France

Paris BN lat. 6265	1515	Paris
Paris BN lat. 12710	1129–1140	Saint-Denis
Paris BN lat. 17656	after 1179	Saint-Denis
Paris B Mazarine 2013	1120–1129	Saint-Denis
Rouen Y 14 (1174)	after 1113	Saint-Evroult

F

Beauvais BM 16	15th c	France
Bern Stadtbibl. 208	12th c	Normandy?
Caen MdBa Coll. Mancel 145	16th c	Normandy
Cambridge Corpus Christi Col. 181	14th c	York, St Mary
Leiden UB BPL 20	c.1139	Bec
Leiden UB Vossius lat. F 77	after 1282	Normandy?
London BL Cotton Nero D viii	12th c	England
London BL Cotton Vitellius A viii	12th c	England
London BL Harley 3679	16th c	Rouen (Paix-de-Coeur)
Paris BN lat. 5997	13th c	Préaux
Paris BN lat. 5997a (+Vatican Reg. lat. 733B fol. 55)	12th c	Mont-St-Michel?
Paris BN lat. 5998	after 1549	Normandy
Paris BN lat. 5999	after 1522	Rouen?
Paris BN lat. 6000	16th c	Normandy
Paris BN lat. 6002	17th c	England (W. Camden?)
Paris BN lat. 6044	1565–1567	England
Paris BN lat. 6217	15th c	Normandy?
Paris BN lat. 12882	16th c	Paris
Paris BN lat. 14663	15th c	Paris, Saint-Victor
Paris BN Nouv. Acq. lat. 1555	17th c	Mont-St-Michel?
Paris B Arsenal 1094	15th c	Paris
Rouen BM Y 11 (1173)	12th c	Jumièges
Vienna ONB 7218	1549	Rouen

Epitome

B	Cambridge Corpus Christi col. 138	14th c	England
B	London College of Arms Arundel 1	14th c	England
E	Bern Stadtbibl. 90	12th c	Fleury?
F	London BL Stowe 56	13th c	England
F?	Paris BN lat. 13817	17th c	France
C	Ralph of Diceto, *Abbreviationes Chronicorum*, ed. W. Stubbs, Rolls Series, London 1876, 241–262. Written 1180/1188.		

The beginnings of the Honour of Clare

RICHARD MORTIMER

'It should hardly be necessary to dwell on the greatness of the Clares,' as Round wrote, yet much that has been written on the greatest baronial family of medieval England has concentrated on its junior members in the twelfth century who accumulated baronies and earldoms with such success, and on the senior line after its acquisition of the earldom of Gloucester.[1] The heights the Clare family achieved were certainly commanding: yet there was never a time when the family was not great, except perhaps for the few years after the murder of Count Gilbert of Brionne in 1040, and the heights were scaled from a position already well advanced. This paper is concerned with the Domesday estate of Richard fitz Gilbert, the ancestor of the later Clares, which lands were the nucleus of the possessions of the senior line, later earls of Hertford and Gloucester. Richard was an important lord in Normandy too, but for practical rather than historical reasons the discussion will centre on his English lands. Nor shall we be concerned with the subsequent acquisitions of this branch of the family: the Norfolk lands of Rainald fitz Ivo, obtained probably very soon after the Domesday inquest, or Cardigan, given by Henry I, or half the Giffard honour which came to them in the 1180s. The honour of Clare was not a static entity created at one moment: in the thirteenth century the demesne lands were administered in geographically determined bailiwicks regardless of the date and manner of their acquisition.[2] Domesday freezes one moment in the long process of expansion.

The Domesday estate of Richard fitz Gilbert, then, was huge: its value was £873, which is greater than any of the monasteries, and all of the bishoprics except Canterbury and Winchester. If one excepts the royal half-brothers, Richard was the sixth wealthiest layman in England. Richard and his wife held land in nine counties, but such a statistic could be misleading if taken to imply an even distribution. Lympstone in Devon, Sutton in Wiltshire, Harefield in Middlesex are Richard's only lands in those counties. His wife Rohese, daughter of Walter Giffard, is entered as a tenant-in-chief in her own right at Standon, Herts., and Eynesbury, Hunts., and neither partner held other land there. Map 1 shows that Richard's estates fell into two separate concentrations: a south-eastern group in Kent and Surrey, and an East Anglian group in Suffolk and Essex. Of the two the East Anglian was the more valuable, accounting for 54 per cent of the total value; the south-eastern group furnished 36 per cent, leaving 10 per cent to come from the remaining lands.

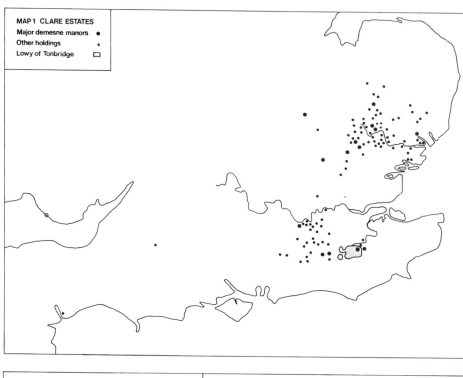

MAP 1 CLARE ESTATES

Major demesne manors ●
Other holdings ·
Lowy of Tonbridge ▭

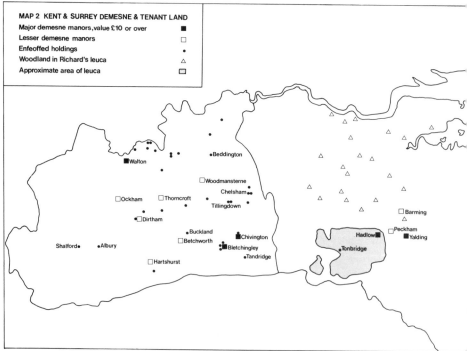

MAP 2 KENT & SURREY DEMESNE & TENANT LAND

Major demesne manors, value £10 or over ■
Lesser demesne manors ▫
Enfeoffed holdings ·
Woodland in Richard's leuca △
Approximate area of leuca ▭

■ Walton
● Beddington
▫ Woodmansterne
Chelsham ●●
▫ Ockham ▫ Thorncroft
Tillingdown ●●
·▫ Dirtham
● Buckland
▫ Betchworth ■● Chivington
Shalford● ●Albury ■ Bletchingley
▫ Hartshurst ●Tandridge
Hadlow ■
●Tonbridge
▫ Barming △
▫ Peckham
■ Yalding

The centre of the south-eastern lands was certainly Tonbridge. Domesday repeatedly refers to Richard fitz Gilbert as Richard of Tonbridge, which makes it curious that there is no separate entry for Tonbridge itself. But Richard's 'leuca' or 'leuum' is often referred to: clearly the 'lowy' of Tonbridge, visible as a baronial franchise later in the middle ages, had come into existence by 1086, at least in some form. It seems most likely that Tonbridge itself was included in the assessment of the relatively populous manor of Hadlow, which contained 47 villeins with 15 bordars and 10 slaves. The boundaries of the lowy were defined in an agreement of 1259—it is these that are shown on the maps—and Hadlow was within them. Domesday also shows Richard in possession of a large quantity of woodland assessed under a number of manors scattered over west Kent, as illustrated in map 2. There has been a tendency to see these as detached portions of Richard's woodland physically situated in the vills concerned, but given what is known about the 'dens' of the Weald of Kent it seems much more likely that the upland manors possessed dens in the vicinity of Tonbridge. One holding is actually called a 'den' in Domesday, and another entry runs 'of this manor there is in Tonbridge wood and land valued at 20s.' ('de isto manerio est in Tonebrige tantum de silva' etc.).[3] In the thirteenth century when the lowy becomes relatively visible, it contained detached dens of upland manors.[4] The manors under which the dens are entered were held by a variety of lords: the bishop of Rochester, Odo of Bayeux or his tenants, the archbishop of Canterbury or his tenants; and were presumably held in 1066 by their predecessors. What these dens had in common was that they were held by Richard fitz Gilbert in his lowy in 1086. The conclusion seems to be that the lowy was a post-Conquest creation. Associated with it was the motte-and-bailey castle at Tonbridge, first mentioned when it was held against William Rufus by Richard fitz Gilbert's sons in 1088, and which formed the centre of a grouping of estates that had been in many different hands in 1066.

Among Robert of Torigni's interpolations in the chronicle of William of Jumièges is a story that Richard accepted Tonbridge in compensation for Brionne ('pro repetitione'), and that the 'leuga' of Tonbridge was measured out with a rope to include the same area as the 'leuga' of Brionne.[5] There are some difficulties in accepting the story as it stands: if the later boundaries of the lowy of Tonbridge, which was not a continuous area, bore any resemblance to those of the eleventh-century, it is quite hard to see how they could have been measured with a rope; and Torigni introduces it as an old tradition from which he remains rather distant ('sunt antiquorum plurimi qui dicunt' etc.). But it is very reasonable to suppose that Richard and Baldwin preserved a claim on Brionne: Torigni's story arises in connexion with an attempt by Roger, Richard's son, to buy it back from Robert Curthose. We encounter more difficulties in respect of the feudal position of the Tonbridge estate. Hadlow in Domesday was held of Odo of Bayeux, yet at least by 1171 it was held by Richard's descendant of the archbishop of Canterbury, for four knights of which he only recognized two.[6] When and how this transfer occurred I have not discovered. Richard's estate in Peckham consisted of two sulungs and a yoke of a larger manor belonging to the archbishop. The other Kentish estates, Yalding and Barming, were held in chief of the crown, Yalding being much the more valuable.

Richard fitz Gilbert was the largest landholder in Surrey. His lands there were worth in total more than three times those in Kent, at £242, and in fact were more valuable than those in any other county, even Suffolk. But they were not as concentrated, showing a fairly even spread across the county. The manors impress by their number rather than by individual size: the most valuable were Shalford, worth £20, Walton on Thames, £14, and Bletchingley, Tandridge and Beddington at between £10 and £12 each.

In East Anglia (map 3) we find a great concentration of demesne manors and tenant land in the area on both sides of the upper Stour centred on Clare, with a more sporadic extension chiefly of tenant land down the river valley and out across the plain of 'high Suffolk' towards the coast. The three great demesne manors in Suffolk, Clare, Hundon and Desning, were each worth some £40, and are instances, not very common in East Anglia, of manor coinciding with vill. The assessment of Desning must include the vill of Gazeley, which is not separately mentioned in Domesday but whose church formed part of the pre-Conquest endowment of the college at Clare;[7] it also includes the valuations of estates in Cavenham, Lakenheath and Herringswell, while sokemen in Mildenhall and Wangford are said to 'lie in' Desning: in fact the Desning

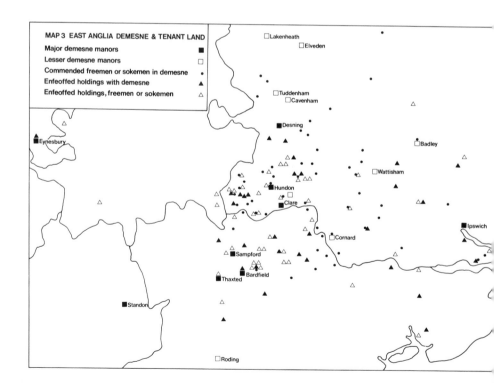

MAP 3 EAST ANGLIA DEMESNE & TENANT LAND

Major demesne manors	■
Lesser demesne manors	□
Commended freemen or sokemen in demesne	•
Enfeoffed holdings with demesne	▲
Enfeoffed holdings, freemen or sokemen	△

estate appears to be a 'soke' by itself. Further east the demesnes at Badley, Wattisham and Cornard were comparatively insignificant, while at Ipswich Richard had come into possession of St Peter's church which had a moderately large estate of six carucates with a number of town houses and burgesses all together worth £15. The demesne manor of Thaxted in Essex at £50 was the most valuable on the entire fee; Sampford and Bardfield came a long way behind, with £17 and £16 respectively, being comparable with some of the larger manors in the hands of tenants, such as Langham or Hempstead. It is an obvious feature of the East Anglian estates that they include a wide scattering of freemen and sokemen, small independent farmers over whom Richard's rights were primarily judicial and financial. In Suffolk, though not in Essex, holdings contributory to Richard's estate on which Domesday shows us demesne ploughs are the exception rather than the rule.

The manors of Standon and Eynesbury belonged to Rohese, Richard's wife, and quite likely formed her dowry. Eynesbury was given complete by Rohese to St Neots priory in 1113; the priory was situated within the manor, apparently, and already held some land there in Domesday.[8] Standon was still an important Clare demesne manor in the later middle ages. The two distant estates in Wiltshire and Devon seem to have no connexion with the rest of the fee: the previous owners contributed nothing else to the Clare lands; in 1086 both were in the hands of tenants, one of them certainly not found elsewhere on the fee. Harefield, in Middlesex, was in demesne and worth £12: it had been held by Countess Gytha in the time of King Edward.

The Clare fee thus falls into compact blocks, a pattern which has been pointed out on quite a number of lay fees.[9] The Tonbridge block immediately suggests comparison with Hugh de Montfort's lands around Saltwood, with the rapes of Sussex, or the lordship of the Isle of Wight. The East Anglian grouping is more scattered, necessarily so given the less generally 'manorialised' social structure of the region, but its centre of gravity is nonetheless a fairly small area which Richard's lands completely dominated. Perhaps it could stand comparison with some of the midland estates such as those around Belvoir or Tutbury. The next questions must be, how many predecessors did Richard have, and how much reorganization has taken place to form the concentrations? These will then involve us in the related problems of how and when the estates were acquired. I shall approach these problems together for each separate block.

Richard's predecessor at Yalding and Barming was a certain 'Alret', a name that presents difficulties as it could represent Aethelraed, Aelfred or Ealdred, so making it virtually impossible to identify individuals. An Alret of 'Ellinges' had sake and soke in the lathe of Aylesford, in which Yalding and Barming lay, and this may well be the one concerned, but even an added name contributes little further to our certain knowledge.[10] His estates were held directly of King Edward, and Richard held them in chief. At Hadlow, and in a single yoke at Tudeley nearby, Richard followed 'Eddeva', who held both of King Edward: Richard held them of Odo of Bayeux. No other Eddeva is to be found holding in 1066 in Kent, so it could be that Richard acquired her whole estate. We have already seen that the lowy of Tonbridge was most likely brought together from the detached dens of upland manors: some of these manors were long-standing estates of the churches of Rochester and Canterbury, others had come into Odo's hands. Richard fitz Gilbert is referred to as 'Richard of Tonbridge' in the accounts of the Penenden plea—or pleas—and so presumably was reasonably well entrenched there by at least the middle of the 1070s.[11]

In Surrey the predecessor who contributed most was a certain Azor, whose estates are shown in map 4. They were the three fairly large manors of Beddington, Woodmansterne and Albury, each worth £10 in 1066, and somewhat smaller estates at Effingham, worth £5, and Tillingdown worth £8; and all of them were held directly under King Edward. The name Azor is fairly common in Domesday: one was a housecarl of King Edward, another (or perhaps the same) was the king's steward; there were Azor the Black and Azor the Red, and among those holding lands closer to those that passed to Richard, Azor of Lessness, who made a grant of land there to Westminster Abbey and was one of King Edward's 'optimates'.[12] One Azor witnessed a charter of the Conqueror given at Whitsun 1068, having avoided disgrace thus far at least.[13] It is certain that our Azor survived into the reign of King William with enough money and enough confidence in the future to buy land: part of the Effingham estate had not been Azor's in King Edward's time, but had belonged, under

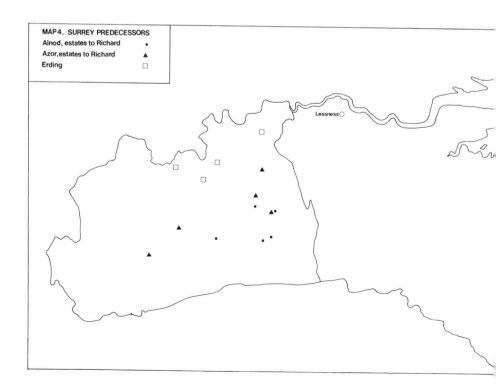

MAP 4. SURREY PREDECESSORS
Alnod, estates to Richard ●
Azor, estates to Richard ▲
Erding □

Lessness ○

the king, to a freeman who had sold it to Azor for some necessity of his own in the time of King William. The expansion of certain Englishmen after 1066 at the expense of their less fortunate or more vulnerable countrymen is a feature we shall meet again. There is another reference to an Azor in Surrey: he held Henley in Woking hundred until he died, and gave it to Chertsey abbey in the time of King William, as the monks said, and they had a royal writ to prove it.[14] Here is a Surrey Azor who never was disgraced or expropriated, or not entirely: it is tempting to identify him with Richard's predecessor, and even with the witness of 1068, but, of course, proof is lacking.

Azor's lands which passed to Richard were quite widely scattered across the county. Those of another predecessor, 'Alnod', were more concentrated near the Kentish border on the slopes of the Downs. This man contributed the demesne manor of Chivington and his share in Bletchingley, where two others had also held in 1066. This had been three manors, but by 1086 was one. He had also held Tillingdown and Chipstead, each worth £7, and Buckland worth £5. All this land had been held directly under King Edward. 'Alnod' is also a name to conjure with, as it could represent Aethelnoth, Aelfnoth, Ealdnoth or even Eadnoth, all of which were common names, which makes any attempt to incorporate him into other Aethelnoths etc. quite impossible. The leading Aethelnoth in this part of England was Aethelnoth 'cild', who survived for a few years after 1066 but whose land eventually went to Odo of Bayeux. Very close to Chipstead was an estate at Banstead, formerly held by an 'Alnod' now held by 'Richard' of bishop Odo. It is possible, but cannot be demonstrated, that this Alnod was both Richard's predecessor and Aethelnoth Cild, and that the Richard was Richard fitz Gilbert.

The third major predecessor in Surrey was Erding, whose lands in the Thames valley were all held of King Edward. These were Walton on Thames, worth in King Edward's time just over half of its value in 1086, Malden and Chessington, and Streatham which by Domesday had been given to Bec. There are no other Erdings to be found anywhere in the vicinity in 1066, and it seems as if Richard had acquired a complete small estate.

These three men, Azor, 'Alnod' and Erding, whose estates were respectively worth some £40, £30 and £20 in 1066, were the largest identifiable predecessors and the lands they contributed accounted for some 40 per cent of the value of the Surrey lands in 1086. The rest of Richard's estate came from seventeen other predecessors, only three of whom provided more than one holding. The question, whether these predecessors had more extensive estates which were split up among several successors is difficult to answer with certainty because of the usual problems of identification. But in the case of six of them it seems fairly certain that they did not have other estates, as no other people of that name occur in Surrey or neighbouring counties. One of these predecessors is worth discussing in some detail. Map 5 shows the lands of one Oswald, who has an entry to himself in the Surrey Domesday.[15] He was a king's thegn in the time of Edward the Confessor, under whom he held Fetcham, which he still held in 1086 of King William. At Wisley he held land worth 40s. of earl Harold, which

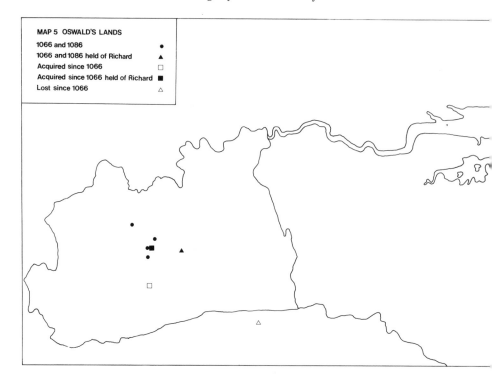

MAP 5 OSWALD'S LANDS

1066 and 1086	●
1066 and 1086 held of Richard	▲
Acquired since 1066	□
Acquired since 1066 held of Richard	■
Lost since 1066	△

he continued to hold under King William. An estate at Wotton is described as Harold's in 1066, but the men of the hundred did not know how he came by it, and by 1086 Oswald was holding it directly of the king. An estate at an unidentified place in the small hundred of Effingham had remained in his hands throughout the conquest period, and was still held of the king in 1086. So far we have a pre-Conquest landowner who had not only survived with his estates, but had even added to them. To his land near Effingham he had been able to add the substantial estate there which had once been Azor's, but which he held as Richard fitz Gilbert's tenant. His relations with Richard were not all advantageous, however, since his estate at Mickleham, which he formerly held of King Edward, he now held of Richard, and he had lost half a hide at Worth in Sussex which in 1086 was in the hands of one Siward. As well as these lands, he held of Chertsey abbey at Effingham an estate worth 40s., which he had held in 1066. This gave him quite a concentrated estate, centred on Effingham, and held of the king, Richard, and the abbot of Chertsey. He had lost one small outlying estate and had had to accept Richard as his lord for another, but in all he appears to have gained land and influence between 1066 and 1086. A thegn called Seman had commended himself to him in King William's time. One entry, though, reveals something of the difficulties he faced in trying to maintain his position: under the unidentified holding near Effingham we read 'the men of the bishop of Bayeux claim on this land for the king's use for each year two marks of gold or two hawks, by the concession of the abbot his brother, that is to say, for the battle he should have waged (pro bello quod . . . facere debuit) against Geoffrey parvus'.[16] Apparently the abbot was, as Round suggested, Wulfwold of Chertsey, which goes some way to explaining his durability.[17] But clearly he was coming into conflict of some sort with the Normans.

The rather scattered Surrey lands, then, represented acquisitions from a large number of predecessors, most of whom passed on single estates, and many of the others had fairly localized holdings. Some of the larger predecessors may have had wide lands outside Surrey, in which case only their Surrey lands went to Richard. Virtually all the land was held directly 'of King Edward' as Domesday expresses it, with only a few of the predecessors able to go with their land where they liked. There has been a process of funnelling many estates into one, and Domesday is replete with hints of orderly transfer, of royal writs and the king's 'liberator'. To the manor of Thorncroft had been joined two further groups of small estates, each 'pro uno manerio', and these are described as 'traditae Ricardo': almost as if Richard had been promised so many manors, and now they were being brought together and assigned to him. If this represents central control of the operation, it was capable of causing some confusion too, in a confusing situation: land at Dirtham had been given by Aluric, who held of King Edward, to his wife and daughter and the abbey of Chertsey; Richard claimed this land and 'liberata fuit ei'.[18] Richard was deeply involved with the abbot of Chertsey, as a number of local landholders seem to have been: Richard's men said abbot Wulfwold had delivered the estate of Apps Court to him in compensation for Walton ('in emendatione Waletone'), but the hundred had never seen a writ or a royal 'liberator', and Richard held it along with neighbouring Walton. On the whole Richard's south-eastern estates are free from accusations of 'invasion', at least in Domesday Book. But it could be that the lowy of Tonbridge was carved out without too much regard to the rights of others: Richard's son Gilbert made an agreement with bishop Gundulf, in the presence of Lanfranc, thus dating c.1087–1089, to pay 50s. annually to Rochester cathedral until he could assign land of that value, 'for the land of St Andrew which Gilbert has'.[19] The dens of Rochester manors which Richard had were all together valued in Domesday at 52s.

The question of when he acquired these lands is not one we can expect to answer more than approximately. Could Richard have endowed himself with Tonbridge by unsupported private enterprise? It seems more likely that he had royal permission at least, and presumably the support of Odo of Bayeux of whom he held Hadlow. In the first four years of William's English reign Richard was clearly a significant figure, called 'princeps' when witnessing a charter in 1068, and witnessing again in 1069.[20] His position in Normandy would have been enough to ensure that. He does not occur as an addressee until after 1070, when a writ concerning the restitution of church lands is addressed to him, Lanfranc, Robert of Eu and the Kentish landholder Hugh de Montfort, and he is found as an addressee in another Kentish context in 1077.[21]

Along with his appearance in the Penenden plea, this suggests that he acquired the Kentish lands in or before the early 1070s. We have seen some evidence of survival among the predecessors in Surrey: a few years would be sufficient to account for this. But there is no reason to suppose that Richard obtained all his Surrey lands at once: he could have gone on gathering the lands of various men over a period of nearly twenty years.

In Kent Richard held a compact area brought together from several predecessors; in Surrey, a large scattering brought together from very many predecessors. The situation in East Anglia, as we see in maps 3 and 6, is apparently rather simpler. Richard had one very great predecessor, one lesser one, and had extended his lordship over a minor multitude of freemen. The greater part of the East Anglian estate came from one Wihtgar, whose father Aelfric son of Wihtgar was involved in the administration of the eight-and-a-half hundreds of West Suffolk on behalf of Queen Emma before they were given to Bury St Edmunds abbey. He was referred to as 'comes famosus' in a Bury document, and was the founder of a college of secular canons at Clare, to which he gave his land there.[22] His son Wihtgar was the 1066 tenant of the rest of a very large estate notable for the number and size of the demesne manors. Cavenham, with a church and five mills was already a berewick of Desning. He possessed the church of St Peter at Ipswich with its estate, and some demesne manors in Essex, especially Thaxted valued at £30. Map 6 shows that Wihtgar

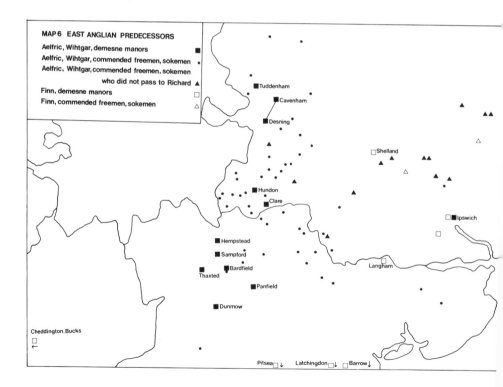

MAP 6 EAST ANGLIAN PREDECESSORS

Aelfric, Wihtgar, demesne manors
Aelfric, Wihtgar, commended freemen, sokemen
Aelfric, Wihtgar, commended freemen, sokemen
who did not pass to Richard
Finn, demesne manors
Finn, commended freemen, sokemen

was the lord of a large number of commended freemen and sokemen, concentrated around his Suffolk demesnes, but spreading a good way eastwards as well. The 'ministerial' position of his father must go some way towards accounting for their success in organizing demesne manors and in attracting the commendation of freemen. Some position of power may have descended to Wihtgar himself: Welldon Finn writes, 'the atmosphere of the entries surrounding him suggests that he may well have been a sheriff's deputy in south Suffolk and north Essex'.[23] The lesser predecessor was Finn the Dane, fortunately a fairly unmistakable name. His estate was very widely scattered, and much smaller than Wihtgar's.[24] He had two manors in the south of Essex and one as far away as Buckinghamshire; his largest estate was the manor of Langham in the Stour valley, and he also had thirteen burgesses in Ipswich and some small estates and commended freemen in East Suffolk. Both these men were described as Richard's 'antecessores'. Among Finn's own tenants was a king's thegn named Thorir who held two small estates worth nearly £3. In addition Richard had acquired some sort of rights over a large number of small farmers, often named individually, and themselves sometimes the lords of demesne lands and collections of tenants. For example, a freeman called Brictric held 55 geld acres at one of the places in Essex called Norton, with one demesne plough, and five villeins and five bordars with one plough between them. In addition there were three slaves, ten acres of meadow and wood for forty pigs. This estate appears to have been held by Brictric quite independently and was worth 40s. in King Edward's time.[25] Generally speaking the freemen and sokemen entered under Richard's fee were those over whom Wihtgar or Finn had commendation or sokeright. Brictric Black and others who do not appear to have been in a subordinate relationship to Richard's predecessors, or indeed anyone, but whose land was held in 1086 by Richard or his followers, are gathered together under the heading 'invasiones super regem' at the end of the Essex Domesday. The theory applied in the arrangement of Domesday is quite obvious, and may well have been intended to apply to the way the estates were acquired, but as is well known it is not entirely reconcilable with what had happened. Not only had Richard and his men 'invaded' certain freemen's estates, which were mostly near to lands more legitimately obtained; but they had also lost the estates of a number to which they could make a claim. Map 6 illustrates the estates of freemen commended to Wihtgar or men over whom he had sokeright, which did not pass to Richard: as one might expect, they are those more distant from the territorial centre of his influence, despite the fact that Richard had acquired, or came to acquire, other freemen in that area.

Given the complexity of East Anglian landlordship and personal relations in 1066, which provided troubled waters in which the acquisitive could fish, there has been surprisingly little reorganization of the pattern of estates. What can be learned of how and when Richard came into possession of his East Anglian lands? Of Clare itself, Domesday says Aelfric gave 'the church and all the place' into the custody of Abbot Leofstan and his own son Wihtgar, and installed a priest and others with him. In fact this was a secular college with prebends, as we know from the documents of the Benedictine priory which succeeded it from 1090. Domesday goes on, 'after King William came, he seised it into his hand'. It must then have been given to Richard by royal grant. Wihtgar kept the remainder of his estate, and cannot have been so dismayed by the advent of the Normans as to lose all acquisitiveness: he is found taking over two freemen at Cornard and thirty acres at Bendysh.[26] But Wihtgar's activities in this line were not as extensive as Finn's, who is found adding freemen to his estate in King William's time at Ringshall and Ashbocking, and taking six acres belonging to Hemmingstone church, while at Badley he had added 26 freemen to the manor by agreement with the sheriff, as the sheriff himself said.[27] It could be that he was helped on his way by some sort of official position: he was associated with Ralph Taillebois in putting some Suffolk land into the king's hand, and Welldon Finn is prepared to speculate that 'he may have been a royal agent'.[28] It seems clear that he was not under too black a cloud when he died, as his widow was holding Pitsea and Latchingdon in south Essex in Domesday, while his Buckinghamshire manor of Cheddington had passed to a certain Swarting. So the impression is that Finn had not been expropriated, that he had profited from the period of the conquest even if much of the profit ultimately went to Richard fitz Gilbert, and that he may even have made himself useful to the conquerors. The same is not true of Wihtgar, who forfeited his estates, as Domesday tells us: 'Wisgarus tenuit quando se fore fecit'. Domesday also tells us of a mysterious agreement with Richard ('conventio Ricardi'), though we have no explanation.[29] The forfeiture of Wihtgar was the capital event in the formation of Richard's East Anglian estate, and it is worth asking when it happened, even if the answer could only be speculative. Apart from a brief appearance at Ely in 1071, our first knowledge of Richard's involvement in the affairs of East Anglia is the part attributed to him by Orderic in the suppression of Earl Ralph's rebellion in 1075.[30] Whether he was rewarded with the forfeited lands of a rebel, or sent to tackle the East Anglian rising because of his lands there, is a moot point. Richard acquired land at Whaddon in Cambridgeshire, which Ralph held on the day when he went against the king, and also two sokemen at Thurlow in the vicinity of Hundon, but not Ralph's larger manor there, which was in the king's hand. Wihtgar could just as well have been involved in the troubles up to 1070, if, as the 'Liber Eliensis' says, Hereward 'versus Estanglos profectus est, cui adhesit iuvenum pars valida'.[31] It is clear that Richard came to occupy an important position in the government of East Anglia: he is the addressee of two writs instructing him and the sheriff to do justice to abbot Baldwin of Bury concerning land in Suffolk, but alas, the writs are not datable even approximately.[32] The evidence of the land pleas is, as usual, difficult to construe at all precisely, but if we accept that there were two stages to the Ely plea, one in the early 1070s and one c.1080, as Professor Miller suggests, then it may be significant that he is not mentioned in the first stage but much in evidence in the second.[33]

Thus Wihtgar had plenty of opportunity to disgrace himself, and could have committed his relatively few 'invasiones' in a day or two. But Finn seems not to have disgraced himself, and to have prospered, possibly for quite a few years after 1066, and passed only some of his estates on to a Norman. Richard is involved in East Anglian affairs more directly from around 1080 than before, but there is simply not enough evidence to justify even a hypothesis.

Richard himself had committed 'invasiones', annexing two freemen in Cavendish previously commended to Harold, and a fairly sizeable estate in Bardfield. He had acquired a manor at Freston formerly Robert fitz Wimarc's, and a freeman once commended to Esgar the Staller. He had encroached on Ely's at Broxted.[34] But he had had considerable difficulty in gaining St Peter's church, Ipswich: the sheriff claimed that some of its alleged possessions belonged to the royal manor of Bramford, though the half-hundred of Ipswich disagreed; while he had had to make good his claim to the church against bishop Herfast—necessarily after 1070 when Herfast was appointed, though that tells us nothing about when Richard acquired his claim.[35] The majority of the 'invasiones' are on tenant land in 1086, which may imply that the lord and his followers were quite well entrenched by then, or that the pace of change was extremely rapid once they arrived. It would make most sense to assume that Wihtgar's estate came first and led to a number of annexations in its vicinity, and that Finn's estate followed. The question whether Richard obtained his south-eastern estates before his East Anglian ones is not one that can be answered, but he could quite easily have acquired both over a period.

One possible approach to this problem is through the process of enfeoffment. If we assume that enfeoffment is a gradual and continuous process, then the greater the proportion of enfeoffed land, the longer Richard had possessed it. And indeed, 67 per cent of the Surrey lands by value was in the hands of tenants, as against 36 per cent of the East Anglian estate. But of course there are obvious objections to this: for instance, that enfeoffment could be gradual and continuous without proceeding at an even rate. Problems of enfeoffment must be considered in their own right, and will occupy much of the rest of this paper. Is there any discernible pattern in the lands held by tenants, or conversely any common factors in the lands held in demesne? I shall assume that lands are in demesne if Domesday does not ascribe a tenant, and use 'tenant land' to indicate estates ascribed whole to named or anonymous individuals, not villein land on estates Richard held in demesne. The frequency of specified tenants makes this seem quite reasonable, but my best warrant for the procedure, in good medieval fashion, is that others have done it before.

To proceed by geographical area: Domesday presents us with an obvious but quite likely spurious contrast between Kent and Surrey, with no tenants at all mentioned in Kent, and a very large proportion of Surrey enfeoffed. We know from later evidence—fifteenth-century, in fact—that much of the lowy of Tonbridge was held by castle-guard, rents in kind, and in fractional knights' fees; the first at least may represent a very early arrangement.[36] The neatness and completeness of the distinction between Kent and Surrey looks much more like the workings of Domesday Book than of an estate; there are enough odd features in the entries covering Tonbridge for the complete absence of specified tenant holdings to be dismissed as yet another. This means that the 51 per cent figure for enfeoffed land in the south-east is probably an under-estimate.

It has been found on other fees that 'the value of the individual manors was a governing consideration in the selection of the places to be retained'.[37] This does not apply to Richard's lands in Surrey, where the only manor to stand out in value was Shalford, which was enfeoffed. Lands not ascribed to tenants in Surrey are distinguished neither by value nor by their position; two of the most valuable are the nearest to the Kentish lands, but Walton was the most valuable and was the furthest away. It is just conceivable that if Richard had wanted to move from Tonbridge to Clare staying in his own houses he would have been able to do so via Walton, Harefield and Standon. Neither is there any neat pattern in the way the estates of the greater predecessors have been treated: all of them provided land for both Richard and his followers. The tenant land is scattered more or less evenly among the demesne manors. Bletchingley was three manors in 1066 and they have been brought into one, which implies a managerial decision though on whose part and for what reason it is impossible to say.

Something similar has happened at Chelsham, where two separate estates, held by different men in King Edward's day, are both in the hands of Robert de Wateville in 1086. At nearby Tillingdown however, two separate estates have passed to two separate Domesday tenants. The united estate at Bletchingley has partly been granted out to tenants: of its ten hides three tenants hold six, valued at 73s. 4d. as against Richard's £12.

The treatment of the south-eastern lands requires more explanation than the evidence provides, but in East Anglia the situation is somewhat simplified by Richard's succeeding to an estate that was already well endowed with demesne manors. Here, quite simply, the most valuable manors, Thaxted, Hundon, Clare and Desning, are all in demesne. The estates where Wihtgar had demesne land which was given to tenants—Panfield, Dunmow and Hempstead— were much less valuable. The only really substantial estate gained from Finn was the manor of Langham, which was in the hands of a tenant in 1086. Of the more distant estates which map 3 shows in demesne, Lakenheath was valued in Desning, while Elveden and Wattisham were of no great significance. Badley and whichever of the Rodings is referred to were slightly more valuable, but still less so than quite a few of the subinfeudated manors.

In a part of the country where manor and vill frequently did not coincide, it is hardly surprising to find a number of separate units in the same vill treated in a number of ways. At Finchingfield we find no less than five separate estates in the hands of tenants, as well as eleven sokemen described as in Richard's demesne. A comparison of maps 3 and 6 shows how often freemen and sokemen of Wihtgar's had passed into the hands of Richard's tenants by 1086, a process we shall come back to later. So Richard has kept a small number of very valuable estates in demesne, all of which were the demesnes of his predecessor; and his followers have mostly been rewarded with the lands of freemen and sokemen. There remained a large number of rent-paying freemen and sokemen: after a long list of Essex sokemen, Domesday says 'all the above pay ('reddent') £15.6s.4d. and are in Richard's demesne'.[38] The centre of these lands was Clare, where, one assumes, Richard built the motte-and-bailey castle which still survives. Had the site been fortified previously, it is possible to doubt that it would have been given to the canons. A few miles away, at Desning, is an interesting sequence of moated sites, and what the Ordnance Survey map shows as another motte-and-bailey castle. The latter was presumably the headquarters of Simon son of Lambert the constable and the 'familia' of Desning, the addressees of an order by earl Gilbert some time in the reign of Stephen. We can hardly say whether the castle they garrisoned was old or new at the time.[39] But it was from Clare that the family took its name, and had started to by 1086, since Domesday once calls Richard 'of Clare'.[40] If the places where the Normans felt most at home were those where they planted vineyards, then Clare and Standon were the favoured residences of the fee.

So far I have been treating Richard's estate as if there was a clear distinction between demesne and tenant or subinfeudated land. When we come to scan the Domesday entries for evidence of how the demesne was exploited we find a number of references which imply that conditions were quite likely similar to those which prevailed on some other estates. Thus Thaxted was worth £30 when Richard received it, and in 1086 £50, as the French and English both said, but Richard gave it to a certain Englishman to rent for £60 ('dedit ad Censum'), and each year he lost at least £10 ('deficiunt illi ad minus decem librae').[41] Thaxted was the most valuable single manor on the entire fee, and if Richard was leasing that, it seems a reasonable guess that the others were leased as well. We have two references to 'reeves', both clearly Englishmen, and somewhat acquisitive. At Braintree Letmar the reeve claimed three freemen as part of Richard's fee, but Richard's own men did not testify to this; and in Chawreth Aethelmaer, Richard's reeve, had encroached on the land of three more freemen and called Richard to vouch for him ('vocavit eum ad tutorem'), but Richard did not come. It could be that the general rise in value between the time the estates were received and 1086 mostly reflects the new landlords putting the rents up, and that reeves who had to pay the increased rents if they were to retain their position were compelled to take rather desperate measures to recoup themselves. If indeed one of the effects of the Norman conquest was the depression of East Anglian freemen and sokemen, it would seem that the Normans themselves were not the sole culprits; while Englishmen such as Finn and Oswald, in bringing other men into their orbit, may have been following the example of their compatriots before the conquest.

Another possible explanation for the rises in value, which we can preceive for the East Anglian lands thanks to 'little Domesday' but not for the southeast, is the great increase in demesne livestock, especially sheep. All the greater demesne manors had more sheep in 1086 than in King Edward's day, except for Sampford (inconveniently for the theory Sampford had lost twelve sheep but gained £5 in value). At Clare the increase had been dramatic, from 60 to 480, at Thaxted from 200 to 320. Demesne sheep-farming was already very well established at Desning under Wihtgar, who had 840 sheep there in King Edward's day: this feature seems to have been extended to Clare and Hundon under Richard, and to Bardfield and Thaxted to a rather lesser extent. If at least some of these demesnes were let out to English reeves the extension of sheep-farming can hardly be attributed solely to Norman business efficiency. Can we assume that the destination of the wool was the Flemish cloth industry? And that the wool was sold for cash? If so, it may have been another policy of the lessees to help meet their increased overheads. However it had come about, the increase was considerable: on the ten demesne manors as shown in map 3 for which figures are available, the total increase is from *c*.1600 to nearly 3000 sheep. Very considerable proportional increases had also occurred on land held by tenants.

Surrey, then, was very largely subinfeudated, and Kent may have been, though if so Domesday conceals it; in East Anglia Richard had a handful of large and valuable manors, with a surrounding cloud of smaller estates held by named tenants. The proportion of demesne to tenant land is greater in the eastern than in the southern group, while the total of tenant land specified for the whole fee is some 40 per cent by value. The distinction may be invalid; but it is perhaps worth comparing with the proportions observed on other Domesday estates. Most work has been done on ecclesiastical lands, but we have three lay fees for comparison. The church lands generally show a lower proportion of enfeoffed land, with the lordship of Canterbury at 15 per cent, Westminster at 18 per cent, Winchester at 20 per cent and Glastonbury at 30 per cent. Peterborough, at 46 per cent, is wholly exceptional and shows a higher proportion than any of the lay fees, but it also had a very high 'servitium debitum' in proportion to its endowment. The lay fees are more comparable to Richard's 40 per cent, and start where the more normal church fees leave off. Hugh de Port's lands are some 30 per cent in the hands of tenants, and the two Lacy honours of Weobley and Pontefract are respectively 40 per cent and 44 per cent enfeoffed.[42]

If we are to attempt to compare the proportion of subinfeudated land with the service due to the king from the whole fee, we immediately run into the fact that no round number of knights due is available. When the earl of Clare drew up his 'Carta' in 1166 there was no figure of knight service that he 'recognised' and an additional figure that he did not recognize. His estate was no longer the same as his ancestor's was in 1086. He had 127 and a fraction 'old fees', 7 and a fraction 'new' ones, and later is found paying scutage on roughly the total figure.[43] Therefore we cannot say on what terms Richard held his fief from William the Conqueror: but if my suggestion about the gradual acquisition of the estates be accepted, then it would seem impractical for the two men to make a single bargain early in the reign to represent the total service due for the future.

The tenants on Richard fitz Gilbert's estate represent such a great variety of income and legal and personal status that sorting them out into categories risks being seriously misleading, but it will have to be done if we are to obtain any sort of general picture, even a false one. The men most demonstrably connected with military service are those whom Domesday actually calls 'milites'. There are only six of them, and they are not well endowed. Two 'milites' followed three sokemen in possession of 36 acres at Alresford near the Essex coast, where there were two ploughs and four bordars; the value of the estate was 60s. Two 'milites' had similarly followed three sokemen at Finchingfield in an estate of exactly the same assessment with the same number of ploughs and bordars, but with three slaves and worth 65s. Another 'miles' was a tenant of another tenant, Robert de Watevile at Malden in Surrey, where he held a hide and a virgate with one plough, a villein and a bordar. The little holding is not separately valued. The remaining 'miles' also held of another tenant, at Albury where his estate, again not valued, comprised one and a half demesne ploughs, a villein and a slave.[44] In ploughs and men, the two Surrey 'milites' held less than the Essex groups of two 'milites'. So if we say that the income of these 'milites' was something of the order of 30s. to 40s. each as ascribed in Domesday, we are unlikely to be drastically wrong. An estate of that kind of value puts them in the upper range of East Anglian sokemen and freemen, where their equals and superiors can be found in individuals such as the freemen of Withersfield together worth 30s., the sixteen freemen of Stradishall ploughs, five villeins, ten bordars and assorted livestock, together with nine further freemen below him, were together worth 60s.[45] But in general such prosperous freemen had had a tier of newcomers imposed on them, and those who remained in Richard's demesne were the poorer sort, such as the nine freemen of Withersfield together worth 30s. the sixteen freemen of Stradishall together worth 20s. or the eight freemen of Brettenham together worth 5s.[46] The terms 'freeman' and 'sokeman' covered a wide variety of incomes, some of them greater than those of men called 'miles'. It is worth recalling here that some Peterborough sokemen are described as serving with the knights of the abbey, not unlike the 'vavassores' of the Bayeux inquest.[47] It seems clear that many of these tolerably prosperous local men had remained *in situ*, but dropped in the social scale. Professor Douglas has printed a charter of enfeoffment from Bury St Edmunds abbey, probably dating from before Domesday, in which the knight's fee is described as the lands of a long list of freemen of Withersfield together worth 30s., the sixteen freemen of Stradishall that the freemen simply stayed on.[48] A number of Englishmen had succeeded other Englishmen in 1086, possibly simply by inheritance: Goding had followed Lefcild at West Bergholt, for instance, and Godart had followed Lefgar at Withersfield, but both estates were very small.

A difficult problem when discussing the estates of tenants is what to do about 'Ralph', 'Robert' and 'Roger'. How often is 'Robert' to be identified with Robert de Watevile? Or are we to assume that all unqualified Roberts are separate individuals? Fortunately these three are the only names that pose difficulties, and I have treated them as if they were all separate individuals. This is likely to be erroneous, but it errs on the side of caution. The name Pagan is not so common in Domesday that one need assume Richard had several tenants of that name, while enough have unmistakable surnames to make the exercise of discussing their estates well worth while. The Clare tenants are a good example of a Norman lord taking his followers from the vicinity of his Norman lands. Orbec and Bienfaite are quite close to one another some 20 km. south west of Bernay. Meules and Le Sap, the castles of Richard's brother Baldwin, are also in the neighbourhood. Four men named in Domesday came from the immediate vicinity, Roger d'Abernon, Picot de Friardel and Roger de St Germain, plus a certain Roger of Orbec. Four more families which made their appearance in the next generation in England also came from close by—Geoffrey de Favarches, the founder of Walsingham priory, from Ferva-ques, and the families latinized as 'de Nazanda', Kersuniere and 'de Waspria' from Nassandres, la Cressonière and la Vesprière. The last four could have descended from men who were unenfeoffed household knights in 1086, or they could have joined Gilbert fitz Richard afterwards.[49]

Some of the named newcomers have even less assigned to them in Domesday than the anonymous 'milites': Roger of Orbec's estate was worth only 18s.—though he may be disguised as a simple 'Roger' in some other Suffolk vill—but Hamo's at Hundon consisted of two bordars, one plough and fifty sheep and was worth 20s. Widard had acquired two sokemen at Thurlow with 25 acres and half a plough, worth 4s. 4d. Fulkered had taken over one freeman and one sokeman in Hawkedon with one plough, three bordars, a slave and five acres of meadow worth £1 6s.8d. One of these minor newcomers, a certain Maskerel, who also occurs as a witness of his lord's charters, held land worth £4 2s.2d.in two Essex vills ten miles apart, one with demesne and one without, and founded a local dynasty which can be pursued through the charters of Stoke by Clare priory. Such men may seem insignificant compared with even some other tenants, but in their own villages they and their descendants were forces to be reckoned with. An interesting example of such a man is one Elinand, who held in the Essex vill of Finchingfield, and in Suffolk at Waldingfield. In the former he succeeded two sokemen in an estate with one and a half ploughs, seven bordars and a flock of 127 sheep; at Waldingfield he followed three freemen with one plough and nine bordars. Neither estate is described as a manor, and there is no distinction between demesne and tenant land. Elinand is chiefly interesting because of his appearance in the Stoke charters, where he is referred to as 'vicecomes': it would take more evidence to suggest him as a sheriff of Suffolk or Essex—it seems more likely that he was a baronial sheriff, perhaps with competence on the East Anglian lands of the fee. To Stoke he granted tithe in Finchingfield, and land and a mill in Waldingfield as well as tithe in Fornham which Domesday does not accredit to him: he could easily have gone on acquiring land after 1086. He died in the second decade of the twelfth century, and two of his five sons became monks of Stoke. The value of his Domesday estate was £4, which puts him in the lower income bracket of Richard fitz Gilbert's tenants. Nearly all the men with similar estates were enfeoffed on the Suffolk lands: the Surrey tenants generally had much higher incomes. It is hazardous to provide figures because of the difficulty of identification, but it seems fairly safe to say that at least nine tenants had Domesday estates worth between £5 and £10, and at least five had over £10. The most valuable estate by far was that of Robert de Watevile, worth at least £62, possibly more. He was followed at a considerable distance by John, Roger d'Abernon, the wife of Salia and Walter Tirel, in the region of £15–£20 at least. Thus there were very great differences between the estates of Richard's tenants. It is worth pointing out that the surviving thegn Oswald's estate was in total worth nearly £20.

Maps 7 and 8 show something of the distribution of these estates. Only the greatest tenants, Robert de Watevile and Roger d'Abernon, held in both the south-east and East Anglia, in both cases only one manor in East Anglia and the great majority of their lands in Surrey. Some estates are well concentrated—Picot's in Surrey, for instance, worth nearly £8, or indeed those of Robert de Watevile. Pagan's estate in Suffolk was very concentrated, and although worth relatively little, £3 3s.4d., had demesne and tenant land of its own. Ernald's rather more scattered estate was chiefly built up of those of sokemen: one of his holdings had two demesne ploughs of its own. Most of Ernald's land by value was held illegally, having been 'invaded' from estates nearby which he held of Richard. Wilard's estate had three centres quite widely scattered, in two of which demesne ploughs are specified. From Withersfield in Suffolk he had 'invaded' over the Cambridgeshire border and annexed a hide worth 40s. Germund possessed the estates of three sokemen near Finchingfield, with no specified demesne lands, and a small self-contained estate at Flowton in Suffolk, thirty miles away, to which he had added 15 acres formerly held freely by a priest.

As well as some quite substantial tenants who appear to have held only of Richard fitz Gilbert, we find a class of men who were tenants in chief in their own right, or important tenants of other lords, holding small estates on Richard's fee. There was a certain amount of interpenetration with other fees. Two causes have been suggested for this phenomenon: simple annexation, taking advantage of political or tenurial confusion to make encroachments which were then covered by a legal formula; and gifts to powerful neighbours to placate them or make them well-disposed. None of the four 'outsiders' held very much on Richard's fee, which may well reflect Richard's power in preventing annexations. Robert Blund, a former sheriff of Norfolk and a tenant in chief in the area north of Bury, had acquired a sokeman worth 3s. at West Stow in the vicinity of his estates, which looks like annexation but is hardly significant. Walter de Caen, the tenant of a large barony on the Malet fee, held the estate of a former king's thegn at Helmingham, closer to his own interests than Richard fitz Gilbert's. This may have been annexation, but is just as likely to reflect mutual convenience. Frodo, the brother of abbot Baldwin of Bury St Edmunds, was much in evidence on the Bury lands, but on the more distant parts towards Norfolk; of Richard he held a small estate at Depden between Bury and Clare, on whose initiative it is not possible to say. Still on the East

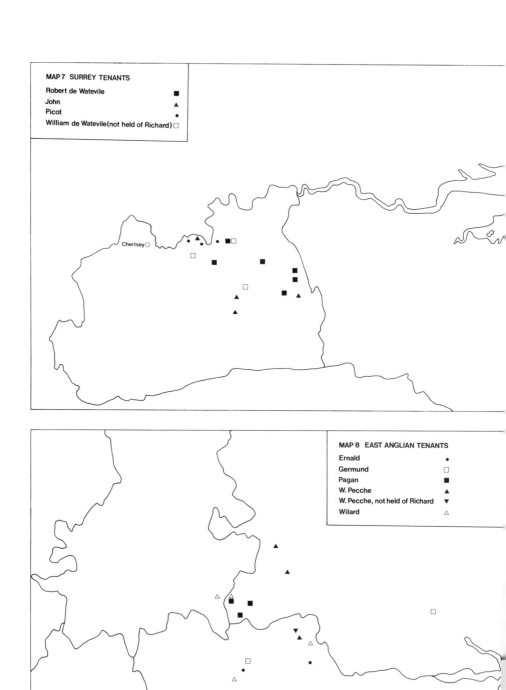

MAP 7 SURREY TENANTS

Robert de Watevile ■
John ▲
Picot •
William de Watevile(not held of Richard) □

Chertsey○

MAP 8 EAST ANGLIAN TENANTS

Ernald •
Germund □
Pagan ■
W. Pecche ▲
W. Pecche, not held of Richard ▼
Wilard △

Anglian lands, we may suspect the process happening the other way round in the case of William Pecche, who held half a hide of Aubrey de Vere in Belcamp, in the immediate vicinity of quite a substantial manor at Gesting-thorpe held of Richard. In Surrey we find William, the nephew of Walkelin, bishop of Winchester, holding a manor worth £6, at Chipstead in the east of the county. His other Domesday estate was on his uncle's great manor of Farnham some thirty miles away. This could hardly be annexation: Richard kept one wood there for himself ('sibi retinuit'), while William had the other. It could well be that the bishop of Winchester, one of the few lords wealthier than Richard, was worth cultivating. Round suggested that this William was William de Watevile, whose estates, shown on map 7, were held of Chertsey abbey and were in the vicinity of those of his namesake Robert.[50] This situation hints at a complexity in the interrelationship of tenant families and the lords they served that the evidence does not allow us to explore.

From this brief and simplified discussion of the first generation of tenants there emerges the central fact that there was no such thing as a uniform 'knight's fee' in landed endowment, which of course is hardly a surprise. We see a spectrum of tenants from Robert de Watevile down to the anonymous 'milites', a continuous gradation rather than a series of discrete groups. The tenant families do not themselves step into the shoes of predecessors with the same estates except in a few minor instances: the configurations of their estates are nearly all new. And if Richard knew enough about his lands to retain one wood in Chipstead while handing the other to a tenant, then there could have been a reasonable degree of centralised control in the distribution. But the fact that the tenants' estates were compiled from those of a number of previous holders implies that here too they could have been put together over a period.

What can we discover of the relationship between the tenants and their holdings? Could they have treated them as economic unities? What sort of services did they receive? Clearly we can hardly think of 'high farming' such as thirteenth-century lords practised. It is evident from map 8 that the lands of Wilard or Germund could not have been treated as units. But they were made up in part from what had been functioning individual estates in King Edward's time, and in all likelihood they were still that: so Wilard's estate consisted of three or four separate economic units, not one. In only two instances does Domesday tell us what tenants did with their lands: a man called Goisfrid possessed an estate at Ringshall in Suffolk; it was derived from three separate freemen of King Edward's day, and on one of them there was demesne with one plough. This was Goisfrid's only Domesday estate, and it seems that there was a home farm. The 'valets' of the three estates add up to 70s.; Domesday says Goisfrid gave it to farm for 70s. but only got 60s. So he was farming out his only estate, apparently. In Surrey, Picot's estate is the most concentrated for its size on the entire fee. His lands had been brought together from three separate Englishmen, and there was demesne land in two places. Yet one of these manors with demesne was at farm for £4. So it would seem that an image of subinfeudated lords living on their estates as a matter of course is at variance with the little evidence available: even when they had home farms to live on they were leased out, like the greater demesnes of their own lords.[51] Map 3 shows what a large number of estates had no demesne at all: the most reasonable explanation is that the demesne-less holdings were sources of cash, and it appears that the holdings with demesne were primarily that as well. This does not mean that the tenants took no personal interest in the lands assigned to them—the large number of 'invasiones' committed by the East Anglian tenants, such as Germund at Flowton, implies quite a lively, energetic concern, and even physical presence on the estate at some stage. The lands appear to have been considered the tenants' own, as well. A few years after Domesday, when Gilbert fitz Richard founded Stoke by Clare priory and his men contributed also, at least three of them were Domesday tenants or their sons, and while they may have been under some pressure to give and the gifts were confirmed by the lord, they appear to be giving of their own.

The question what service Richard obtained from his tenants is impossible to answer from strictly contemporary evidence relating to this fee. In the 1166 Carta a number of tenants obviously the descendants of those in Domesday are shown owing knight service. Their estates could have changed complexion in the intervening eighty years, and the terms of tenure could as well. Such a question can only be answered by analogy with other fees. To take evidence from fees neighbouring Richard's own, though both ecclesiastical: in the 'Feudal Book' of abbot Baldwin we find King William granting land to Bury St Edmunds when the Anglo-Saxon holder died, 'so that the abbot might give it to his Frenchmen to go in the service of the saint when and where necessary', while on the lands of the Archbishop of Canterbury in west Kent a number of knights held in fee and also for an annual render to the monastic treasury.[52] Again the evidence is very scanty, but it does not suggest that military service was limited in time or place, or that it could not be supplemented by money payments. The nature of the service rendered can only be discussed in terms of probabilities with so little evidence available. It could be that some of the estates of lesser men were held for serjeanty service, or even some quite menial household task, such as seems to have been the case on the Warenne fee. It has also been suggested that knights could be assigned to outlying estates as managers: Stenton pointed out fifty years ago that we are talking now of 'knights', not of 'chevaliers' because the English assimilated the French newcomers to their own 'cnihts' who were primarily household retainers, especially those concerned with administering property.[53] If this was the case then their functions may simply have been to assign lands to the farmer who would pay the most, perhaps collect the money, and perhaps keep it. But maps 2 and 3 show that tenants' land was even more common close to the greater demesne manors than far from it, and that some Frenchmen were enfeoffed on the demesne manors themselves; and if they started as managers they soon came to consider the land their own.

This pushes us towards the conclusion that the estates were intended as remuneration for those to whom they were assigned. In which case we can only be struck by the enormous differences between tenants. Some of the greater ones clearly represent the honorial baronage of the twelfth century, and would be expected to furnish knights themselves—one such has already been enfeoffed by Robert de Watevile. Attention focuses on the lesser men, 'the undistinguished stipendiary knighthood of the conqueror's reign', as Stenton called them.[54] It could be that the lesser estates represent an English version of the 'feudum loricae' such as can be found on the honour of Mortain's lands in England. But it is not necessary to suppose that the lower levels of endowment represent the social status of one grade of early knights. For one thing, not all the lesser French tenants need have been knights, though some were. But if tenants such as Goisfrid and Picot were leasing their lands, it seems reasonable to suppose that they normally lived in Richard's household, and in a world of knights living in households their status relative to the outside world would not be determined by their individual income but by the style in which they were maintained by their lord. Their life-style need not have been maintained out of their own resources alone. There is thus no necessary connection between individual economic resources and social status. It seems that the lord rewarded his men with money: one recalls the young knights inciting Robert Curthose by saying 'you scarcely have a penny to give your dependants'.[55] Giving an estate to a follower would thus be like assigning him a rent, which perhaps he would then have to collect. But such an assigned rent could easily have been supplemented by further gifts which would leave no record. So we cannot deduce from the size of his Domesday estate how much a follower of Richard fitz Gilbert was actually given.

But once assigned, an estate soon became the grantee's. A few years after Domesday some of Richard's tenants were free to grant property to their lord's religious foundation, though they may not have been equally free to withhold it; and some of them passed estates on to their sons. The difference between an enfeoffed knight and a household knight would begin by being a matter of where their reward came from, though it would not remain that for long. It is clear from the evidence of leasing that Richard's cash income was large, and it may have been underpinned by the increase in demesne sheep-farming. Such quantities of ready money would help explain the siting of the castle at Clare, where there were burgesses in 1086, and perhaps even the growth of a town at Tonbridge. Land may have been the ultimate source of wealth, but it was not the only form in which wealth could be held.

The impact of Richard fitz Gilbert and his followers on England had been to establish a new tenurial geography. He has amassed the estates of many predecessors, carved out a new lordship in Kent, and extended his sway over a number of East Anglian freemen. He has distributed lands among newcomers in new configurations. But it could have taken nearly twenty years for this to happen, during which time some Englishmen had been able to prosper. The nature of Richard's estates varied from region to region, reflecting what was there when he came.

The Making of the March: Aspects of the Norman Settlement in Dyfed

I. W. ROWLANDS

The March of Wales—the sum and total of Marcher lordships which were to assume their mature form by the end of the thirteenth century—was directly the result of the Norman impact on Wales and its borderland and essentially the creation of the Anglo-Norman aristocracy. Where the documentation and the work of the castle-builder survives, the role of the Anglo-Normans in the making of this March can be illustrated and interpreted, its chronology and narrative established.[1] More often than not, however, the uneven nature of the source-material, together with the insecure and ephemeral existence of many an Anglo-Norman lordship, make it difficult to focus on the peculiarly Norman contribution to the evolution of Marcher society as revealed by the comparative fullness of later documentation. Mindful of such a qualification, this study is an attempt to identify and illustrate some of the formative elements in the making of the March in West Wales by the Anglo-Norman conquerors of the native kingdom of Dyfed.

That the first Norman incursions into Dyfed, undertaken in 1093 by Roger of Montgomery, earl of Shrewsbury and William fitz Baldwin, sheriff of Devon, were swift and unopposed may be gathered from the somewhat terse entry in the native annals: 'the French overran Dyfed and Ceredigion—which was not in their power before that—and made castles in them and fortified them'.[2] Their ferocity and disruption moved another witness to pen a memorable lament: 'The people and the priest are despised by the word, heart and work of the Normans. For they increase our taxes and burn our properties. One vile Norman intimidates a hundred natives with his command, and terrifies (them) with his look . . . Families do not now delight in offspring; the heir does not hope for the paternal estates; the rich man does not aspire to accumulate flocks.' The first castles were built and garrisoned—the process of occupation and exploitation was ready to begin.[3]

There were, however, to be no easy pickings in Dyfed and, consequently, one formative strand in the fabric of Norman colonial society there was to be its very precariousness. Periodic Welsh offensives from 1094 onwards made this province no place for the faint-hearted. In 1096 only the steadfastness of its castellan saved the Montgomery fortress of Pembroke—and with it the Norman hold on western Dyfed—upon the desertion of its knightly garrison;

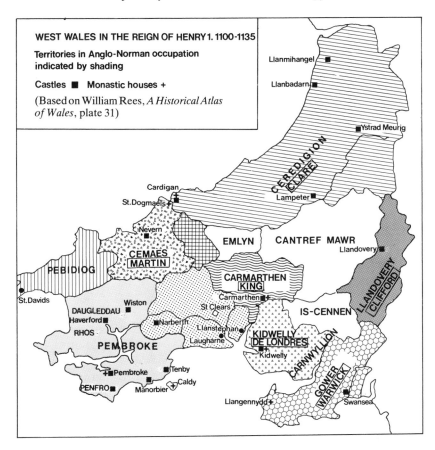

WEST WALES IN THE REIGN OF HENRY 1. 1100-1135

Territories in Anglo-Norman occupation indicated by shading

Castles ■ Monastic houses +

(Based on William Rees, *A Historical Atlas of Wales*, plate 31)

farther east, in the Tywi valley, the death of their lord prompted his followers to abandon his castle at Rhyd-y-gors.[4] The vulnerability of these early settlers is strikingly illustrated by the manner in which their fortresses in eastern Dyfed huddled around the Tywi estuary and Carmarthen Bay and, farther west, around the mouth of the Cleddau rivers or along the Castle Martin Peninsula at Pembroke, Carew and Manorbier where, as a boy, Gerald de Barri (*alias* Gerald of Wales) remembered the night alarms occasioned by the Welsh capture of nearby Tenby in 1146.[5] So unstable could the military situation become that it is possible to understand how one settler in Daugleddau could make the same grant to two different religious houses in England—the eventual recipients, suitably enough, were those *milites strenui* of the Church, the Hospitallers.[6] Early reverses were, however, made good and the reign of Henry I marked a notable extension and consolidation of Anglo-Norman settlement in Dyfed as elsewhere in Wales. But the momentum was not maintained once his masterful presence was removed and by the 1150s much of this achievement was undone. The Welsh recovered their hold over most of eastern Dyfed while the Norman position in the west seemed seriously threatened—for the men of Pembrokeshire, it had all been a close-run thing. Perhaps it wasn't simply wishful thinking which induced the annalist to describe Maredudd ap Gruffydd of Dinefwr as 'lord of Ceredigion and Ystrad Tywi and Dyfed' on his death in 1155; the stage was set for the remarkable successes of his brother, Rhys, in the decades that followed.[7]

Unlike the thegns of Anglo-Saxon England, the Welsh warrior class faced no single military calamity; they thereby possessed the vital element of time—time to withdraw, to submit, to calculate, to regroup. The Anglo-Norman settlers in Dyfed therefore encountered many difficulties. To the north, across the Teifi river, the Norman hold on Ceredigion was fitful and uneven and their occupation therein was marked, it would seem, by almost chronic instability.[8] Furthermore, the dynasty of Rhys ap Tewdwr, last native ruler of the whole of Deheubarth (of which Dyfed was part) had not been extinguished or entirely dispossessed. The Normans had to contend therefore with a displaced princely family which still retained a territorial base and maintained a resilient presence within their patrimony in Cantref Mawr. Moreover, the scions of such a house were ever potential leaders for the adventurous or the malcontent ('young hot-heads' as the followers of Gruffydd ap Rhys were called in 1116) and always the centre of a whole web of lineage and kindred ties which a royal house counted among its strongest assets. Such ties could of course, extend to many a native lord in areas subject to Anglo-Norman domination as well as to major dynasties outside the confines of Deheubarth itself.

The alien lordships most immediately vulnerable to any *revanchiste* impulse from Cantref Mawr were those in Cemais and Emlyn and the complex of lordships in eastern Dyfed dignified in the royal accounts for 1130 by the title of 'honour of Carmarthen' and for most of the twelfth century the soft 'underbelly' of the Norman position in West Wales. In addition, conflict and faction within colonial society in Dyfed itself could, at times, weaken both its fighting capability and resolve.[9] The latter however was most seriously undermined by the death of Henry I and the subsequent succession dispute which removed any effective royal commitment to Welsh affairs: the *sine qua non* for co-operation between the king and his lords of the March had, in the course of that conflict, been dissolved. Such conditions were not conducive to a 'Darwinian' determinism in the evolution of Marcher 'liberties' and 'regalities'—the reign of Stephen, when Marcher lords had to fend for themselves, may be the critical period here. In Dyfed, where there had been a royal presence at Pembroke from 1102 to 1138 and at Carmarthen (though intermittently) from *c*.1109, the priority must surely have been military security and the expectation that of royal intervention when needful.

The fate of the Anglo-Norman settlers in Dyfed rested ultimately, not upon royal protection, but upon their own resources and the resource of their leaders. The greatest of these were powerful figures such as Arnulf of Montgomery, the first Norman lord (and probably earl) of Pembroke whose father and two brothers were in turn earls of Shrewsbury. Though a member of a family with a tradition of Marcher responsibilities, both in Wales and

Normandy, Arnulf also possessed estates in Holderness—a necessary reminder of the fact that many a lord of the March had lands and therefore interests outside it. Like many a Welsh prince of Dyfed before him, he sought an Irish alliance when he married into the royal house of Munster, but neither this nor his possession of the lordship of Pembroke could save him from forfeiture and exile in 1102.[10] His eventual successor at Pembroke, Gilbert fitz Gilbert, likewise belonged to a family with wide Marcher connections; while he himself followed his uncle as lord of Netherwent, and Chepstow, his father and brother were successively lords of Ceredigion. His son, Richard fitz Gilbert, known to posterity as 'Strongbow', went one step further than Arnulf of Montgomery; not only did he contract a royal marriage in Ireland, he went on to make extensive conquests there. The success enjoyed by the Clares in Wales was, however, denied to the other branch of the family. Neither William nor Richard, sons of Baldwin de Meules, were able to gain a permanent foothold in eastern Dyfed in the 1090s. If they had, the descendants of Gilbert of Brionne would have dominated West Wales.

These were great men whose horizons extended far beyond Dyfed and we may doubt whether they were settlers in the sense that they would have been permanent residents within its bounds. Having staked his claim in 1093, Earl Arnulf apparently left for England. The true *marchiones* of Dyfed were the local magnates, the men on the spot *(viri probi prudentiique)* such as the castellans at Pembroke, Haverfordwest and Wiston and the families they founded such as those of fitz Gerald, de Barri, de la Roche, de Brian, fitz Wizo, fitz Tancard and fitz Martin. It was these men and their descendants who provided the military leaders of the settler contingents in their engagements with the Welsh and represented their community before the royal officers.[11] The origins of such families are obscure for many of their ancestors came westwards as younger sons, landless and household knights in the retinues of Norman or Flemish lords. About the first de Barri at Manorbier, a later descendant, Gerald of Wales was uncharacteristically reticent though he seems to have moved along the South Wales coast before eventually settling down in southern Pembrokeshire.[12] More is known about Gerald of Windsor. As the younger son of William the Conqueror's constable at the castle of that name, his ministerial career was, it seems, a family tradition. He began it as steward to Arnulf of Montgomery, survived his lord's fall and exile and ended it as royal constable of Pembroke and substantial local magnate with lordships at Carew and Emlyn. Gerald had done well. 'To put roots down,' as his grandson put it, he married into the princely dynasty of Deheubarth. He established in Pembrokeshire a lineage whose members were influential men, providing a bishop and two stewards for the see of St David's and in the second half of the twelfth century, leading participants in the conquest of Ireland.[13] It was the activities and ambitions of such men that gave to Anglo-Norman society in Dyfed its own particular identity and dimensions.

To the Welsh annalist, the Norman intrusions into his homeland were but another chapter in the *gesta Francorum*; to the native cleric, their conquests were the *opus Francigenarum*. In fact, in one version of the *Brut*, the Normans are referred to by that name on but two or three occasions.[14] Among the conquerors of Dyfed the Normans and Norman seigneurial leadership assuredly predominated but the non-Norman element cannot be neglected. Together with those lords on the Welsh border by the late eleventh century who bore the names of their Norman patrimonies, such as Montgomeri, Lassi, Candos and Escouis, were the men from Brittany, Flanders and Maine.[15] While the personnel of the seigneurial class can be sketched, that of the vital groups in the early colonisation of Dyfed, namely the knights and the sub-tenants, remain largely unrecorded although something may be recovered from place-name evidence. It can be surmised that a good number of them came from their lords' English estates and that a major recruiting area lay across the Bristol Channel in south-west England.[16]

Although common elements were provided above all else by feudal lordship, knight's fee, manor and castle, from this long and oft-interrupted process of colonization there emerged in Dyfed a settler society hybrid in origin, language, dialect and custom. Such a society might experience a two-way assimilation—on the one level (and more selectively) with the native Welsh community and, on the second, within that society itself. If that historically silent process of assimilation was a prolonged one as it was, for instance, with regard to Breton and Flemish elements in the English shires of Lincoln and Cambridge, then how much less hurried in the March of Wales where diversity of custom and institution was the necessary result of piece-meal and private conquests?[17] Even if we allow, as we must with the genealogies of the de Barri and fitz Gerald families before us, for the leaven of intermarriage, contemporary sources of the twelfth century and beyond still reflect this diversity. The range of such sources is impressive, ranging as it does from native annals, episcopal and royal *acta*, private charters and place-names to a *chanson de geste*, inspired if not composed by a settler in Dyfed. The many 'diverse folk' of Dyfed were listed by the author of one version of the *Brut*, *sub anno* 1116, as 'Flemings and French and Saxons and their own (i.e. Welsh) folk', and in a royal charter, Henry I's subjects in the honour of Carmarthen are distinguished as *fideles sui: Franci, et Anglici, Flamingi et Walenses*.[18]

The distinction drawn here between *Francigenae* and *Flandrenses* is but one of many indications of a substantial Flemish settlement in Dyfed and, in particular, in its western *cantrefi* where it was most concentrated. Certainly, many prominent Flemish lords, together with their followers, took part in the Norman Conquest of England and were duly rewarded in the ensuing distribution of land by William the Conqueror, whose queen was, of course, daughter to the Count of Flanders. Concentrations of Flemish enfeoffments can therefore be traced in the folios of the Domesday Book, and there is early evidence also for Flemish immigration into shires not included in the survey.[19] But the closest parallel to the Flemish colonization of western Dyfed is provided by the planting of Flemish settlers in parts of Clydesdale and Moray from the second decade of the twelfth century onwards by successive kings of Scotland, a process expertly illuminated for us at last year's Battle Conference by Professor Barrow.[20] It may well be that the Flemings early enjoyed that reputation as vigorous and doughty colonizers which finds many an echo in the twelfth-century accounts. Their appearance in Dyfed, then, fits within a well-established context for their activities elsewhere; in west Wales, it is paralleled by their presence in the neighbouring lordships of Kidwelly and Ceredigion.[21]

The chronology and narrative of the Flemish migration into western Dyfed are complex subjects and many of the difficulties that surround them will not be resolved until the relationship between certain sources can be satisfactorily explained. The sources in question are, on the one hand, the Latin versions of the *Annales Cambriae* and the Welsh translations of the *Brut* and, on the other, annalistic and chronicle writing at Worcester and other centres in western England.[22] All are unanimous however in associating the initial immigration with the reign of Henry I, and the different dates which they provide still enable us to focus the event within the narrower limits of 1107–1111. While the arrival of the first Flemish settlers in any numbers might elicit a single date or occasion from the annalist, it is inherently likely that an original *adventus* would have been followed up by successive and probably intermittent groups of settlers over a period of many generations—the varying dates in our authorities would thus be explained. In any event, a *terminus ante quem* is provided by a writ of Henry I which confirms the presence of Flemings, at least in Daugleddau, before the election of Bernard as bishop of St David's in 1115.[23]

That the Flemish settlement in Rhos and Daugleddau (two *cantrefi*, we may note) was a deliberate act of policy by Henry I is confirmed by virtually all our sources, annals and chronicle alike. With regard to Rhos, it is unequivocally asserted by all the extant versions of *Brut y Tywysogyon*, by William of Malmesbury and the Worcester chronicle; with regard to Daugleddau, a non-monastic source (a comital charter of *c*.1139–48) provides the next-best evidence to a royal grant itself: *Hunc locum a tempore Henrici regis ex ipsius dono Flandrenses incolunt.*[24] Royal control and supervision is underlined by the Pipe Roll account for Michaelmas 1130 which strongly suggests that these two cantrefs were under the direct responsibility of the royal agent at Pembroke.[25] Among the considerations behind this royal initiative, the defence of a newly-acquired lordship and the need to find men to colonize it must have been paramount, for a number of Earl Arnulf's followers may well have followed him into exile. Henry I was in this respect no different from other Marcher lords (save that his range of contacts was wider). The right kind of men to settle in such regions and able to fight to stay there would always be at a premium and lands there would have been offered on attractive terms:

> Whosoever shall wish for land or peace,
> Horses, armour or chargers,
> Gold or silver, I shall give them
> Very ample pay;
> Whosoever shall wish for soil and sod
> Richly shall I enfeoff them.[26]

Although there is no firm evidence on this point, it is probable that many of these Flemish settlers came to Dyfed in small groups under their own leaders (or *locatores* perhaps) who contracted with the king or his agents to bring a specified number of men. Such a leader, it would appear, was Wizo, a *princeps Flandrensium*, who was permitted to obtain a substantial and compact group of estates in Daugleddau.[27] A similar role may have been played by such Dyfed Flemings as Tancard, castellan of Haverfordwest, Letard 'Litelking' (the sobriquet, at the very least, is pretentious) and William of Brabant, whom a Latin version of the Welsh chronicle described as a *primas* of the local Flemish community. The continental Germanic personal names attached to many a twelfth-century vill, manor and farmstead in southern Pembrokeshire may also be those of such local notables. We know that some, like Wizo, came directly from Flanders; others may have travelled from estates in England and it may be significant that a substantial number of Flemish tenants-in-chief and others held lands in north Somerset and parts of Devon.[28] Some of the Dyfed Flemings may have begun their careers as mercenaries in the English king's armies. While it is not known whether the treaty between Henry I and the Count of Flanders in 1101 (renewed in 1110) actually had for its effect the arrival of Flemish knights in England, one of its clauses stipulates that the Count should not deny permission to those men of his land who wished to enter the English king's service.[29]

A discussion of the continued vitality of a separate Flemish identity in Dyfed—a subject which much engaged the attention of later local historians—lies beyond the scope of this study, but there are indications that, in some areas at least, the Flemings were still a distinct element within Marcher society there into the second half of the twelfth century and beyond. Gerald of Wales certainly found them so and he further distinguishes them by including comments on certain of their customs and by highlighting the fact that, on one occasion at least, they were still special recipients of royal protection. More unusual interest perhaps is attached to the almost casual manner in which the archdeacon relates how his brother was addressed in *Flandrensica lingua* by a gentleman of Haverfordwest: does this passage suggest that Philip de Barri, lord of Manorbier and a leading magnate of southern Pembrokeshire, was bilingual?[30] That there was an identifiable Flemish group among the lords and knights who left Dyfed for conquest in Ireland from 1168 onwards is recognized by the thirteenth-century account of their exploits in the Song of Dermot.[31] If the Flemish language or dialect had for the most part been extinguished by the late fourteenth-century, its existence for many generations after the initial settlement of its speakers would have prolonged rather than accelerated the process of assimilation within the lordships of Anglo-Norman Dyfed.[32]

The particular personality of Marcher society in Dyfed was shaped also by the connections, primarily personal and tenurial, that linked it to southwestern England. Contacts between these two maritime regions astride the Bristol Channel long antedated the twelfth century but the Normans were the first, since the Anglo-Saxon penetration into Devon and Cornwall, to exercise the earlier British domination of both sea-boards. The actual formation of the cross-channel connections that resulted is difficult to illustrate from surviving records but there exist sufficient indications of their existence. Undoubtedly, it was the careers and endeavours of individual Anglo-Norman conquerors that forged the initial links. The first moves, as we saw earlier, were made by the fitz Baldwin brothers, hereditary sheriffs of Devon and major tenants-in-chief in the county, although their attempts to establish themselves in the lowlands around the Tywi estuary ultimately proved abortive.

Where they—grandsons of Count Gilbert of Brionne—failed, some of their Devon tenants persevered and prospered. One such was the ancestor of the de Brian family whose successors have emerged by the thirteenth century (and probably earlier) as lords of Walwyncastle in Pembrokeshire and of the commote of Laugharne in Carmarthenshire. A 'Wido de Brian' who occurs as a landowner at Rosemarket near Haverfordwest in a mid-twelfth-century charter may safely be identified with the 'Wido de Brionna' of the 1166 *carta* of the honour of Okehampton once held by the fitz Baldwins.[33] The link established by the earliest de Brians (one of whose Devon holdings—Tor Bryan—still bears their name) was maintained for most of the mediaeval period. Onomastic evidence in support of similar cross-channel holdings is notoriously difficult to deploy and in many cases no more than intuitive coincidence can be established such as that between the Gilbert de Grenemara' of the Carmarthen Pipe Roll account for 1130, his namesake in the 1166 *carta* of William, earl of Gloucester and 'Grenmere' on the Somerset coast.[34] Without postulating such a West Country connection, it would be difficult otherwise to explain the origin of, for example, Puncheston and Morvil in the lordship of Cemais—the former perhaps connected with the Punchardon sub-tenants of the honour of Okehampton, the second with the Moreville tenants of the Reviers earls of Devon.[35] Even more speculatively, it is tempting to look across the same stretch of water for the first Norman lords of St Clears; the early history of this lordship is obscure but does its name suggest a connection with the St Claire lords of Stoke Trister in Somerset? Further support for this West Country origin is supplied by the tiny Cluniac priory at St Clears whose mother house was St Martin des Champs at Paris—a distinction it shared with only two other communities in England, namely St James's of Exeter and Barnstaple, both in county Devon.[36]

A more notable cross-channel family was that of the fitz Martin lords of Cemais and tenants-in-chief in Devon and Somerset. J. H. Round long ago disposed of the shaky pedigree of Martin, the original dynast, through his descendants faithfully retained his name. His son Robert was the first of the family to acquire their *cantref* in north-western Dyfed though he appears to have held lands in Gwent and in south Pembrokeshire also.[37] The fitz Martins never surrendered their Somerset and Devon interests and wisely so for Cemais was a vulnerable lordship for much of the twelfth century. Significantly enough, when the neighbouring lordship of Emlyn fell to the Welsh in 1165, its Anglo-Norman ruling family was compensated with lands in north Devon.[38]

Fitz Martin's Cemais tenants likewise appear as landowners in Devon as do the abbots of the family's major foundation in Dyfed, St Dogmael's.[39] Another Dyfed monastery, the Cistercian abbey of Whitland, profited from the generosity of a Devon magnate, namely John of Torrington, custodian of Pembroke and Carmarthen castles under King John; he endowed the monks with extensive lands in the lordship of St Clears.[40] Further research will, I am sure, extend our knowledge of such personal and tenurial links, strengthened as many were by intermarriage: a later example of its operation in this cross-channel context is aptly provided by the marriage of Nicholas fitz Martin to Maud, daughter of Guy de Brian of Laugharne and Eva, daughter of Henry de Tracy, lord of Barnstaple. When such connections traversed the Irish Sea, the resulting tenurial pattern could become very complex indeed, so much so that when William de la Roche's Pembrokeshire estates were claimed by four heirs, one was resident in Pembroke, another in Cornwall, a third in county Cork and the fourth (according to the Irish return) 'was supposed to be living in England'.[41]

If the south-west of England provided brides and husbands for the Anglo-Norman settlers of Dyfed, it also provided contingents for military campaigns against the Welsh and, it is likely, outlets for the trade of such emerging boroughs as Pembroke, Tenby, Haverfordwest and Carmarthen whose merchants may well have provided the shipping necessary for cross-channel traffic.[42] The English peninsula also provided the tenants essential for the cultivation of Dyfed's manorial estates; as in English Gower, so on the vills and manors of the lordship of Pembroke, the size of the customary acre was identical to its measurement on Devon and Cornish estates.[43] It required the immigration of a goodly number of such peasant settlers over many generations, in the wake of acquisitive lords, to account for the English character of much of lowland Pembrokeshire, most starkly revealed in its place-names. It is indeed striking how the Marcher lordships of South Wales share with Devon alone among English counties such a high proportion of the *tun* place-name element—an indicator of vigorous primary and secondary colonization.[44] Settler society in Dyfed, then, developed not in peninsular isolation but influenced by contacts not only with native Welsh traditions and institutions but also with those of south-western England. Moreover, from the 1170s, a third dimension was added as a result of conquests in Ireland—yet broader horizons now unfolded before the Anglo-Norman families of Dyfed.

All the various factors discussed hitherto operated within units of feudal lordship and authority created by the Marcher lords of Dyfed and their knightly followers. That the March of Wales was established by private enterprise and its institutions nourished by seigneurial control has, by constant reiteration, become an inflexible and barren truism. A study of Anglo-Norman Dyfed suggests, however, that royal initiative and intervention were factors for which too little allowance has been made. The *licentia regis* cannot always have been a mere formality for tenants-in-chief departing with their valuable retinues to campaign against the Welsh: there was always the example of Baudri fitz

Nicholas before them.[45] That the Conqueror permitted an entirely free hand to would-be Marchers is contradicted by his dealings with Robert of Rhuddlan in North Wales and, more notably, with Rhys ap Tewdwr, to whose fragile provincial kingdom in the south he appears to have extended his protection against the avarice of his own subjects.[46] This protection may not have extended to the border region of Brycheiniog; Rhys's death there in 1093 in a skirmish with a Norman force led to a sudden extension of the Norman presence in South Wales and one sufficiently massive as to suggest to certain historians some degree of co-ordination by the Crown. While William Rufus' interventions in Wales indicate a more immediate concern for the defence of the English border, a tantalizing entry in the *Brut* asserts that William fitz Baldwin's castle-building in eastern Dyfed had been undertaken by this king's command.[47]

A new chapter opens with the accession of Henry I 'who had subdued under his authority all the island of Britain and its mighty ones; . . . and the man against whom no one could ever avail save God himself'. It is to him alone of all the English kings that the *Brut* accords the title 'the Great'.[48] For the next thirty-five years the same authority regards it as axiomatic that only a very courageous man or a fool omitted the royal will or the king's friendship from his political calculations. Henry I was the only constant in the Balkan-like fragmentation of political alliances that followed upon the fall of Rhys ap Tewdwr and the Norman incursions into his erstwhile dominions; this instability was compounded by the humbling of the house of Montgomery-Bellême, the ambitions of the dynasty of Powys and the restlessness that a legacy of disinheritance had nurtured in Rhys's descendants. The king used such opportunities skilfully by manipulating dynastic rivalries and seeking to isolate the 'hot-headed'. His shrewd calculations were assisted by the use of limited force, sound intelligence (what better informant than the royal chaplain, Bernard, bishop of St David's?), the distribution of 'gold and silver' and above all, it seems, by fear. The odour of his overlordship percolates through the entries in the *Brut* though only once is it specifically enunciated: if it was so widely accepted, its outright assertion was superfluous.[49]

'And he will honour and exalt you over and above any of your fellow landholders. He will make all your kinsmen envious of you.' Such were the benefits of royal friendship offered, we are told, to a Welsh princeling; they were, of course, equally attractive to Henry's vassals in England and Normandy.[50] For the new king, Wales proved to be a providential source of patronage; he did not have to give away what was his own and some lordships such as Ceredigion still had to be won and paid for.[51] From 1102 onwards Henry virtually created a new March, as it were, in his own image. A brief list is sufficient indication of his impact on its personnel, and hence on its character: Brecon (Miles of Gloucester), Abergavenny (Brian fitz Count), Chepstow and Netherwent (Walter fitz Richard), Glamorgan (Robert of Gloucester), Gower (Henry de Beaumont), Kidwelly (Roger of Salisbury), Cantref Bychan (Richard fitz Pons) and Ceredigion (Gilbert fitz Richard). No less impressively did Henry I dispose of lordships among the native princes, sometimes by redemption or purchase, at other times by free grant 'without tribute and without castles'.[52]

To this list must be added the 'grant' to Bernard, the queen's chaplain, of the lordship of Pebidiog or Dewisland (the temporal estates of St David's) in Dyfed where Henry's hand was felt more firmly than elsewhere in Wales. Here, the king himself became a lord of the March, for he retained the lordship of Pembroke, forfeited by Earl Arnulf, in his hands for the remainder of his reign. This is worth stressing because it is often held that Carmarthen was the only royal fortress in Wales at this time. He may have kept Pembroke with its mint and borough because it was worth having: in 1130 its farm was set at £60 and it paid almost £100 into the royal coffers. Among other considerations may be reckoned the military and political advantage of a royal presence in the March and, more negatively, the danger signals in Arnulf's Irish adventures. The more appropriate question perhaps ought to be 'Why not?' rather than 'Why?') That Pembroke was subject to a full and vigorous exploitation of the king's fiscal and jurisdictional rights is clear from the account presented by its sheriff at the Michaelmas Exchequer of 1130. In this document, the 'normality' of its entries (e.g. the *firma*, a visitation by royal justices, *oblata* for royal intervention in matters of inheritance and succession) suggests a long period of firm royal control which owed something perhaps to the earlier *comitatus* of Earl Arnulf.[53] As lord of Pembroke it is probable that Henry exercised a feudal and personal overlordship over the lords of Cemais, Emlyn, Rhos (Haverfordwest), Narberth and Daughleddau and that his direct lordship extended essentially over the Castle Martin peninsula: here, in later records, were the demesnes (including Kingswood) and knightly tenants of the Earl of Pembroke and, significantly, the castle-guard fees of Pembroke castle.[54] Comparative support for such an arrangement comes from the lordship of Glamorgan with its two component parts of *comitatus* or 'shire-fee' and member lordships— likewise the end result of piece-meal conquest and consolidation.[55] Elsewhere in western Dyfed Henry's influence was felt less directly but to much effect. His patronage of Arnulf's steward, Gerald of Windsor, was the basis of that family's fortunes while, farther north, he protected the interests of Robert fitz Martin. His plantation of Flemings radically altered the character of the lowlands north of Milford Haven. His support of Bishop Bernard ensured that St David's emerged virtually unscathed and indeed much strengthened in terms of its temporal lordship and diocesan boundaries by the end of his episcopate. Bernard was given a great deal but not an archbishop's pallium, and one suspects that Henry I's inclinations in this regard were as crucial and decisive as the Conqueror's on the matter of York's subordination to Canterbury. A metropolitan province in the March would, if achieved, have been inherently more separatist than the most powerful Marcher lordship.

In eastern Dyfed Carmarthen emerges from 1109 onwards as a centre for royal administration but what was administered from its castle is problematical. The 'honour' attached to it has a distinctly more makeshift appearance than that of Pembroke; here, a historian seeking a symmetry in the pattern of government in a newly-conquered (and more importantly, half-conquered) region may mistake the nomenclature of authority for its mature institutions.[56] A more modest conjecture would be that Carmarthen castle was a convenient centre for an assemblage (often contracting or extending) of territories, Anglo-Norman and native, dependent upon the king. Whether the lordships of Laugharne, St Clears or Llanstephan were ever parts of this aggregation in the Anglo-Norman period is impossible to determine with any certainty and later practice is no sure guide to earlier arrangements. Certainly in 1130 the royal agents at Carmarthen collected revenue (Anglo-Norman lordship was ever fiscal) from a very extensive area but the Pipe Roll presents only an ephemeral glimpse of their activities.[57] In western Dyfed, Henry I's role was decisive for its contemporary form as a Marcher region; in its eastern half his intervention, at the very least, determined the framework within which its future history was to unfold.

By the thirteenth century this and other factors had conspired to reproduce within the native kingdom of Dyfed that *morcellement* that was so typical of the March as a whole. More than a dozen lordships jostled within its former bounds and amongst them were the smallest in Wales. This plurality of lordships ensured that there was to be no successor state, no Norman honour of Dyfed, on the model of Brecon and Glamorgan where Marcher lordship was, ultimately, co-terminous with the Welsh *gwlad*. Early Dyfed had long enjoyed the status of an 'over-kingdom', containing within its seven *cantrefi* the skeletons of still earlier kingdoms now fossilized as units of royal administration. From the tenth century, it formed part of a larger unit, the provincial kingdom of Deheubarth—the great political prize in the dynastic struggle that dominated politics in South Wales on the eve of the Norman conquests.[58] Won by Rhys ap Tewdwr, in 1081, and retained by him until his death in 1093, this dynastic creation was, it seems, a brittle thing which individual vigour alone could sustain. In Dyfed it rested uneasily on a long-established particularism and sense of *pays*, reflected in contemporary verse, in its own body of laws and customs, and in its very name (inherited from its Iron Age overlords) which contrasted sharply with the purely locative Deheubarth, *dextralis pars* or 'right-hand' Wales.[59]

Although its name survived, Dyfed's territorial integrity was an immediate casualty of the Norman assaults. The activities of Arnulf of Montgomery in the west and of the fitz Baldwins in the east led to its partition, to become the '*Dyfed ddwycawn*' (Dyfed of two laws) of a late eleventh-century poem.[60] The easternmost *cantref* of Gwarthaf, was effectively detached. Henceforth, the major centres of authority were to be Carmarthen and Pembroke respectively, and the boundaries of the archdeaconries of St David's and Carmarthen set the church's seal on this fracture. The active survival of native units of authority (and, it would seem, of much else), the *cantref* and commote, is the most difficult of the formative elements in early Marcher history to interpret. Our ignorance as to their identity, boundaries and, in many cases, their very existence before the Norman conquests needs to be vigorously professed. This ignorance extends to much of the Welsh legacy to their Norman supplanters and any conclusions drawn from the Dyfed evidence are tentative and the illustrations highly selective.[61]

The tradition that the conquest of Dyfed had been achieved by the acquisition of *cantrefi* remained vigorous at the end of the twelfth century. In its western part, perhaps because it was the earliest to be won and the most securely held, the *cantref* appears to have provided a workable framework for the new lords. A measure of continuity is indicated by the emergence of lordships in Penfro and Emlyn while the Flemish settlements are invariably associated in the sources with the *cantrefi* of Rhos and Daugleddau. The re-organization of the diocese of St David's that followed upon Bishop Bernard's election in 1115, both with regard to the lordship of Pebidiog and the establishment of rural deaneries, point in the same direction. More revealing is the description (*c.*1121) of Robert fitz Martin's grants to St Dogmael's in his lordship of Cemais, wherein are noted, in some detail, the bounds between the *cantrefi* of Cemais and Emlyn.[62] Eastern Dyfed once again provides an apparent contrast for, when its component lordships appear in our records from the mid-twelfth century onwards, it is the commote that defines them. In this respect, Gwarthaf, the nearest of the Dyfed *cantrefi* to the caput of the Deheubarth dynasty at Dinefwr, may have been subject to earlier sub-division, although the fact that it was retained as the basis for the rural deanery of Carmarthen suggests that it may have been the sphere for initial Norman activity in this area and that its extinction resulted from later and more piece-meal conquests. In any event, military necessity and the wishes of individual Norman lords were always sufficient to counter a slavish acceptance of native institutions. As with the northern shires of England, it may have taken decades of assimilation and assertive lordship for the commote to emerge as compatible with feudal notions of authority.[63]

When, towards the end of the twelfth century, a third-generation settler enumerated his gifts to the priory of Pill, he did so in language redolent of the feudal order of things: lands *in villa de Nova Mota, in eodem feodo de Mota*, the use of woods *circa nominatim motam*, the church of *Novum Castellum* and *omnes ecclesias totius conquesti mei*. The reality was however more complex for among those churches granted by Adam de la Roche were two with Celtic dedications.[64] For, even after making due allowance for the disruption to settled agricultural activity in Dyfed wrought by Viking raids, the ravages of princely warbands and the violence of the Norman incursions themselves, this new order was not everywhere triumphant.[65] Recent studies, tracing the broad pattern and chronology of Anglo-Norman settlement, have not only identified the novel elements but have also indicated the extent of native survivals in tenure, custom, place-name and church dedication. In certain parts of Dyfed, notably the lowland *cantrefi* of Rhos, Daugleddau and Penfro, vigorous and ruthless colonization, of old and new lands, ensured the ubiquity of manor, English customary tenant, knight's fee and non-Celtic place-name. Elsewhere, in Cemais, Pebidiog and the eastern lordships, a more hybrid pattern emerged, apparent above all perhaps in the partible Welsh knight's fee. The demarcation line between the two did not however correspond rigidly to highland and lowland zones and Welsh place-names and tenants survived even in the most Anglicized arena.[66]

Many factors, ranging from self-preservation and opportunism on the one side to incomplete conquest on the other, encouraged a measure of accommodation and collaboration between the new arrivals and the doubtless bewildered leaders of the Welsh community. Frustrated dynastic ambition is the most likely explanation for the support given to the Normans at Carmarthen in 1116 by the dynasty of Rhydderch ap Iestyn, once ruler of Deheubarth, whose son had been defeated by Rhys ap Tewdwr at the battle of Mynydd Carn in 1081.[67] A survivor of a different sort was Cuhelyn Fardd, the 'ruler of Britons' of an early twelfth-century poem, whose descendants in the thirteenth century served fitz Martin and king in a variety of local offices. He retained his authority and patrimony in Cemais and, like Maredudd ap Rhydderch in Cantref Bychan, relieved his lord of the difficulties of ruling Welsh communities directly; it is fitting, then, that the most forthright statement of the view that these were best governed by native office-holders should have emanated from the settlers of Dyfed.[68] Another collaborator in 1116, as custodian of Laugharne castle, was Bleddri ab Cydifor of Newchurch, the king's official interpreter at Carmarthen, patron of the Augustinian foundation there and a Welsh landowner who, in the Pipe Roll of 1130, appears in the novel guise of contributor to *auxilium militum*—though even Bleddri couldn't stop his men from killing Flemings. His son, with a castle of his own at Cilsant in the lordship of St Clears, confirmed his father's grant to Carmarthen and, *à la mode*, was a patron of the knights of St John at Slebech.[69] Other, if more fitful, instances of collaboration between settler and native families, most notably between the fitz Geralds and the house of Dinefwr, are explained by ties of kinship.[70]

The kindred, of course, impinged on almost every aspect of life within Welsh society but the importance of family connections, of *affinitas et consanguinitas*, for the Anglo-Normans cannot be discounted. In a hostile environment, the renown and strength of one's lineage were as important a foundation and manifestation of local power as land, castles or money. Its role is apparent, for example, in the lands granted and the marriages arranged by Bishop David fitz Gerald, the first Welsh bishop who was a member of a local Marcher family.[71] Both he and his cousin, Gerald of Wales, belonged to one of Dyfed's most formidable lineages and the archdeacon rarely permits his readers to forget the fact. He lets slip few opportunities to mention his kinsmen, invariably *magni et probi homines*, their protection of him during the discharge of his duties and, on one occasion, the vulnerability he felt during their absence. The Flemish branch, I suspect, inspired little affection but was respected for its power.[72] This lineage, with its network of local connections between Norman, Welsh and Fleming, is in itself a commentary on the history of Anglo-Norman Dyfed.

Gerald's pride in it may perhaps explain why we find expressed for the first time, in his works, a consciousness of a separate Marcher identity, of being a *gens inter gentes*. Does it betray a sense that the March was essentially the creation of such local lineages, of men who had come to stay and came to terms with their frontier role?

Such a role informed settler society with a duality of aspect and a certain creative tension which stemmed from contact with institutions of political authority, social organization and religious observance so different to its own. In Dyfed these elements are most apparent perhaps in the history, under Anglo-Norman domination, of the church of Saint David's—'the nerve-centre of Welsh ecclesiastical and patriotic loyalty'.[73] The last Welsh bishop was roughly handled by the conquerors of Dyfed but he also received the protection of Archbishop Anselm. Some of the church's lands were alienated and seized but its territorial claims against Llandaff were vindicated. The cathedral was re-dedicated to Saint Andrew but the name of David was retained. The secular *clas* was disbanded but the *claswyr* emerged as prebendary canons on the Norman model. Its bishops eventually became Marcher lords in their own right but the basis of their temporal power was the old *cantref* of Pebidiog. Non-Welsh bishops were elected throughout the twelfth century but two of them vigorously propounded the claims of 'Archbishop' David before king and pope. Canterbury's primacy and claim to obedience were enforced but the cult of St David was given official recognition.[74] Rhigyfarch ap Sulien may have lamented the cruel oppression of the Normans but his *Vita Davidis* encouraged Norman clerics to support the metropolitan protensions of the see.[75] In these ways, then, St David might become a focus for the loyalties of settler and native alike. When, from the 1170s onwards, the Marcher lords and knights of Dyfed charged against their Irish enemies, the battle-cry that issued from their lips was *Sein Daui*: 'For he was their lord'.[76] Thus did the Celtic Saint of Dyfed claim as his own the descendants of those alien *conquistadores* who had first invaded his see and patrimony a little over a century before.

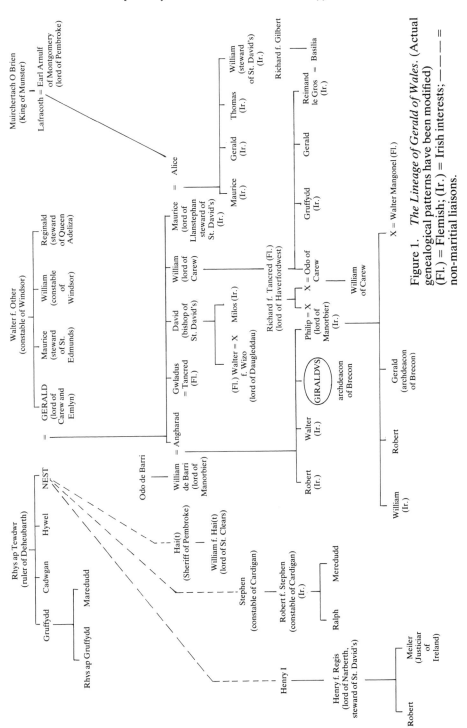

Figure 1. *The Lineage of Gerald of Wales*. (Actual genealogical patterns have been modified) (Fl.) = Flemish; (Ir.) = Irish interests; ————— = non-marital liaisons.

Women and the legitimisation of succession at the Norman Conquest

ELEANOR SEARLE

Historians are faced not only with the search for new data, but with the continual need to re-examine the assumptions they bring to their interpretation of data. This is peculiarly necessary for medievalists. Men do not necessarily articulate the logic of their social choices, and we are in constant peril of attributing our own assumptions to men and women unlike us, and thus misunderstanding the normal operation of their institutions.

For several years now, I have been trying to look anew at some problems in inheritance in feudal society through the light thrown on the institution by control over women's marriage.[1] Henry I's coronation charter of 1100 takes the matter very seriously; it is the third *capitulum*, coming after control over the church and male inheritance. 'If any baron or any of my men should wish to arrange a marriage for his daughter, sister, niece or cousin (*'cognatam'*) let him speak to me about it. But I will not take anything from him for this permission, nor will I forbid him to give her, save if he should wish to marry her to my enemy.' He then of course promises to arrange the marriage of any orphaned heiress with the counsel of his barons.[2]

I propose taking the statement very seriously too, as an expression of good lordship—and not just of good royal lordship. A male with a claim to inherit could be controlled directly, for he would one day present himself for acceptance as vassal and peer. A woman, if she was ever to be declared an heiress, had to be controlled at the moment of her marriage—from the first to the last of them.[3]

Now, the chronicles of the Norman conquest take marriage very seriously. Indeed, once one begins to examine them, marriage is a continuing theme of the Norman settlement in England. I would argue that if we too take their theme seriously, we will see a modified picture of the politics, perhaps even something new about the chronology and the means of reducing the violence, of that settlement. Let me first sketch the configuration of marriage/ inheritance/security that I propose as an approximation to the assumptions with which men faced the complex problems of legitimacy in the England of the late eleventh century.

Inheritance in the seignorial world of the eleventh century could be neither automatic nor governed by rigid rules. From the lord's point of view this is easy enough to see, for he could not afford an ineffective, hostile or even unreliable vassal. But it is as true of the vassal group. A lord's vassals—the claimant's prospective peers—had an anxious interest in the claimant's qualities. No vassal group could well afford to have members who were in themselves incapable, or unable to inspire and hold the loyalty of their own men. The unstable man, even the unknown man, was unthinkable as an heir, because he was unthinkable as a peer. We concentrate on the lord when we think of the warrantor of a vassal's land. But, by the very logic of feudal power, he did not act alone. A unilateral decision by a lord was a dangerous matter for him because ultimately his group of vassals were the strength of his arm. The vassals relied upon one another as a court where their advice and assent made them as well as their lord the warrantors of one another's secure possession and of the peaceful succession of their children. Admittance to membership in such an interdependent group was the only right a man could possibly have to a share in the resources by which that group protected itself. A man did homage to his lord for his land, but no wise lord would take homage without a decision of his court of vassals: their declaration that X is *heres*.

Inheritance is recruitment, then. Security implied the necessity of continuing to demonstrate the qualities that secured acceptance. Just as the rules of inheritance were of necessity flexible, so tenure could not be unquestioned. It is important to remember this lest we overestimate the seriousness of the fault that might lead to dispossession. The fault of Mabel of Bellême's father, William Talvas, was not that he was disloyal to his Norman lord and peers. It was that he could not control his disloyal son, Arnold. We do not know why his son Oliver was unacceptable as his heir—but he was so. The sister, Mabel, was the heir, and Oliver was thereafter maintained within the family until old age when he became a monk. Oliver may have been moved by the example of his merry uncle who had resigned the lordship and part of its lands, and had preferred to be bishop of the lordship's diocese. The cost of inheriting was not low, and there must have been sons who preferred not to pay so dearly. To the Norman duke and his magnates, Mabel was perhaps the preferable heir because she could be married to the formidable and loyal Roger II of Montgomery.[4] The distribution of resources was a decision in which many needed to participate.

In such a world we cannot continue to imagine that men could lay down rigid rules for the purpose of defining a unique heir, nor even a male heir. But they could, and did, insistently define legitimate claimants, a 'pool' of heirs. Battles over succession could, in this way, be limited. The castle of Roger de Mortemer of the 1050s was taken from him—not because he had betrayed his lord, but because he had received into that castle his lord's enemy. But Roger was left a powerful baron, quite powerful enough to make trouble. He did not. And part of the reason must be that the castle was not given out again to just anyone. William de Warenne, who succeeded Roger, was carefully called 'consanguineus eius, tiro legitimus': of the acceptable pool of heirs.[5] Neither Mabel's father, brother nor uncle made trouble when the great Bellême lordship was channelled through a female. We think of broilsome Norman lords—and so they were—but in their broilsomeness and insecurity they sought, and even abided by, tenure decisions lent legitimacy by the elevation to the inheritance of one of a finite number of 'rightful' heirs. It was as true in the Anglo-Scandinavian kingdom they were shortly to conquer. King Cnut's loyal Dane, Siward, married the daughter of the older Anglo-Saxon house that had been earls of Northumbria. In Earl Waltheof and his brother, their sons, true legitimacy was achieved. The in-coming of the foreigner was a moment of great danger to such fragile polities. Even as late as the fourteenth-century the necessity of, and means of, legitimising such entrance was understood. In the legend of the 11,000 virgins we read that Conan, conqueror of Brittany, caused their tragedy because he wanted wives for his men, and was foolish enough to object to their marrying Breton girls even

> To have cleym thorow heritage,
> Ne dowarye thorow mariage.[6]

Rights of inheritance can, this realizes, be channelled through women, whether or not men exist in the 'pool' of heirs. If so, then we must revise our notions, and look at the women of the Conquest for new evidence of continuity or discontinuity.

The group that conquered England faced there the old problems of legitimacy in ways that exacerbated their difficulty. These are problems faced not by William, but by his vassals, the group on whose cohesion and mutual trust would depend the success of the conquest and their own enrichment. Let me identify what I take to be some major aspects of the problem of legitimacy faced between 1066 and 1100. First there was the problem of allowing entrance to their group to men—especially Englishmen—who accepted their lord and were accepted by him—for here their lord's interest differed from his vassals'. This is related to the more obvious legitimisation: the acceptability to the English of new lords. And this in turn is related to the third problem, that of the dispossession of families from land. The conquest was a brutal business, but total disinheritance in the eleventh-century was more dangerous than we may imagine: indeed so disruptive that it was avoided whenever possible.[7] Finally, the conquerors faced the problem of their own heirs. For them, in large measure, England had been conquered. But every generation had required much testing and some rejecting before trust could be established. So it would be for the heirs of the conquerors. Let us look at these problems of vassalage and legitimacy through what I propose as the traditional means of their solution—the control of family—and we shall see why marriages, achieved and failed, are such an important theme in the tale of the Norman conquest.

The theme of arranged and controlled marriage begins, appropriately, in the negotiations preceding the death of Edward the Confessor. Harold, earl of Wessex, had a wife, Edith Swan-neck, no less a wife and the mother of no less legitimate children because their union was 'more Danico'.[8] But Harold had not yet married 'in matrimonio Christiano more', in Robert of Torigny's phrase.[9] And so he was free to entertain the proposal of such a marriage to Duke William's daughter, as the early sources agree he did.[10] They agree, too, that marriage involved a formal relation between the giver and the receiver of the woman, that it was a channel of claims to property, and as such, necessarily subject to control. William of Malmesbury puts in Harold's mouth a version of marriage-formation that his hearers would have recognized as necessary for so great an earl. When he breaks off the betrothal Harold denies that it could have been binding on him: just as it would be judged ineffectual for a girl in her parents' custody to vow the disposal of her body in marriage without her parents' knowledge, he says, so would such a promise be pointless for him who lived *sub regis virga*, under the discipline of the king.[11] The greatest earl, because his family would be so great, had, in the way of marriage, no more freedom than the littlest girl.

This is dwelling long upon a marriage that never took place and may never have been planned, but the earliest versions of the supposed arrangements tell us clearly just now significant such arrangements were thought to be. Such a marriage entailed the acceptance by William as lord, of Harold as vassal, and would have been the visible sign that William had warranted Harold's possession of Wessex. It was in keeping with William's own early conception of himself as English king, attempting to rule through Englishmen and English institutions, altered to fit his conception of lordship.[12] I think our evidence will help to show one of the rocks on which that attempt foundered.

This attempt of William to be an Anglo-Norman king as Cnut had been an Anglo-Scandinavian one, was surely one of the reasons why the Normans met virtually no widespread, organized resistance in the three or four years after Hastings. Perhaps another lies in the age of the remaining English earls and the Aetheling. Waltheof of Northumbria had been too young to succeed (*adhuc parvulus*)[13] when his father died in the mid-1050s, and his claim to the earldom had been on that account passed over. He could have been little older than his mid-teens in 1066 and was without experience as far as we know. The other earls Edwin and Morcar were also in their teens, and the Aetheling was but a boy. All were unmarried. Only one was ever to be married.

Waltheof's and Edwin's marriages are the first to concern us here and there is too little time in such a paper as this for any detailed analysis of the circumstances surrounding them. Waltheof's signified his acceptance as a member of the magnate group who regarded one another as legitimate peers and landholders. He had shown himself dangerous in 1069/70, he had demonstrated that he had the loyalty of men in the North, he had submitted, and he received his Huntingdon estates as the dowry of Judith ('nomine pacis dotae')[14] his Norman wife and neice of the Conqueror. Whether or not the Norman magnates were unanimous or even cheerful in their assent, it cannot be that they were unconsulted.

Earl Edwin's marriage into the group and the ducal house was another matter. For a while he remained earl in a diminished Mercia, and no new

Norman earldom was established in the western marches during the 1060s. If Edwin were to be accepted into the Conqueror's family western Mercia would be closed to William's magnates and England would become as it was under Cnut. The matter came to a head, if we accept the explanation of Orderic and the hints of other chroniclers, over this question of Earl Edwin's marriage. If this is right then we can observe a side of the political genius of the Conqueror we are seldom aware of: he knew when to be persuaded and when his trust in his vassals must be proved by allowing them to take the lead. He was then willing to risk his life fighting for their advantage. From the moment when the Normans denied a Norman woman to the English earl, the conquest became theirs more than their duke's. Orderic says, '. . . the noble youths Edwin and Morcar, sons of Earl Alfgar, rebelled . . . For when King William, had made his peace with Earl Edwin, granting him authority over his brother and almost a third of England, he had promised to give him his daughter in marriage; but later, listening to the dishonest counsels of his envious and greedy Norman followers, he withheld the maiden from the noble youth, who greatly desired her and had long waited for her. At last his patience wore out and he and his brother were roused to rebellion.'[15] After a long wait for acceptance either the Norman court had made a formal decision or Edwin realized that he would forever wait in vain, his position slowly eroding. From that moment Edwin and Morcar had no more choice than Hereward.

How long it took to hunt the brothers down we cannot say. Their legends and that of Hereward merge—quite rightly, for they are the same tale of the desperation of the totally disinherited, the unaccepted. We do know that by 1071 Morcar had been captured. A few months later Edwin was dead at the hands of murderers. Orderic makes this the moment of the push into Mercia: 'After King William had defeated the leading Mercian earls as I have related— Edwin being dead and Morcar languishing in prison—he (William) divided up the chief provinces of England among his followers'.[16] The dismemberment of Mercia had begun.

If marriage meant acceptance and meant property rights, it was an important thread weaving the peace among an interdependent group. The marriage pursued in the face of prohibition was a cause for disseisin quite as compelling as receiving an enemy into one's castle. And so the 'fatal bride-ale' of 1075 can be regarded. Florence of Worcester tells us that the marriage between Ralph of Gael, earl of Norfolk, and Emma, sister of Roger, earl of Hereford, had been forbidden.[17] The earls persisted, and after the wedding withdrew to their strongholds. Both were summonsed, judged and disseised, easily and without the necessity of the king's presence, as Lanfranc's letter to his lord in Normandy assures him.[18] The whole 'rebellion' can be reduced to the defiant disobedience of a notably ineffectual young man, as Lanfranc's letters to Earl Roger show him to have been. William fitzOsbern's heir had shown himself unworthy of continued acceptance, as had Ralph the Staller's.[19] The disseisin was done 'judicali sententia'. Of the great men only the English guest Waltheof lost his life.

There was a second pattern of marriage that makes sense, not as a recognition of legitimate membership of a vassal group, but as recognition of legitimate succession to lands being held: legitimate not only in the eyes of Norman lord and peers, but as a claim to hold in something less than constant fear. This second pattern was not the usual magnate one, for their claims were secured by membership in their family/vassal group that spread across the Channel. It was the pattern of those who would hold only in England, and who could not hope to hold forever as occupying troops in a land of Herewards and Edrics. 'Castlemen' they were for a time, as the Anglo-Saxon kenning for them tells us, but they had not risked their lives to huddle forever in castles. And they could not—let us admit it—murder the whole of the English thegns. 'Manormen' we see them by 1087, and as is so often remarked, they appear as the heirs of their Anglo-Saxon *antecessores*, holding so often exactly the same estates, however inconveniently those estates might straggle across counties. Scant though the evidence is, if we look at that evidence accepting that marriage was a moment of inheritance quite as important as any admission into a fief, and that marriage was one of few ways of legitimately effecting a property-transfer, we shall see that it tells a consistent story.

A significant fact about the few Englishmen of importance who were allowed fiefs is that they seem to have left heiresses only. Thus Colswein of Lincoln left an heiress, married to Robert de la Haye, a Norman. Turchil of Arden did leave a son, but that son did not inherit—his lands went to the Earl of Warwick, under whom the Ardens continued in possession as vassals—a family tradition indeed recorded that the Norman earl had married the daughter of the English family.[20] If so, it is the precise circumstance of Oliver de Bellême, his sister Mabel and Roger II de Montgomery. We know too that Robert d'Oilli, castellan of Oxford, married the daughter of Wigot of Wallingford and 'inherited' her father's lands, and Geoffrey de la Querche married Alfgeofu, heiress of Leofwine, thegn of Warwickshire.[21] Even at a higher level, we know of the Countess Lucy, the English heiress of Bolingbroke, Lincolnshire, who carried her estates and her ancestors' earldom/shrievalty to her Norman husbands, Ivo Taillebois (d. ca. 1094), Roger fitzGerold, and Ranulf le Meschin earl of Chester.[22] Lucy's grandfather, William Malet, had fought among the Conqueror's closest companions at Hastings, and was of an important Norman family. Yet he was 'partim Normannus et Anglus, compater Heraldi'.[23] His widow was still alive in 1087, arguably herself an English heiress.[24]

The problem of the continuation of English families after the Conquest is not so much one of evidence that Norman fighters, particularly at the lower levels, married Englishwomen, as in realising that inheritance through the female would have been an acceptable arrangement to men of that time—that they felt differently about family constitution than we assume they must have. Yet the pattern is so common that we must be wilful not to see it. From the marriage that channelled the Norman Count Rodolf's great landholdings through his daughter to the ducal steward Osbern in the early eleventh-century, while his two sons were pensioned off with bishoprics, to the great Berkeley marriage in the 1150s whereby one baron was dispossessed in favour of another, but in such a way that the sons and daughters of the two were married and mingled the blood and lands of Berkeley of Berkeley and Berkeley of Dursley, there is a continuing pattern by which the polity was strengthened, resources redistributed and families were mingled in fact without violence.

One Englishman had a special claim to Norman attention, and his case is sufficiently documented to provide an instructive example of the peaceful satisfaction of English claims through marriage. He is Harold, son of the pre-conquest Earl Ralph of Hereford. His mother had the Anglo-Danish name, Gytha. His grandmother had been Goda, Edward the Confessor's full sister. He was in fact as directly an 'heir' of the Old English kings as was Edgar Aetheling, and he was therefore particularly dangerous. His father, Earl Ralph is so often thought of as a 'Norman favourite' of Edward the Confessor, that we are apt to forget that he was half-English, was married to an Anglo-Dane, and had given his son the name of the greatest of the Godwinssons. In the circumstances, this Harold was fortunate to survive. He did not of course inherit. But he was eventually allowed to marry the daughter of Alured of Marlborough, the Domesday holder of Ewias, in the most dangerous western corner of Hereford, and to become Alured's *gener et heres*, to use Oderic's term in a different context.[25] He called his own son Robert. He was one of the tenants of a wild corner in the honour of Boulogne, the huge honour associated with the marriage of his grandmother and Eustace of Boulogne. Harold, sole living descendent of this princess, and one of only two males of the lineage of Athelred to survive, was content to live as a Norman vassal holding of a Norman in-law. By 'content' I mean that he had been satisfied to the extent that he did not rebel, and that, I take it, was the point. Men had different thresholds of contentment, but here we see a significant one—for a man of high birth and no poltroon. It took a brave man with a cool nerve to hold Ewias Harold. His acceptance tells us much about his assessment of reasonable options.

The curious letter about Englishwomen written by Archbishop Lanfranc belongs, I would suggest, to the mid or late 1070s, and must be seen in the context of the legitimisation of the Norman settlement.[26] Lanfranc had been asked: which Englishwomen in nunneries are to remain as nuns and which are to be sent home? The answer was that nuns who had made profession or who had been offered as oblates were to remain such. Those women who fell in neither category were to be sent away *ad presens* until their wishes about living as nuns might be minutely investigated. Now why should this category of women concern the king and his justiciars? Many girls were brought up and educated in nunneries or boarded there and left freely. Many widows retired to them. Why send them away? I would suggest that they concerned Lanfranc and his fellow-governor because they were wanted at home as peace-weavers and channels of inheritance. Send them home, Lanfranc is saying, and it will be closely examined after a short time whether they might wish to make their lives among Norman men or to return to the cloister. A sub-set of these Englishwomen might choose to leave without investigation—those who had fled not out of love of God but out of fear of the French. If we put the letter in the mid-1070s, then the land was growing peaceful, because as Orderic bitterly says, 'foreigners grew wealthy with the spoils of England, whilst her own sons were either shamefully slain or driven as exiles to wander hopelessly through foreign kingdoms'.[27] Despite sub-enfeoffment many were made exiles— Simeon of Durham, perhaps one himself, speaks movingly of them.[28] But their sisters were wanted at home.

Whatever the motivations of the men and women involved, Lanfranc was dealing with a general problem. Some twenty years later, in 1093/4, his successor Archbishop Anselm had the problem still to deal with, in two specific, and I would argue, clear cases: those of the great ladies Edith and Gunnilda. Their cases can be reconstructed and we can be sure that we are either seeing strange passions shaking heretofore solid and middle-aged barons, or looking at women with the legitimising effect of heiresses.

In 1068 Malcolm of Scotland had given refuge to many nobles of the North and to the English royal children, Margaret, Christina and Edgar. He had subsequently married the young Margaret.[29] St Margaret's dowry could be as large and vague or as specific as suited Malcolm. At its most specific, it provided a legitimate claim to Lothian, annexed years earlier.[30] In 1091 he met William II on or near the Lothian border to begin the process of negotiating areas of recognized influence in the uncertain North.[31] In his revealing account of Malcolm's claims, Orderic puts these words in Malcolm's mouth: 'I acknowledge that when King Edward gave me his great-niece Margaret in marriage he gave me the county of Lothian. King William later confirmed what his predecessor had given me . . .'[32]

St Margaret's dowry, then, was Malcolm's justification of claims in the North. Her daughter's dowry was as expandable and as significant. This is the reason that the dispute over this daughter's marriage in 1093 was so bitter. Her case is the subject of the first of the letters of Anselm concerning runaway nuns.[33] It is addressed to the bishop of Salisbury, asking him to use his authority to compel Malcolm's daughter to return to the abbey of Wilton where she had laid aside her religious veil and returned to the world. Anselm has, he says, delayed his condemnation of her sin for fear that it had been prompted or condoned by the king. But, he writes, he has spoken with the king and found to his satisfaction that such was not the case—the king wished Malcolm's daughter in a nunnery. Let us put the whole story of Malcolm and his daughter into the context I propose and we shall see that there is nothing so obscure in the final break between Rufus and Malcolm, nor in the circumstance that a twelve-year-old girl should have been the centre of the quarrel.

The girl Edith (later of course, Queen Matilda) was in England in the summer of 1093 at Wilton where she was awaiting the husband for whom her father intended her.[34] Malcolm had come to the king at Gloucester to continue the settlement they had begun in Lothian two years earlier. As part of that settlement Malcolm intended a marriage between his daughter and Alan the Red, lord of Richmond. Now Alan was more to a Scots king than the greatest baron of Yorkshire and one of the greatest in Lincoln and East Anglia. His greater attraction perhaps was that his territory lay immediately to the south of the disturbingly effective Robert de Mowbray, earl of Northumberland. Mowbray's arrival upon the Tyne in *ca.* 1080 had brought for the first time since the Conquest a force that neither Malcolm nor the previously unmanageable Northumbrians could dislodge. His presence there promised a check to Scots' activities south of Lothian—and at the same time to Count Alan's activities north of the honour of Richmond. A marriage that would give Alan claims to Lothian and Malcolm a grandson in Richmond would suit them both very well indeed. It was what strategists call a 'pincer movement', and the phrase graphically describes the geography of Mowbray's situation. If Rufus contemplated for a moment sanctioning it, he must have been quickly recalled to his duties as a lord by his vassals, led by Mowbray. In August of 1093, I would argue, Rufus acted much as had his father in 1070 and yielded to his vassals. When Malcolm arrived at Gloucester the king refused even to talk to Malcolm except in his own court according to the judgement of his own barons and of them only.[35] It was an act of flamboyant good lordship. Malcolm however would have none of being treated as merely another vassal whose family planning was subject to his fellows' agreement. He was willing to abide by the judgement of a joint court made up of magnates of each realm and convened on the borders. The two kings parted (if one may use the term after a non-meeting) in great enmity and Malcolm went north, where Mowbray of course was left to deal with him. By November Malcolm had been killed, either ambushed or raiding.[36] But he had first gone to Wilton for his daughter, had torn the veil from her head, as she later testified, telling her that he had intended her as a wife for Count Alan rather than for a community of nuns, and taken her away. Anselm's letter of February, 1094 did not get her back.

Seen so, Edith's 'place in all this' is anything but 'obscure', as it has been called. Rufus wished her back and veiled; only after he had heard this did Anselm write his directive. The king, indeed, is the likeliest source of Anselm's information, to judge from the memory of Herman of Tournai, who heard, and later recounted, Anselm's story that Rufus had thought himself satisfied by having seen a veil on the princess' head.[37] A girl with such a potential was best kept behind stout walls.

At the same time another woman best kept incarcerated was taken from Wilton: Gunnilda, daughter of Harold Godwinsson. At the angry breakup of the Gloucester court, King Malcolm and Count Alan had ridden off, angry men both, and, as it happened, men doomed to die within months. As if they rode together—as well they might—King Malcolm snatched his daughter from Wilton, while his chosen son-in-law rode off with Gunnilda from the same nunnery. In her case Anselm knew she had willingly worn the veil, for he himself had once talked to her.[38] The facts as we know them are few. Count Alan abducted Gunnilda within a day or so of the breakdown of negotiations at Gloucester, as I have said. Shortly, and without having married her, he was dead. But Gunnilda did not return to Wilton. Instead Count Alan's brother

Alan Niger 'succeeded not only to his estates but to his matrimonial plans', in Southern's phrase.[39] Anselm wrote her then a bitterly physical letter, horrible to read, attempting to disgust her with the world and man's embrace. What happened to her eventually we do not know, but she left no legitimate children, and another of the Breton family succeeded to the lands of his brothers.

The facts of the story, few as they are, are clear enough, but the interpretation must be part of the pattern the historian believes he sees. Let me contrast two – one that does not see property and succession claims inhering strongly in women, and another, the one I am putting forward for your consideration, that assumes that such attributes in their women were rarely out of the minds of contemporaries.

Professor Southern, assuming that eleventh-century baronial marriage was of such relatively minor importance that it could be both freely contracted and romantically motivated, infers from Alan's abduction of Gunnilda that the union with Edith foundered because 'Count Alan Rufus saw a young woman whom he liked better'. He reminds us that Alan was a tough, practical warrior in his mid-fifties. 'The result', he writes, 'was a strange and passionate romance . . .' Stranger still that his brother and heir should be smitten by the same passion: 'Why these important barons, in the face of ecclesiastical censure and as an alternative to the important political alliance proposed by King Malcolm, should have preferred the daughter of Harold is a question we shall never answer . . . the secret of her power died with her.[40]

Looked at as I propose, the strange and passionate romance of the grizzled veteran of Hastings evaporates. Nor is the affair an enigma. Instead it joins the other evidence in making sense of the many post-Conquest unions of which contemporaries were so conscious. Reading Orderic, Florence of Worcester and the Anglo-Saxon Chronicle as I propose, it was not Count Alan who broke off the marriage, but Rufus' insistence that it be considered by his magnates assembled. Malcolm, we are told, left in a fury. He had been insulted and his interests disregarded. Was Count Alan's situation any different? Was there a second-best for this long-unmarried Breton, who knew better than to go ahead with the marriage on his own?

Count Alan held four hundred manors in England. Nowhere was he more independent and powerful than in the 'magnitude and solidity' of his great honour in the north of Yorkshire. But his power extended through the eastern part of the old Danelaw: in Lincolnshire, Cambridge, Norfolk, Suffolk, Essex.[41] Gunnilda's name is of the Danelaw, and her mother Edith Swan-neck had been one of the great Danelaw powers. Many lands had been under her soke and many men commended to her. Edith Swan-neck had been a wife *more Danico*, but for a Dane that meant no lowly position. Nor did it denote a woman of low birth. Only the daughter of a great war-leader's lineage could have commanded so many and held so much. When we realize this we can see something of Gunnilda's utility to Alan and to his heir after him. She was the Swean-neck's heiress and heiress to whatever legitimacy remained of the old Danish war-lineage. And the Breton honour of Richmond (like Lacy of

Pontefract) was unusual in the continuance of pre-Conquest Anglo-Danish men on their old estates.[42] Second-best the union undoubtedly was to the chance for Lothian, but not so far behind it perhaps, especially to an angry man. I do not think that the secret of Gunnilda's power died with her.

Gunnilda's fate provides us with evidence that at least makes a coherent picture. There was no marriage *more Normannico* and therefore no children with claims to inherit and to be seated beside their father's peers. Nor need there necessarily be. The woman herself passing the cup in the new lord's hall was important as a bridge to the old form of lordship, and the children could be provided for. Thus a bizarre tale of strange and ruinous passions, full of the most unlikely coincidence and quite out of character for the actors, is transformed into reasonable, if unromantic, baronial 'politics'. It requires merely a slight shift in our perceptions of the significance to these men of their own and one another's marriages.

It might seem fitting to conclude with the great marriage of 1100 as the ultimate in legitimising succession to England and claims to Lothian, which it is.[43] Edgar Aetheling's inheritance went through his sister. It is even more enlightening to look at Henry's sexual politics long before his marriage. A more unmarriageable young man than Henry can scarcely be imagined. Having cheated him out of his inheritance, his elder brothers were hardly likely to make his fortune for him by a marriage. Yet the shrewd Henry was not to be done out of children whose marriages could be useful supposing better days were on the way. William of Malmesbury was not being quite a fool when he recorded that Henry copulated only to get children, 'effundens naturam ut dominus, non obtemperans libidini ut famulus'.[44] When Rufus died Henry already had a quiverful of potential barons, earls, heiresses and queens for his nobility and neighbours—and loyal supporters for their legitimate siblings.[45] And not a single one carried dangerous claims to the crown. I would maintain therefore that, while individuals were inconvenienced by the church's growing definition of marriage as monogamous, the seignorial world in fact welcomed and encouraged clerical aid in reducing the 'pool' of legitimate claimants, and thereby reducing the dangers and violence of succession-disputes.[46] The baronage soon went beyond the Church in England, and denied legitimacy even to 'mantle children' whom the Church accepted. They were not converted to a new morality of marriage. They were making use of a new control over inheritance.

I have tried in this paper to do no more than propose a new way of looking at evidence we all know of, and to convince you only that it produces at least a consistent picture, and one that has the merit of not underestimating the long-term difficulties of eleventh-century conquest and colonisation. Marriage and the control of inheritance are, in this reading of the evidence, the very heart of the solution to the conquerors' problems. The pattern of marriage at the knightly level was necessarily to marry Englishwomen, to become the lords of their male in-laws, and to produce children who were legitimate heirs of English grandfathers and legitimate claimants to the fiefs of Norman fathers.

At the magnate-level the pattern was quite different, for marriage 'Christiano more' within that exclusive group involved Normandy as well as England. Control over one another's marriages was for them a powerful control over one another's wealth and power. Looking back, as we do, through statal preconceptions, we can forget that the overmighty subject was quite as dangerous to his neighbours as to his king. Looked at in this way, the decision-making powers of the vassal-group of the eleventh century assumes rather more importance than is generally given it. Much of William I's political success looks to be in knowing when to yield to his vassals' insistence that they, as well as he and the church, define the legitimacy of aspirants to their women's hands and property.

Land and power in the eleventh-century: the estates of Harold Godwineson

ANN WILLIAMS

It is one of the ironies of history that the bulk of the evidence from which an estimate of the landed wealth of Earl Harold can be made comes from the great record compiled by the clerks of his successful rival. Without Domesday Book, it would be impossible to discover where Harold's land lay, or how much he held. Neither Harold himself, nor his brothers—Tostig, Leofwine and Gyrth—were in a position to make a will, and if Godwine did so, it has not survived. Royal charters to laymen are rare in the reign of Edward the Confessor and royal charters in favour of any beneficiary, lay or ecclesiastical, are few in number for the reigns of his Danish predecessors. There is not a single royal charter in favour of Harold (though as we shall see, he did hold several royal estates) and only three in favour of Godwine, one of which is a fabrication.[1] Two East Anglian wills include bequests to Harold and one of them contains a bequest to Godwine also.[2] One private transaction of Cnut's reign concerning land in Kent has been traditionally ascribed to Earl Godwine.[3] Other scraps of information can be gleaned from the Anglo-Saxon Chronicle or from material in the surviving records of the great Benedictine houses like Abingdon. But these sources on their own would be quite inadequate to provide any picture of Harold's landed possessions. For this—as for so much else—we must turn to Domesday.

I have therefore attempted to extract from Domesday every reference to land held by or from Harold, or by those who in some sense were regarded as his men. I cannot claim to have succeeded, and since I am almost completely innumerate, I cannot pretend that the figures presented here are more than approximately correct. But the accompanying table is a rough estimate of the hidage of Harold's lands in 1066, in each of the shires where he appears as a landowner. I have used the hidage assessment as a basis of calculation rather than the value expressed in money for two reasons; firstly, virtually all the estates are assessed either in hides, carucates or sulungs (though there are exceptions in special cases), whereas the money value is not always given, and secondly, in order to compare Harold's landed wealth with that of his predecessors in the Old English period, for whose estates only the assessment and not the value is recorded.

Harold, then, held something more than 1,900 hides, nearly 500 carucates and 3 sulungs of land; his men held about 430 hides, 86 carucates and 2½ sulungs of land. To these totals must be added the lands in East Anglia assessed in acres; and in addition it must be borne in mind that Harold's estates in the western shires of Wessex are quite clearly preferentially assessed, as comparison between the hidage and the ploughland assessment (shown in brackets on the table) will show. The table shows, then, not the actual size of Harold's landed endowment (though it may reflect this), but his tax liability. If the rate of geld in normal circumstances is taken to be two shillings on the hide,[4] Harold's land would have yielded something in the region of 4,800 shillings—a sum equivalent to the wergild of four thegns.

Shire	*Estates* (No.)	*Assessment*	*Estates held by Harold's men* (Assessment)
Wessex			
Kent	2	3 sulungs	2½ sulungs
Surrey	7	183 hides	33 hides
Sussex	14	319 hides	41 hides
Hants.	5	51 hides	30½ hides
Berks.	10	200 hides	18½ hides
Dorset	14	130½ hides	2 hides
Wiltshire	14	220 hides	
Somerset	7	59 hides (158 ploughlands)	
Devon	14	36½ hides (334 ploughlands)	
Cornwall	17	72 hides (362 ploughlands)	
Mercia			
Worcesters.	1	15½ hides	
Staffords.	1	3 hides	
Shropshire	1	7½ hides	
Cheshire	4	4½ hides	
Warwicks.	0		
Gloucesters.	4	35 hides	41 hides
Herefords.	38	172 hides	55 hides
Oxfordshire	5	50 hides	
Leicesters.	3	35 carucates	
Derbys.	0		
Nottinghams.	3	2½ carucates	
East Midlands			
Hertfordshire	2	39½ hides	77½ hides
Middlesex	2	31 hides	22½ hides
Bedfordshire	1	(see Herts.)	
Cambridges.	3	21 hides	18 hides
Buckinghams.	5	74½ hides	82 hides
East Anglia			
Suffolk	2	20 carucates	34 carucates, 700 acres
Norfolk	10	20 carucates	52 carucates, 280 acres
Essex	37	194 hides, 166 acres	10 hides, 14 acres
Northumbria			
Yorkshire	4	88 carucates, + 86 carucates of sokeland	
Lincolnshire	8	48 carucates, + 197 carucates of sokeland	
Rutland	1	2 carucates	
Huntingdons.	1	10 hides	
Northamptons.	0		

Of course this figure standing on its own is of only limited interest. To put it into its proper perspective, we should need to know at the very least the total wealth of the king, with that of the earls of Northumbria and Mercia respectively, and that of 'typical' representatives of the groups of royal thegns, median thegns, and lesser ranks of society. It would probably be possible to obtain such information, but I have not yet done so. In defence I can only plead that one has to start somewhere, and that Harold seemed an appropriate starting-point; adding in mitigation, that my next project will be a similar exercise regarding the earls of Mercia. Meanwhile a comparison of the wealth of the king and queen and the three great earldoms has been provided by R. H. Davies, in an unpublished thesis quoted by Professor Barlow in his biography of Edward the Confessor.[5] Mr. Davies used the monetary value of the estates as a touchstone of comparison, calculating the wealth of the king at 5,000 pounds, that of the queen at 900 pounds, that of the sons of Godwine (excluding Tostig) at 4,000 pounds, of the Mercian family (excluding Morcar) at 1,300 pounds and that of the Northumbrian earls (the lands of Tostig and Morcar combined) at another 1,300 pounds. The dominance of the West Saxon earls is very striking. Comparison of Harold's estate with that of previous earls and ealdormen is perhaps fruitless, since his father was the first man to hold the whole of Wessex as a single earldom; but for the sake of completeness, Ealdorman Aelfheath, who held the central shires of Wessex from 959 to 971/2, possessed something in the region of 686 hides in seven shires.[6]

The question which immediately springs to mind is, how was this huge estate acquired? One contributory factor is immediately suggested by the uneven distribution of Harold's lands. The greatest concentrations lie in those areas of which Harold was at one time earl; the West Saxon shires of Sussex, Surrey, Berkshire, Dorset, Devon and Cornwall; the East Anglian shire of Essex; and the shire of Hereford. Possibly connected with the earldom of East Anglia are the large holdings attributed to him or to his men in Buckinghamshire and Hertfordshire, and possibly connected with the earldom of Hereford are his substantial estates in Gloucestershire. Outside these areas, Harold held a respectable amount of land in Yorkshire and Lincolnshire, but in the remaining shires, especially those of western Mercia and the Danelaw, his holdings were negligible. It is interesting that the three counties where he had no land—Warwickshire, Derbyshire and Northamptonshire—were connected either with the Mercian or Northumbrian earldoms. This pattern of distribution recalls the suggestion made long ago by Maitland, that a large proportion of the estates held by the family of Earl Godwine were *comitales villae*—lands connected with the office of earl.[7]

To turn to a closer examination of the lands concerned, this suggestion is amply borne out. Harold's first public office was the earldom of East Anglia to which he was appointed in about 1044.[8] His sphere of authority certainly included Norfolk, Suffolk and Essex. It was presumably during his tenure of this office, which, apart from his exile in 1051-2, he held until his father's death in 1053, that he acquired the huge estates in Essex and the smaller but still substantial lands in Norfolk and Suffolk attributed to him in Domesday. Some at least were royal estates, presumably granted to Harold as earl; such were Necton in Norfolk, which was not assessed in hides, and rendered 6 night's feorm, and four estates in Essex, three of which, Brightlingsea (with Harkstead), Lawford and Newport (with Shelstead) are said to have rendered 2 night's feorm each, while the fourth—Writtle—rendered *x noctes de firma.* As Round pointed out, 'this archaic system of providing "feorm" for the household was normally characteristic of "ancient demesne" of the Crown and the only other Essex manor on which it is found was that which Earl Aelfgar held at Baddow'—Aelfgar, of course, being Harold's successor in the earldom. Round also noted that a hide at Writtle held by the bishop of Hereford is entered in one place as belonging to the king's fee and in another as *in feudo Haroldi.*[9]

In the tenth century the ealdordom of East Anglia also included the shires of eastern Mercia,[10] and at the very end of the century, the shires of Oxford and Buckingham, which had been administered by the ealdormen of Mercia, were under the jurisdiction of the ealdormen of Essex.[11] It is therefore interesting that Harold seems to have held royal estates in Hertfordshire and Buckinghamshire. It was again Round who pointed out that Hitchin, Herts., bears all the marks of having been at one time a royal manor. It was preferentially assessed, and it rendered 60 pounds 'assayed and weighed out'—forms of payment particularly associated with royal estates.[12] On the analogy of Hitchin, Round suggested that the three estates belonging to Harold in Buckinghamshire whose value, unlike that of his other estates, was expressed as *reddet*, not *valet*, were also royal or comital manors. The three estates were at Princes Risborough, Swanbourne and Upton near Slough.[13] Hertfordshire at least was part of the earldom given in 1045 to Beorn Estrithson, Harold's cousin, who was later murdered by Swein Godwineson. It is possible that Harold acquired his interests in the area after his cousin's murder in 1049, but given that Beorn's career seems to have been closely bound up with that of Harold, it is perhaps more likely that Beorn's authority was subordinate to that of Harold as earl of East Anglia; such subordinate commands are known in the tenth-century.[14]

Harold renounced the East Anglian earldom in 1053, when he succeeded to that of Wessex on his father's death. In 1057, he also became earl of Hereford on the death of Earl Ralph 'the Timid'. His position as earl of Hereford is clearly reflected in Domesday. He held the earl's third penny of the borough of Hereford, and two of his estates in the shire, Cowarne and Burghill, are clearly comital manors. To Cowarne was attached the third penny of three unnamed hundreds and to Burghill was attached the third penny of the hundreds of Stradford and *Chistetornes.* But the Burghill entry is of even more interest, for it records that this manor and that of Brinsop, also held by Harold, had previously belonged to Osbern Pentecost 'when Godwine and Harold had been exiled'.[15] The language clearly implies that it was because of their exile that Osbern held the estates and it is therefore possible that they formed part of the comital endowment of Swein Godwineson, for whom an earldom including Hereford was formed in 1043.[16] Osbern Pentecost was one of the Normans forced to flee the country after the reinstatement of Godwine and his family in 1052, whereas another Norman castle-builder in Herefordshire, Richard fitz Scrob, was allowed to remain.[17] The particular animosity of the family against Osbern is understandable if he had been holding some of their forfeited estates.

As earl of Hereford, Harold regained some of the wealth and power which his eldest brother had held intermittently for eight stormy years. It seems that the earldom included at least part of Gloucestershire, for the third penny of the borough of Winchcombe was held by Harold.[18] Gloucestershire had been part of Swein's earldom, but the family's connections with the area go back even further. Jarl Eilaf Thorgilson, brother of Godwine's wife Gytha, held an English earldom in the early years of Cnut's reign, which must have lain in the western midlands, since he led an expedition against the Welsh in 1022, and probably included Gloucestershire.[19] Jarl Eilaf is not recorded to have had any descendants, and it is possible that some of Harold's land in Herefordshire and Gloucestershire come ultimately from this source.

When we turn to Harold's lands in Wessex itself, the comital character of some of them is immediately evident. Maitland himself pointed out that the Exon. Domesday for Somerset enters the lands of Godwine's family as a separate section of the *Terra Regis*, headed *mansiones de comitatu*. At least two of Harold's Devon manors must fall into this category; Molland, to which was attached the third penny of three named hundreds, and Moreton, to which was attached the third penny of the hundred of Teignbridge. Over Wallop, Hants, must be another comital manor, for it commanded the third penny of six named hundreds; this estate, however, was held not by Harold but by his mother, Countess Gytha. The many estates in Somerset, Devon and Cornwall preferentially assessed for geld were probably also either comital manors, or old royal manors assigned to the earl. The Dorset manor of Puddletown, the only one in the shire preferentially assessed, was certainly a comital manor, for attached to it was the third penny of the whole shire of Dorset.[20] Crewkerne, Somerset, which was not assessed in hides and did not pay geld had been a royal manor in the ninth-century, since King Alfred had bequeathed it to his younger son, Aethelweard. It was held in 1066, however, not by Harold, but by a lady called Edith. Round conjectured that she was Harold's handfast wife, Edith Swan-neck.[21]

Chance references in the pages of Domesday and elsewhere hint at the ways in which Harold's personal as opposed to his comital wealth was built up. The tradition preserved in the twelfth century by the canons of Waltham asserts that Waltham itself was given to Harold by King Edward, after being forfeited by its previous owner; and Domesday itself tells us that Lees in Essex was given to Harold by Ansgar the staller.[22] In her will, the East Anglian lady, Wulfgyth, gave an estate at Fritton (either in Norfolk or Suffolk) to Earls Godwine and Harold, and her son Ketel left Harold an unidentified estate at *Moran* (probably in Norfolk).[23] Some land was probably acquired by purchase. This cannot be illustrated with regard to Harold himself, but Domesday records that Godwine bought an estate in Woodchester, Gloucs., for his wife Gytha.[24] He also bought an estate at Stoke, Kent, from two men who held it of the bishop of Rochester, but without the bishop's knowledge.[25] This dubious transaction reminds us that both Godwine ·and Harold were accused of despoiling the church, and indeed Domesday records a number of estates seized from ecclesiastical bodies and persons by Earl Harold 'through force and injustice'. Harold's relations with the church will be discussed later, but some of his estates may well have been acquired through outright theft. Harold's influence, though not his actual demesne land, was also extended through the various men who commended themselves to him. There are numerous references, notably in East Anglia, to men who were Harold's *commendati*, and one Suffolk thegn, Stanwine, sought Harold's protection after his previous lord, Eadric of Laxfield, had been temporarily exiled.[26] It is also possible that some of Harold's estates in the north midlands came to him by his marriage with Ealdgyth, daughter of Earl Leofric. Both Maitland and Stenton suggested this possibility, more or less simultaneously, though Stenton commented that had this been so, Harold would not have been in possession within the term of the Domesday enquiry, 'the day when King Edward was alive and dead'. He added, however, that Domesday is not entirely consistent on this point, and Professor Barlow believes that the marriage agreement at least must have preceded Edward's death.[27]

The question of Harold's first wife, Edith Swan-neck, needs further investigation. If, as suggested by Professor Eleanor Searle in her paper to this conference, the lady known to Domesday as Edith the Fair *(pulchra, faira)* and the Rich *(dives)* is in fact Edith Swan-neck, Harold's wife *more Danico*, two conclusions follow. Firstly Harold's lands in the eastern midlands would be complemented by those of his wife, who, with her men, held nearly 280 hides and 450 acres of land in the five shires of Suffolk, Essex, Cambridgeshire, Buckinghamshire and Hertfordshire, most of which passed first to Earl Ralph, and then, after his forfeiture, to Count Alan. Most of her land lay in Cambridgeshire, where Harold's possessions were small. Secondly, and perhaps more significantly, Harold would join the group of noblemen who married influential women in the Danelaw; Cnut, whose marriage to Aelfgifu of Northampton produced King Harold I; Edmund Ironside, whose marriage to Ealdgyth, widow of Sigeferth, against his father's will, brought him the allegiance of the Five Boroughs; and the Mercian earls, Leofric and his son Aelfgar, whose marriages to Godgifu and Aelfgifu respectively brought them estates and therefore influence in the Danelaw and northern Mercia. Though, like Harold's, the marriages of Cnut and Edmund were *more Danico*, the offspring were regarded as legitimate enough to claim, or transmit a claim to, the English crown.[28]

It is when one looks at the vast accumulation of land in Sussex belonging to Harold and his family that one is driven to the conclusion that most of his land in the south-east came to him by inheritance. The family of Godwine held over 1,200 hides in Sussex, about a third of the shire. These lands were divided in Domesday's reckoning between Harold, his father, his mother, his three surviving brothers (though Tostig's share is negligible) and his sister Gunnhildr. Edith also held land in Sussex, though it is almost impossible to distinguish between her possessions as Edward's queen and those held as Godwine's daughter. This concentration of land, no less than the fact that the whole family (or virtually all of it) are represented as landholders, is one of the strongest pieces of evidence for the South Saxon origin of Earl Godwine.[29] The appearance of Godwine himself as a pre-Conquest tenant deserves mention. He or his men are said to have held over 660 hides in Surrey, Sussex and Hampshire, and 120 sulungs in Kent, besides smaller amounts of land elsewhere. The information on pre-Conquest tenures is supposed to reflect the position on the day of King Edward's death, January 5 1066, and Godwine, of course, died in 1053. It is mainly, though not exclusively, in the shires of the south-eastern circuits that Godwine appears as a pre-Conquest tenant, but even if his appearance was a peculiarity of the commissioners associated with this circuit, the practice would still require explanation.[30] Earl Aelfgar, who also predeceased King Edward, also appears frequently as a pre-Conquest tenant, though in his case, the matter is more understandable, since his death, whenever it occurred, was much closer to the Domesday term; he may not have died until 1065.[31] A closer parallel is the occasional appearance of his father, Earl Leofric, who died in 1057.[32] Some-one must have been holding Godwine's land between 1053 and 1066. One possibility is suggested by an entry in the Exon. Domesday for Dorset, which records that the third oak in the wood of Burton Bradstock had belonged by custom to Earl Godwine, and was attached to the manor of Frampton. Turning to the Frampton entry, we find the estate held in King Edward's day not by Godwine, but by his wife Gytha.[33] Did she hold all Godwine's estates in 1066? Two circumstances suggest that she did. Firstly, Countess Aelfgifu, Earl Aelfgar's widow, is recorded in the Domesday description of the borough of Colchester as the holder of three hides attached to the manor of Shalford. But in the entry relating to Shalford, the pre-Conquest tenant is given as her husband.[34] Secondly, the wills of some Old English noblemen, after listing various requests, leave the residue of their estates to their wives, either for the term of the widow's life, or unconditionally.[35] This suggests that Gytha held at least a life-interest in the lands attributed to Earl Godwine, in addition to the land entered in her own name.[36] If William of Poitiers is not simply exaggerating when he tells us that Gytha offered the victorious William its weight in gold for Harold's body, she was clearly a very rich lady.[37]

From whatever source he acquired his land, Harold as earl of Wessex was a wealthy man, the richest noble in England after the king. But his power of course did not rest simply upon the possession of land, but upon the network of patronage and influence which such possessions enabled him to exercise. Domesday allows us to catch a glimpse of the dynamics as well as the structure of Old English society by naming some of the *commendati* and sub-tenants of the greater lords. But there are various problems in the interpretation of this information. Firstly, although the general framework of the Domesday enquiry was fixed for the whole country, each group of commissioners had their own idiosyncracies; for instance, the south-eastern circuit (Circuit I, covering Kent, Surrey, Sussex, Hampshire and Berkshire) gives details of pre-Conquest sub-tenures, whilde the south-western circuit (Circuit II, covering Dorset, Wiltshire, Somerset, Devon and Cornwall) does not. Moreover the actual compilation of the Domesday text is uneven in quality; the account of the north-east midlands is hastily compiled and comparatively uninformative, whereas the shires of western Mercia are very fully described, with a wealth of detail not found elsewhere. A related problem is what Round called 'the singular laxity of the scribes in their use of formulae'.[38] He was speaking of the problems experienced by those trying to unravel the mysteries of commendation, but his strictures apply equally to other matters. In this particular context, it does not help identification that a man may be described indifferently as a thegn, a housecarl, a free man or by some surname or bye-name or patronymic. Such a circumstance exacerbates the final problem, one experienced by anyone working in the field of Old English nomenclature, the problem of names. The English had no regular system of patronymics or surnames and since some English names, Godwine for example, are very common, identification can be a hazardous, not to say exasperating task. If a man is called something like Aelfric, Eadric, Leofwine or the like, it is virtually impossible to be sure that one has traced all his land 'on the day when King Edward was alive and dead'.

However, despite the problems, no study of Harold's wealth can avoid dealing with his resources in men as well as with those in land. A glance at the table will show that it is only in some areas—the south-east, East Anglia and the eastern midlands, and the shires of Hereford and Gloucester—that the details of the men who acknowledged him as their lord are given, and all examples have therefore to be drawn from these regions. Harold's men varied considerably in rank and wealth, from the unnamed sokemen, some with only a few acres, in the eastern districts, through local thegns prosperous enough to have acquired men of their own, to those who could legitimately be described as powerful noblemen in their own right. Of the first type one can say little; usually not even their names or individual holdings are provided. Typical of a lesser thegn is a man who held of Harold in Essex and Suffolk and bore the uncommon name of Skalpi—a name of Norse origin, though of course we know nothing of the origin of its bearer. Skalpi had received from Harold the 2½ hide estate at Lees, Essex, given to Harold by Ansgar the staller. The entry gives something of the history of the estate and its holders. Skalpi gave it in dower to his wife, apparently after the Conquest, since one of the witnesses was Roger the marshal, a post-Conquest landowner in Essex. Skalpi continued to hold the land after King William's arrival until 'he went where he died in York *(Ehroica)* in outlawry',[39] presumably during the northern risings of 1069-70. Apart from Lees, he held another small estate in Essex and two in Suffolk, amounting to 3 hides and 3 carucates, plus some smaller amounts of land held by men commended to him. Virtually all his land seems to have come from Harold. In the Lees entry he is described as Harold's housecarl, and one of the Suffolk entries calls him Harold's thegn; he exercised soke over his two Suffolk manors under Harold.[40] Because Skalpi's name is unusual, we can be virtually certain that all the Domesday references are to one man, and that he held no other land. Skalpi may stand as an example of a thegn of very modest standing, who owed everything to Harold's patronage. It is interesting that he managed to retain his land for a while after the conquest, though some of Harold's men were even more successful at maintaining and even improving their positions under King William.[41]

Another of Harold's men in the same area was Leofwine of Bacton. Like Skalpi, he held land in Suffolk and Essex, being variously described as Leofwine of Bacton, Leofwine *cild*, Leofwine the thegn and Leofwine a free man. All these references have been supposed to refer to the same man because the estates concerned passed to one Norman tenant-in-chief, Walter the Deacon.[42] On this assumption, Leofwine held 9 hides and 13 acres in Essex and 8 carucates and 175 acres of land in Suffolk. In Suffolk also, men commended to him held another 104 acres of land. However he only acknowledged Harold's lordship for a small proportion of this land. It is only in respect of his manor of Bacton itself that he is described as 'under' Harold. Another of his estates was 'in the soke and commendation of the abbot of Bury' and in respect of Milden, he is described as King Edward's thegn.[43] Leofwine may be taken as a fair example of a number of Harold's men. He was a substantial local landowner, with men of his own, a *commendatus* of Bury St Edmunds, and perhaps most importantly, a king's thegn. Several men described in one place as Harold's thegns appear as king's thegns also. The most obvious example is Tunmann, described as 'King Edward's thegn, Harold's man by commendation', but more interesting is Eadric, who held an estate at Blakeney in Norfolk, 'under King Edward, freely, from Harold'.[44] He also held at Bradiston in the same county, but here he is described as *rector navis regis Edwardi*. The Bradiston entry also provides the information that 'after King William came into England, this Eadric was outlawed to Denmark'.[45] Eadric the commander of King Edward's ship can be identified with Eadric the steersman, who gave to St Benet of Holme 'five estates in the neighbourhood of North Walsham' including Honing.[46] The Domesday entry for Honing says that the abbot had given Eadric half the estate and that Eadric had made a reversionary gift of the other half to the abbey, so that he held the whole estate of the abbey and did service *(deseruiebat)*.[47] It is possible to suggest what his service was. The abbot of St Benet was Aelfwold, who is said to have been entrusted by Harold with a naval command in 1066 and in consequence to have suffered 'tribulations' in King William's time. Indeed he was forced for a while to seek refuge in Denmark, and though he himself eventually returned to his office, at least one of his men died in exile.[48] It seems likely that Eadric had been under Aelfwold's command, and that we have here the occasion of his flight to Denmark. It is even possible that the royal ship commanded by Eadric was provided by the abbey, like those vessels provided by other shipsokes. Eadric's support must have been a valuable asset to Harold. It would be equivalent to access to a 'unit' of 60 men serving in the host by land or sea.

All three of the men so far discussed were of thegnly rank. Skalpi belonged to the class of lower or median·thegns; Eadric and Leofwine were royal thegns.[49] Service to the king was one of the distinguishing features of status in Old English society, as elsewhere. Another was possession of land. A reference in the *Liber Eliensis* suggests that possession of 40 hides was required to raise an ordinary thegn to the rank of the *proceres*.[50] Since Leofwine and Eadric bear very common names, we cannot tell if they held estates in addition to those mentioned equivalent to this amount, but some of Harold's men did. A clear example is Azor, one of his men in Sussex. He held at least 86 hides of land, 27½ hides of Earl Harold, 20 hides of Earl Godwine and the remainder as a king's thegn. Three of Azor's estates, amounting to 8 hides, were held of him by a man called Brihtmær. We are not told Brihtmær's status, but possession of 8 hides would entitle him to thegnly rank.[51] Azor is thus in the position of the king's thegn described in the writings of Archbishop Wulfstan—'the thegn who prospered (so) that he served the king . . . (and) had a thegn who served him, possessing five hides of land . . .'[52]

Obviously it was advantageous for Harold to have good relations with the men who were prominent in their localities, for without them he would have found it difficult to discharge his duties as earl. But in the case of his East Anglian *commendati*, the relationship survived the surrender of his earldom. This is true of his men in the east Midlands also. On the eve of the conquest, Berkhampstead, where the victorious William was to receive the submission of the English, was held of Harold by Eadmær *attile*, called here a thegn of Earl Harold, but elsewhere described as a king's thegn. He was a rich man; his lands in Hertfordshire, Buckinghamshire and Middlesex passed to Robert of Mortain, and he may have held land in the south-west also.[53] Wing in Buckinghamshire, an ancient royal manor and site of one of the finest surviving tenth-century churches in the country, was held by Edward *cild*, a man of Harold, elsewhere called a king's thegn.[54] It is interesting to see the number of king's thegns who were also commended to Earl Harold (or indeed to other great noblemen), for from the ranks of the king's thegns were recruited the royal officials—sheriffs, high-reeves, military commanders and envoys—on whom the king's government depended. They correspond, as Ganshof noticed, to the royal vassals of Carolingian Frankia.[55] It was in part the breaking of the direct relationship between the Carolingian kings and their vassals which consolidated the power of the counts, and led to the rise of territorial principalities in France. In the attraction of such men into the orbit of Harold and other nobles, one can see a foreshadowing of a similar process.

None of the thegns mentioned so far seems to have been of more than local importance. However Domesday gives us a glimpse of Harold's relations with men of wider influence. One is Aethelnoth *cild*, also called 'of Canterbury'. He was one of a group of landowners in Kent from whose estates the king did not take the usual heriot. In return, these landowners had to provide a royal bodyguard, either at Canterbury or Sandwich, at the king's choice.[56]

Aethelnoth's importance can be gauged from the fact that he was one of the hostages taken by William to Normandy in 1067; Florence of Worcester, who gives this information, calls him *nobilis satrapem* (a term not infrequently applied to ealdormen).[57] He possessed extensive estates in Kent, Surrey, Sussex, Hampshire, Buckinghamshire, Northamptonshire and Oxfordshire, totalling over 180 hides.[58] But from the point of view of this study, the interesting estates are two tiny manors in Kent, which Æthelnoth had taken from the canons of St Martin's, Dover, for inadequate compensation. This transaction had been achieved *per violentiam Haroldi*.[59] An exactly similar case can be quoted from the other end of Wessex. Eadnoth the staller's estates were scattered over the shires of Wiltshire, Dorset, Somerset, Gloucestershire and Berkshire. His title indicates a king's thegn with 'a seat and special office in the king's hall', with a part to play in royal government. Eadnoth served three kings, Edward, Harold and William himself, and died in 1068, leading the western fyrd against the sons of Harold.[60] His son, Harding fitz Eadnoth, was an important landowner before and after the conquest and ancestor of the Berkeleys.[61] Eadnoth held a small estate in Berkshire of Harold, and in Dorset he had received two hides at Ilsington, which Harold had taken from an unnamed clerk.[62] Though Domesday does not say so, the land in Berkshire (a couple of hides at Draycot) was probably also ecclesiastical land, belonging to Abingdon.[63] Such favours must have helped to draw the powerful nobles into Harold's sphere of influence. That Harold's favour was worth having we can deduce from the gifts made to him, not only by the East Anglian lady Wulfgyth and her son, but also by Ansgar the staller, another great landowner, who appears in the *Carmen* negotiating with William for the surrender of London.[64]

Since Aethelnoth and Eadnoth both appear as despoilers of the church, they form a convenient bridge to a discussion of Harold's relations with the church. He and his father are usually regarded as irreligious plunderers of church property, and this reputation is borne out by Domesday. According to the commissioners' informants, Harold's 'victims' included the Benedictine nunnery of Shaftesbury, the bishoprics of Rochester and St Petroc, and the secular canons of St Guthlac, Hereford, St Mary Chatteris, and St John Sussex.[65] Other sources reveal that he was at odds with Leofric of Exeter and Giso of Wells.[66] Similar—and even more serious—charges are levelled at his father and his elder brother Swein is accused of seizing three estates from the church of Worcester, while the Anglo-Saxon Chronicle accuses Tostig of 'robbing God'.[67] In most of the cases concerning Harold, the amounts of land were small,[68] but he held some 30 hides of land belonging to the church of Hereford, 43 hides belonging to Shaftesbury abbey, and two estates in Somerset amounting to 50 hides which were claimed by Bishop Giso.[69] What lay behind Harold's seizure of the Shaftesbury estates we do not know. Giso's quarrel with Harold has been discussed elsewhere and seems to have been concerned with the ratification of his predecessor's will, a matter which would have involved Harold as president of the shire court.[70] Harold's seizure of the Hereford estates is puzzling, for between 1056 and 1060, at least, the see was administered by men with whom he was on good terms; Leofgar his priest, who 'wore his moustaches during his priesthood until he became a bishop' and then 'gave up his chrism and his cross, his spiritual weapons, and took his spear and sword . . . and so went campaigning against Griffith the Welsh king' until he was killed on June 16 1056, and Ealdred, bishop of Worcester and another campaigner against the Welsh, who administered the bishopric of Hereford from Leofgar's death until his own appointment to the archbishopric of York in 1060. After 1060 the Lotharingian Walter, a royal clerk and Queen Edith's chaplain, became bishop.[71]

All these allegations against Harold are detailed by Freeman, who attempts to absolve his hero of blame.[72] Without repeating Freeman's arguments, I should like to make a rather different point, though one mentioned by Freeman in passing; that the difference between a pious benefactor and a ruthless spoliator is not necessarily that between one man and another, but between one ecclesiastical commentator and another. One monk's benefactor is another monk's despoiler. For instance, King Edward is usually portrayed as a saintly and pious patron of the church, yet Hugh Candidus accuses both Edward and Edith of attempting to rob the abbey of Peterborough. Harold, on the other hand is listed as a benefactor of the abbey, which may help to explain the presence of its abbot Leofric, Earl Leofric's nephew, at Harold's side in the Hastings campaign.[73] Edward's royal abbey of Westminster was also in possession of lands belonging to the abbey of Pershore, though attempts have been made to clear the king of the charge of robbing Pershore of these estates.[74] Leofric of Mercia, often contrasted with Godwine as a model of piety, had a very different reputation at Worcester, where he, his father, his brother and nephew and his grandsons are represented as spoliators of the church's lands.[75] Indeed there is a strong contrast between the treatment of Harold by the Domesday scribes and their treatment of Leofric and his family, which bears out Freeman's assertion that the discredited Harold was a convenient target for vituperation. For instance, the Domesday entry for the Worcestershire manor of Salwarpe says only that it was held in King Edward's day by one Aelwine *cild*. For the full story, we must turn to Heming's Cartulary, which records that the estate had been disputed between the church and Earl Leofric's brother Godwine, and that Godwine on his deathbed had restored it and renounced his claim. But his son Aethelwine 'who had his hands cut off by the Danes while a hostage' overturned his father's will and retained the estate with the help of his uncle, Earl Leofric.[76]

None of this of course excuses Harold's spoliation of the church, but merely puts it into its proper context. A pious man in the eleventh century was one who founded, endowed or protected those churches with which he or his family was particularly associated. Such piety could go hand in hand with indifference or even hostility to other foundations. For an example one has only to look back to the years of the monastic reform movement in the late tenth-century. Aethelwine *Amicus Dei*, the co-founder and *advocatus* of Ramsey abbey, seized estates from the church of Ely, while his rival Aelfhere of Mercia, castigated by the *Vita Oswaldi* as an enemy of the reform movement, was a benefactor of the reformed abbey of Glastonbury.[77] Harold was no Odda of Deerhurst, but he appears to have been no better and no worse than other powerful laymen of his day. His own particular favourite was the college of secular canons at Holy Cross, Waltham, of which he was regarded as the second founder, since he extended so considerably the very modest establishment set up by Tofig the Proud. The extensive estates held by Holy Cross in 1066 seem to have been acquired either from Harold, or through his efforts, and it is not therefore surprising to find that Harold had a good reputation in the records of this house. The twelfth-century author of the tract *De Inventione Sanctae Crucis* describes Harold treating the foundation as if he were its brother, born from the same womb *(quasi uterinus filius ecclesie)*.[78] His reputation at Worcester is also good thanks to his veneration for Bishop Wulfstan so eloquently described in the *Vita Wulfstani*.[79] Wulfstan, like Leofric of Peterborough, supported Harold in 1066, as, not surprisingly, did his uncle Aelfwig, abbot of the New Minster, who was killed at Senlac, though not necessarily as a combatant. As we have seen Aelfwold of St Benet of Holme was also one of Harold's supporters, and though Harold himself is not recorded as a benefactor of this house, his handfast wife, Edith Swan-neck, is.[80] Another house which experienced Harold's patronage, not only as a benefactor but on a wider scale, was Abingdon. According to the thirteenth-century cartularies of the house, it was at Harold's suggestion that Edward, after the death of Godwine, gave Sandford-on-Thames to the abbey. This may in fact have been a bequest of Godwine himself, since the estate was given to him by the king in 1050.[81] Harold did not lose all interest in the estate, since it was held of the abbey by Blacmann the priest, who also held two other estates of the abbey, one of which he held through Earl Harold. The estates were granted to him because of a church in honour of St Andrew which he built on the island of Andrésey, south of the monastic buildings. Blacmann lost his lands after the conquest and fled to Denmark, apparently in the company of Harold's mother, Countess Gytha.[82] His lands, with those of other tenants of the abbey, were later used to endow the military tenants of Abingdon and are said to have belonged to 'those tenants of the church who were called thegns and who died at the battle of Hastings'. Whether or not this implies Blacmann's presence at Harold's side in the final campaign, it suggests that the abbey's contingent fought with him *en masse* at Senlac.[83] Other entries in the Abingdon records suggest why they should have given him such support. Harold is said to have assisted abbot Ordric to recover the abbey's estate at Leckhampstead. This case has already been discussed by Miss Harmer, but since it shows Harold in his capacity as earl of Wessex—and such glimpses are rare—perhaps it might be recounted again. The estate had been leased in the time of Cnut for the usual three lives to one Brihtmund. After his death it passed to his wife and thence to his eldest son, and on the death of the latter, it should have reverted to the abbey. But the younger son, Brihtwine, persuaded abbot Siward to extend the lease in his favour. By some means, Brihtwine managed to acquire the charter relating to the land, and thus could claim to hold it *in iure hereditario*. Siward made a formal statement of denial, swearing 'by the oath which I owe to God and my lord king' that Brihtwine had a life interest only. But it seems that while Brihtwine held the charter, nothing could be done, for, as the Abingdon account puts it, 'anyone who held such a document could with confidence claim the land'. Ordric appealed for help to Harold, who prevailed upon Brihtwine to disgorge the charter, and in the case which Ordric was then able to bring before the witan, the land was adjudged to the abbey.[84] Domesday reveals that the estate was still held in 1066 by Brihtwine, but as the abbey's tenant.

Moreover it was by Harold's advice and in his witness that another local magnate, Thorkell, did homage to the abbey for his estate at Kingston Bagpuize. Though no details are given, one suspects that Thorkell's situation was not unlike that of Brihtwine, and that, having acquired one of the abbey's estates, he was brought by Harold to acknowledge Abingdon's ultimate ownership and his own status as a tenant. Abingdon lost this estate after the conquest, for Thorkell died at Senlac, and his lands were confiscated.[86]

Abingdon was a rich and powerful house and previous ealdormen in Wessex had found it politic to secure the friendship of its abbots with gifts. Eadric, the donor of Leckhampstead, is likely to have been the brother of Aelfheah, ealdorman of central Wessex from 959 to 971/2. Aelfheah himself was also a benefactor of the house, as was his brother Aelfhere, ealdorman of Mercia, 956, to 983, and Eadwine, ealdorman of Kent and Sussex, 977 to 982, was buried in the monastery.[87] This background helps to explain Harold's interest in the house and his willingness to help in its difficulties. Not that Abingdon benefited in the event by its association with him. The abbot at the time of the Conquest was Ealdred, who made his submission to William, but subsequently the abbey became a centre for the disaffected English. Ealdred was arrested on charges of treasonable dealings with the Danes; he himself was imprisoned and the abbey plundered of its treasures.[88] Abingdon seems to have been a lesser Ely, whose abbot, Thorkell, entertained the invading Swein of Denmark in 1069. Thorkell had been placed in office by Harold in his brief reign, and the language of the Abingdon writer, though circumspect, suggests that Ealdred was also Harold's appointee; at least, his succession to the abbey is linked with that of Harold to the crown.[89]

Harold's wealth and power enabled him to gather friends and supporters among both lay and ecclesiastical magnates. It remains to consider the more tangible uses of his huge estates. They must have taken some administering, and it is unfortunate that we have no information as to how they were managed. Incidental references in Domesday mention the reeves in charge of particular properties, but there is nothing that would provide a picture of Harold's household.[90] Individual estates, however, seem to have played a part in the political calculations of Harold and his family. For instance, it is at least of interest that Harold's estate of Catton in Yorkshire seems to have included Stamford-bridge, the site of his greatest victory.[91] When we discover that Earl Morcar held land at Gatefulford, another fitful gleam of light is shed on this obscure and little-known campaign.[92] It may also be of importance that among his estates in Sussex, Harold held land at Whatlington and Crowhurst, the one just north and the other just south of the site of Senlac.[93] But the manor which most people associate particularly with Harold is not entered in his name in Domesday. Bosham, according to the Domesday text, was held by Earl Godwine in King Edward's day.[94] This manor is closely bound up with the fortunes of Harold's family. It was at Bosham that Swein Godwineson's ships were lying in 1049, when he abducted and subsequently murdered his cousin Beorn Estrithson.[95] It was from Bosham also (which seems to have included the neighbouring Thorney Island) that Godwine, Swein and Tostig fled to Bruges in 1051.[96] The Bayeux Tapestry shows the hall at Bosham where Harold feasted before his ill-fated journey to the continent in 1064/5.[97] In fact the family held sizeable amounts of land in the general area. Godwine himself held land at Westbourne (now part of Portsmouth), Singleton in the Downs north of Chichester, and Climping, a few miles to the east. Harold had land at Eastergate, between Climping and Chichester, and Tostig not only held land at Fishbourne, just adjacent to Bosham, but also lands in the Isle of Wight and the New Forest area which, as Round pointed out, constitute 'a far more valuable estate than we should have been led to expect from the distant sphere of his power and one which may have prompted his descent upon the isle in 1066'.[98] It is clear from the Chronicle entry for that year that Tostig was able to count upon support in the area, for not only were 'both money and provisions given to him there' but he was able to use the Isle of Wight as a base to launch a raid all along the south coast as far as Sandwich.[99] It was off the Isle of Wight also that Godwine waited in 1052 for the arrival of Harold and his ships from Ireland. The campaign waged by the family in 1052 shows clearly which areas they could rely upon for support. Godwine's first attempt at a come-back took the form of a landing in Dungeness. He quickly gained support from the men of the eastern shires. Two versions of the Chronicle ('C' and 'D') say that an oath was sworn to him—'they all said that they would live and die with him' *(þa cwædon ealle þ hi mid him woldon licgan 7 lybban)*. The serious purpose of this oath is shown by the fact that it was also sworn in 900 by the ætheling Aethelwold, when he raised a rebellion against his cousin Edward the Elder.[100] However, Godwine did not feel able to resist a combined landfyrd and shipfyrd sent against him by the king's supporters and withdrew to Pevensey, whence he returned to Bruges. It was at Pevensey that he had lain with his ships and his nephew Beorn in 1049, and once again we discover that the family held land in the district; Godwine himself had a huge estate (50½ hides) at Willingdon to the west, and Harold held a small amount of land at Bowley in Hailsham, on the edge of the Pevensey levels.[101] From Pevensey he returned to Bruges and thence came to the Isle of Wight, where he undertook some extensive raiding while waiting for Harold, including a raid on the royal estate of Portland in Dorset. After their meeting, however, they were careful to do no damage off the south coast 'except that they lived off the country', but concentrated upon gaining support as they moved eastwards.

Harold's experience in the west was very different. It is not clear why he with his brother Leofwine should have gone to Ireland in 1051 while the rest of the family fled to Bruges. The ship in which he went had been prepared by Swein for his own use, but it seems he changed his mind, and his brothers went instead. When Harold returned in 1052 to land at Porlock on the Somerset-Devon border, he met fierce resistance. His invasion was countered by a force drawn from both shires, and a battle took place in which thirty of the local thegns were killed. Harold nevertheless seized what provisions he needed and made off round Lands End to meet his father.[102] The general lack of sympathy in the south-west for the house of Godwine was demonstrated once again after the Conquest when Harold's sons made two unsuccessful raids on the south-western shires, in 1068 and 1069. In 1068, when Bristol was besieged, the invaders were opposed by a force headed by Harold's one-time protégé, Eadnoth the staller (who was killed); the 1069 attempt was driven off by Count Brian. The son who led the attack on Bristol is not named, but the attempt may be connected with the fact that the only estates said by Domesday to have been held by Godwine Haroldson were two small manors in Somerset, one of them lying on the Somerset-Devon border, south of Bristol—this is Langford in Burrington.[103]

The general support given to Godwine in the south-east, coupled with the enormous amounts of land held by him and his children in Sussex combine to suggest that the family was South Saxon in origin. Godwine's father was probably Wulfnoth *cild* 'the South Saxon' who in 1009 was accused of some unspecified offence and raised a rebellion among the ships gathered in that year. It is said that Wulfnoth persuaded twenty of the king's ships to support him against his detractors, which indicates a man of considerable local importance.[104] South Saxons do not seem to have played a prominent role in the royal government before the eleventh-century. It is true that we can rarely determine the origins of the great ealdormen and earls, but where we can they tend to be either West Saxons (in the reign of Aethelred and before) or, in the reigns of Cnut and his sons, Danes. The rise to power of a South Saxon family may be connected with the growing importance of the south east in the same period. Sussex had been something of a backwater in the eyes of the West Saxon dynasty, whose power was based on Winchester, Wessex and southern Mercia. We know little of the history of Sussex in the tenth-century. With Kent, it formed the ealdordom of eastern Wessex, but its ealdormen are shadowy figures, and no continuous sequence of them can be established. It seems that the eastern shires were often administered by the ealdormen of central Wessex.[105] In ecclesiastical terms also, Sussex was a neglected area. The monastic reform movement seems to have passed it by. It has no great Benedictine abbeys such as those re-founded in Wessex, Mercia and the east midlands. Indeed lands in Sussex were used to endow such establishments to the detriment of South Saxon houses and even in 1066, Selsey was one of the poorest sees in England.[106] But in the eleventh century Sussex and Kent begin to play a role in the political history of England. This increasing importance may be connected with the fact that from the early eleventh-century, Danish armies began to enter England through the south-east. The English kings responded to the threat, and Sandwich became the assembly point for royal fleets when the campaigning season began every year.[107] Perhaps these circumstances may explain Godwine's rise to prominence; a man whose influence and wealth lay in this area would be of particular use to a king who, like Cnut, was interested in control of the North Sea and the Channel. In more general terms, the re-orientation of English interests towards Normandy and Flanders, which marks the eleventh-century, seems to have brought Sussex into the limelight and enabled a South Saxon family to gain wider influence.

In conclusion, perhaps it should be said that the study of pre-Conquest noble families is in its infancy. Professor Loyn observed in a note to his study of Harold's career produced for the commemoration of the Conquest that 'there is need for a modern critical study of the holdings of the Godwine family in 1066'.[108] It cannot be claimed that this paper fills that vacuum. But it is to be hoped that it shows at least the value of such studies to an understanding of Harold's career in particular, and Old English society in general; and that it will encourage others to undertake the examination of the careers and families, not only of Harold and his brothers, but of other Old English noblemen.

Danish kings and England in the late tenth and early eleventh centuries—economic implications

DAVID M. WILSON

The problem of the eleventh century in this country is not just the story of England, nor of the Conqueror. It also has to do with the Danes—with kings like Sven and Knut who made a great deal out of England and who brought at least one Scandinavian kingdom properly into the forum, even the cockpit, of Europe.

The theme of this note is, 'Who gains?'. And perhaps of greater interest, 'What and where gains?'. Too often we see the raids and conquests of Sven and Knut as episodic—reflecting the staccato phrases of the Anglo-Saxon Chronicle. Rather we should see them as a whole, against their background in Scandinavia and more particularly against their social and economic background. During the reign of Knut's grandfather, Harald Bluetooth, Denmark became a united kingdom and the attempts of Sven and Knut to keep that kingdom together led to wild adventures overseas. Why were these adventures necessary? Whilst money is not necessarily at the base of all human endeavour, it can have a lot to do with it and I wish in this paper to indicate some possible economic causes, implications and reasons for Sven's invasions and Knut's conquests. This cannot be the whole story—rather an element in it.

The main burden of my argument is that Harald, in his consolidation of the Danish state, practically bankrupted it and that Sven, following the example of his rather uncertain subject Olaf Tryggveson of Norway, sought to profit from the wealth of England by raiding and taking Danegeld in order to repair the results of his father's extravagances. I would further argue that Knut, following Sven's example, used the money raised—initially at least—for the ends of Denmark and only later for those of England. These ends are far from clear, but the establishment of towns and the reorganisation of land-holding may be part of the story. In painting a very impressionistic picture of this almost protohistoric period I shall largely use the evidence of archaeology (which has been subject to considerable reassessment in recent years) together with the results of detailed source-criticism recently produced by Danish historians. I must acknowledge long hours of discussion with Olaf Olsen, Else Roesdahl, James Graham-Campbell and Raymond Page which helped to form, for better or worse, some of the ideas expressed here.

It is important to understand the basis of Danish history of the tenth and early eleventh century up to the death of Sven Forkbeard. What follows immediately is the sort of thing a Danish schoolchild or an English archaeologist must use and is not for specialists. The family from which Knut stemmed was the Jelling dynasty, so named after their necropolis at the Danish village of that name, where a carved runic stone provides the first major indigenous historical statement concerning Denmark:

> King Harald had this monument made after Gorm his father and Thyre his mother, that Harald that won all Denmark and Norway and made the Danes Christian.

Our knowledge of the Jelling dynasty is thin and often obscure. We do not know when Gorm died or when Harald Bluetooth became king. Adam of Bremen says that Harald reigned fifty years: if, then, he died *c.* 985 (not later than 987), which seems likely, it is possible, but no more than possible, that Gorm died *c.* 935. Nor do we know when Harald 'made the Danes Christian', although we can be reasonably certain that it would have been a gradual process. According to the German cleric Ruotger the conversion took place between 953 and 965, approximate dates which are confirmed by the chronicler Widukind.

Again, knowledge of political events in Denmark in this period is so slight that the meaning of the phrase 'won all Denmark and Norway' is obscure. We may assume that the first element refers to the consolidation of the Danish state. Indeed, the fact that Harald was buried in Roskilde may indicate an eastward shift in the centre of gravity of the Danish state. This might be the time when the southern provinces of Sweden, for example, became part of the kingdom of Denmark in more than formal terms. Further, the borderlands with the Germans and Slavs to the south were almost certainly consolidated during Harald's reign. The reference to Norway in the inscription is obscure, but we do know that there was an earl Hakon in Norway *c.*960 who may have been, in theory at least, a dependant of the Danish king. The Norwegian reference may also be related to an involvement in the English Danelaw until the fall of York in 954. But to this we shall return.

Summarising the surviving evidence, we can see that Harald Bluetooth was King of Denmark for a longish period in the middle of the tenth century, that he strengthened—at least in his own eyes—the Danish kingdom and probably consolidated it, and that he conquered Norway. He himself presumably became Christian—the first Christian king of Denmark—and presumably by political act ordered the Danes to become Christian. From the monuments, burial mounds and memorial stones at Jelling we know also that Harald was not afraid of public works—the construction of the great monuments there was itself a major engineering and economic burden—and it seems likely, from the results of recent excavations by Knut Krogh, that Harald built the first church at Jelling, having translated the bodies of the king and his wife from one of the great mounds that now dominate the village.

Sven Forkbeard was Harald's son and successor. He had led some sort of rebellion against his father, who had, according to Adam of Bremen, died in exile. Sven succeeded his father in the late 980s and our knowledge of the state of Denmark and of the activities of its king grows swiftly so that we are able to sketch in the outlines of a portrait of the Danish royal house of this period. For thirty years Sven ruled in Denmark as a military king and died abroad at Gainsborough on 3 February 1014 on one of his expeditions. But it is easy to dismiss Sven simply as a warlike national leader. He was skilful in his control of his country and of its external politics. His adventures abroad laid his kingdom open to attacks from Swedes and Slavs, but Sven turned all this to his advantage by marrying the widow of King Eirik of Sweden, a woman surrounded by mystery and romance. She was sister to the powerful Boleslav Chrobry of Poland and the mother of Sven's two sons Knut the Great and Harald. Later she separated from Sven and her sons were brought up in Poland. By this marriage Sven gave himself considerable interest and power in both Sweden and among the Slavs. After the death of the Norwegian king Olav Tryggveson in 1000—in whatever circumstances this took place—Sven's position as the senior Scandinavian king, hitherto rather shaky, became unquestioned, and shortly after this he appears in the chronicles as the chief leader of the foreign host in England.

After this summary we can more clearly discern Denmark during Harald's reign. When he came to the throne Viking power in England was on the wane. The battle of Brunanburh was the culmination of a number of campaigns which were effectively to restore the Danelaw to the English kingdom. The fall of York and the expulsion and death of Eirik Bloodaxe in 954 put a formal end to the political power of the Scandinavians in England which had been rocky for a number of years. Edgar's brilliant reign is seen with hindsight in Professor Loyn's words as 'a fitting climax to this hard century of Christian resistance and Danish attack'.[1]

The Scandinavians remained in England as anglicised farmers or as foreign traders, but few benefits (other than the strictly commercial) filtered back to Denmark. There had obviously been internal trouble in Denmark as is shown by Harald's boast on the Jelling rune-stone that he had 'won all Denmark and Norway'. Harald had by the 960s created a kingdom, seemingly stable and probably well defined, yet this collapsed around his ears: his son led a rebellion against him and he was even exiled for a short time in the Slav lands (although perhaps in a Danish enclave there). What had caused this rebellion? Was it just that he was, to use Sir Frank Stenton's words,[2] 'an autocratic master' who had imposed the Christian religion on a pagan country? Or was it something more?

I think something more. Stenton was certainly right in his description of Harald as an autocrat, but his autocracy had bled the country economically by the very process of consolidating it. Although such fine economic judgements would be foreign to Harald and his contemporaries, I think that in his public works programme we have an indicator of the line which Harald followed, a line which at times perhaps went over the border of cool thinking about a power base into royal extravagance, the expense of which was difficult for the small realm of Denmark to bear, especially as Norway perhaps became more powerful and as trouble was hinted at from the south.

The indicators of this extravagance are to be seen largely in the archaeological record, the interpretation of which has recently been subject to considerable revision. Harald seems, particularly in his last years, to have indulged a passion for military and civil works on a scale never previously seen in the North, a passion clearly revealed by archaeological excavation.

Harald was not the first Danish king to indulge a taste for expenditure on great military works. Of these works the most famous is the series of linear fortifications across the neck of the Jutland peninsula which form a boundary between the Danes and the Germans. Few, if any, Viking graves are found south of this line, a line which delimited the ancient Danish state. The Danevirke has been investigated in detail by Danish archaeologists in the last few years. The *Annales regni Francorum* record a phase in its history, *sub anno* 808, when Godfred, the Danish king,

> decided to fortify the border of his kingdom against Saxony with a rampart, so that a protective bulwark would stretch from the eastern bay called Ostersalt (as far as the western sea) along the entire north bank of the River Eider, broken by a single gate through which wagons and horsemen would be able to leave and enter. After dividing the work among the leaders of his troops he returned home.[3]

The Danevirke consists of seven elements (together some 30km in length) which link the valley of the Rheide with the Schleifjord and the Schwansen peninsula—thus, as the Rheide valley was marshy and impassable, it effectively separated the Jutland peninsula from Germany. Three main phases have been recognised. Firstly, a line consisting of the Main Wall, the North Wall and probably the East Wall (which cuts off the Schwansen peninsula); secondly, the Kovirke (literally 'the cow work'); thirdly, a strengthened Main Wall, the Crooked Wall and the Connecting Wall (which links the Danevirke to the semi-circular fortification of the town of Hedeby). The first phase is dated by dendrochronology *c.*737, more than seventy years before Godfred is said to have built his wall. The fortification attributed to Godfred in the Frankish annals cannot, however, be recognised on the ground.

The earliest wall was repaired and the Crooked Wall and Connecting Wall added in the period after 968 (a date provided by dendrochronology) probably during the Danish wars with the Ottonian empire. This series of earthworks was kept in repair throughout the eleventh and twelfth centuries and in the reign of Valdemar, in the 1160s or 70s, parts of the rampart were faced in brick. The Kovirke is closely paralleled in the details of its construction by the Trelleborg series of fortresses to which we shall return and which date to the late tenth century, so the Kovirke like them almost certainly belongs to the reign of Harald.

One feature mentioned in the Frankish annals was the single gate to allow the passage of animals and carts. This traffic passed along a road, the Hærvej (army-road) which can still be traced in parts of the Danish countryside as far south as Viborg.

Possibly related to the ancient Hærvej is the single-period wooden bridge across the marshy valley of the River Vejle at Ravning Enge, which was about 1km in length and between 5 and 6m wide.

The bridge was built with astonishing accuracy on exactly squared piles—each 1 foot square in section actually 11.6 inches or 29.5cm—which is the unit used in all the construction. The piles are set in lines of four—eight feet apart—and the four piles span sixteen feet. Some 1700 such piles must have been used, together with some 800 raking piles which flank the road and obviously helped to support the trackway above the valley floor. The timbers were pointed and sunk by their own weight into the marshy subsoil. The structure of the roadway is not known, but it would have carried weights of up to 5 tons. A similar but slighter causeway was found at Risby and the structure is paralleled in the Slav lands of the modern GDR.

The Ravning bridge is dated by dendrochronology to *c.*979 within one or two years. Perhaps its most remarkable feature is the accuracy, almost pedantry, of the engineer who designed it.

Almost contemporary with the bridge at Ravning Enge is the Kanhave Canal which cuts the island of Samsφ in two. Samsφ is an island, some 18 miles long, which lies north of Fyn between Sjælland and Jutland. 1.25m deep, 1km long and 11m broad, it allows access from the east side of the sound between Samso and Jutland to the large natural harbour of Stavnsfjord. Where it passes through sand, the sides of the canal are battered and protected by longitudinal planks of oak, regularly pegged into position through square holes in the boards, which are themselves retained by raking posts driven into the subsoil. Where it passes through clay there was apparently no need to shore the sides.

The wooden portions of the structure show no signs of repair—it is a one-period project, presumably built for a specific purpose. It is without parallel in western Europe although considerable lengths of waterway were constructed or reinforced at this time. The canal could have had an economic function in that it might cut two or three hours from the sailing time by avoiding the northern tip of the island. Equally it could have had a military function in that it might have controlled the straits on either side of Samsφ. The canal smacks of central authority and one might suggest that it was built by Harald when the Norwegians threatened the heart of Denmark; folk memory also ascribes its construction to Harald.

Central authority was, however, certainly behind the planning and execution of one of the most remarkable phenomena of Viking Age Scandinavia: the well-known group of circular fortresses erected in the late tenth century, Trelleborg in Sjælland, Nonnebakken in Fyn and Fyrkat and Aggersborg in Jutland.

Although Nonnebakken in the suburbs of Odense is not capable of a great deal of archaeological investigation, and despite the fact that Trelleborg had an outwork and that Aggersborg was three times the size of Fyrkat, the similarities are obvious. The ramparts in all cases form a perfect circle, are strictly concentric with the external ditch and have four entrances joined by axial streets. The buildings within the rampart form square courtyards and each courtyard encloses a smaller building. The large buildings within the fortresses have the same form—each has bowed sides. All measurements used in the construction of the fortresses are based on the foot. Many constructional details—the structure of the rampart (at Aggersborg and Fyrkat but not at Trelleborg); the shape of the ditch; the form of the berm; the wood paved streets—are similar. But there are differences, of which size is the most obvious. Aggersborg for example, has a diameter of 240m compared with 120m at Fyrkat; and Trelleborg has an additional outer ward enclosing fifteen houses. But similarities outweigh differences. Only a powerful central authority could possibly have organised the building of such uniform structures; surely only a king could have invested such capital of labour and money in these elaborate structures?

The timbers of the fortresses are dated by dendrochronology to the reign of Harald Bluetooth, although Olaf Olsen has recently made a gallant—if unconvincing—attempt to date them to the reign of Sven. They must have functioned within the defensive strategy of Denmark, either as places of refuge or as fortified royal centres, not I think as barracks.

The late tenth century was important in the development of Scandinavian fortification, presumably under the centralising influence of the newly consolidated state. Towns were first properly fortified at this time. Hedeby, the famous merchant town mentioned much earlier by Alfred the Great, was first fortified in the late tenth century. Hedeby was not to survive for long; but other towns had defensive works thrown around them and lasted longer. Aarhus is perhaps the best known archaeologically; it probably had a semi-circular defensive work, similar to that at Hedeby, by the end of the century. Archaeological evidence for the fortification of other towns in Denmark is unknown, but place names help us to identify (however tentatively) other fortified places: both Hälsingborg and Aalborg include the place name element *borg*, which may betoken a fortified place, and both these names were at least known in the early eleventh-century. No evidence as yet has been found for any fortification of the important old town of Ribe; its topography (despite recent excavations of Mogens Bencard) is unclear, but it may well have been easily defendable by water. Similarly the ancient town of Viborg has not produced any sign of fortification (the element *borg* here has a different root). Roskilde was certainly fortified against attack from the sea in the early eleventh century, but no evidence has yet been found of landward defences. The seaward defences of Roskilde consist of five ships which had been sunk in the early years of the eleventh century across the bar of the Peberrenden channel. Weighed down by stone, the vessels had been carefully scuttled to close the channel which formed the easiest approach to the town. Surprise attacks from the sea were thus made less easy.

The sunken ships at Skuldelev are but one type of sea defence. More elaborate underwater barriers were constructed elsewhere for this purpose, as at Hominde, in Rødby Fjord. A C14 analysis gave a tenth-century date to this palisade-like defence. Other Danish sites with underwater fortification include Hedeby (where a sea palisade protecting the sloping beach and delimiting the town's harbour has been known since 1953), Helnæs (in south Fyn), dated by C14 to the eleventh century, and the blockades at the mouth of the Haderslev fjord in southern Jutland, the strengthening of one of which is dated to a similar period by the C14 method. A number of other sites which have not yet been dated properly are known. There is clearly then a fairly obsessive attention to defence in the late tenth and early eleventh century in Denmark, identified by centralised planning emphasised and indicated in the conception and execution of the fortresses, the Kanhave Canal, the bridge at Ravning Enge, possibly the straight line of the Kovirke and at least some of the underwater fortifications.

Despite protests from Olaf Olsen it is difficult not to see Harald as the man behind most of this remarkable series of engineering achievements, of splendour comparable to the necropolis which he built—at no mean cost—for his parents at Jelling. All dating evidence points in this direction and it might then be little wonder that Harald was in such trouble with his rebellious subjects towards the end of his life. Power was concentrated in his hands, engineering works of some expense were expected by the king from people who were by no means wealthy. There may even be some possibility that the Danish state had stretched its economic resources to the limit, especially as the flood of eastern silver was beginning to dry up at this time.

Sven, on his accession, came to a well organised kingdom, centralised and with a tough fortification system which he hardly needed to use, although he was almost certainly responsible for at least some of the underwater fortifications—possibly that at Roskilde which is dated to his reign. After a year or two of consolidation, however, he was deeply involved in the plundering of England. Olaf Tryggveson had been successfully raiding in England for a number of years and in 991 had taken the first Danegeld—a sum of £10,000. Olaf was already doing well by the time that Sven (perhaps still formally the overlord of Norway and therefore of Olaf who was only at this time a petty king in Oppland) joined in the fray in 994, when the sum received was £16,000. This was Olaf's last appearance in England; he returned with his money to Norway to claim and establish a kingdom, having been confirmed a Christian in the presence of Aethelred at Andover. Olaf returned with wealth and experience and with the aid of the men of the Lade earldom, gradually established a kingdom in Norway, although his hold on it was short. He was killed in battle in 999 or 1000 by an alliance of Sven, Haakon Jarl's son Eirik, and Olaf Skötkonnung, the Swedish king. Sven became master of Norway, setting Haakon Jarl's son Eirik and Sven as earls to rule that country.

By Olaf's actions Sven of Denmark may well have become conscious of the wealth of England and of its potential use in Scandinavia. Certainly he returned to raid in England with a will. The raids on England increase dramatically after Sven had established power over Norway. In 1002 £24,000 was paid by the English, and from 1003 Sven's name appears frequently in the Anglo-Saxon

Chronicle as leader of the host. The geld was paid in 1006 and again in 1007, while in 1011 the immense sum of £48,000 was levied. Even after Sven's death in 1014 great booty was taken and gelds levied, culminating in 1018 in that immense payment of £72,000 (plus £10,500 from London) in Knut's first year as king.

All these sums seem rather petty when listed like this. What do they actually mean? It is difficult to gain any real view of this, but let us consider the £72,000 Knut gained in 1018. This is equivalent to some 17 million silver coins. This was no minor sum and could be used for much more than merely to pay and placate the mercenaries who fought in the army.

These are the gelds we read of in contemporary Swedish sources on the great rune-stones. A stone from Väsby in Uppland reads, for example, 'Alle had this stone raised to his own memory. He took Knut's geld in England. God help his soul'. Another from Yttergärde in Uppland has an inscription which ends with the words 'And Ulv has taken three gelds in England. The first which Tosti paid. Then Thorkel paid. Then Knut paid'.[4]

The remains of this silver is to be seen in the great Swedish hoards. There are nearly 34,000 Anglo-Saxon coins known from Sweden. A mere drop in the ocean compared with the vast number paid out by the hapless English, but a mighty sum when compared with the 3,300 found in Norway and the 5,300 found in Denmark. And yet Norway and Denmark were the chief receivers of the geld, and particularly Denmark.

One might interpret the figures thus: that the Swedes served as mercenaries in the Danish and Norwegian armies. They took their money individually and went home to live off it for the rest of their lives. Some of it was buried in the ground. In Denmark the story was different. The Danish leaders paid their foreign mercenaries well, but, having more control over their own country-men, could afford to pay them less and plough back at least some of the profits from the Danegeld into royal projects at home. The wealth of England con-tributed to the centralisation and establishment of the Danish state. The fortification of towns, the seaward fortifications, the establishment of mints, the resettlement of villages all happened in Denmark during this period and could only have taken place with the great influx of money into the country from England. In days of complicated—if rather ineffectual—economic plan-ning it is tempting to see this as a conscious and deliberate policy of the Danish king. But this would be far too sophisticated an idea for a medieval tyrant, the results presumably came about without formal planning. Sven had seen how well Olaf was doing and set out to benefit himself and his state in a somewhat similar way. He allowed his father's great military works to crumble where necessary (few of the works traced archaeologically show much evidence of repair) and put his effort into constructing an effective state with fortified towns and different (?more logical) land-holding. When then his son came to the throne, *rex totius Angliae et Denmarciae et Norreganorum et partis Suanorum*, he had both a policy, a power base and a treasury to help keep his impossibly large kingdom together. He held on to his father's nation state but, like his

Norman successor, he perforce had to turn to the much more interesting and formidable task of keeping England together and governing a country much richer than his original homeland.

Note on sources

Much of the material concerning the engineering and fortification is published in books with summaries in English or German. References will be found in D. M. Wilson, *Civil and Military Engineering in Viking Age Scandinavia,* (National Maritime Museum, London 1978). Most of the other information is easily available in the standard sources and text books.

Notes

[1] R. Allen Brown, *The Normans and the Norman Conquest*, London 1969.

[2] The principal modern accounts and discussions of the Battle of Hastings are those of E. A. Freeman, *The Norman Conquest*, iii, Oxford 1869, Chapter xv, 377–507 (Cf. J. H. Round, 'Mr Freeman and the Battle of Hastings', *Feudal England*, London 1909, 332–98); W. Spatz, *Die Schlacht von Hastings*, Berlin 1896; F. H. Baring, *Domesday Tables . . .*, London 1909, Appendix B, 217–32; H. Delbrück, *Geschichte der Kriegskunst im Rahmen des Politische Geschichte*, iii, Berlin 1923, 150ff; Sir Charles Oman, *A History of the Art of War in the Middle Ages*, 2nd. ed., London 1924, 151–66; F. Lot, *L'art militaire et les armées au moyen âge en Europe et dans le proche Orient*, Paris 1946, i, 282–5; F. M. Stenton, *Anglo-Saxon England*, 2nd. ed., Oxford 1947, 583–8; A. H. Burne, *The Battlefields of England*, London 1950, 19ff; Richard Glover, 'English Warfare in 1066', *EHR* lxvii, 1952; G. H. White, 'The Battle of Hastings and the Death of Harold', *Complete Peerage*, xii, London 1953, Pt. i, Appendix L; J. F. C. Fuller, *The Decisive Battles of the Western World*, London 1954, i, 360ff; D. C. Douglas, *William the Conqueror*, London 1964, 194–204; C. H. Lemmon, 'The Campaign of 1066' in *The Norman Conquest, its setting and impact*, ed. D. Whitelock and others, London 1966; John Beeler, *Warfare in England 1066–1189*, Cornell U.P. 1966, 11–33; Brown, *Normans*, 158–76.

[3] One thinks especially, in this country, of the work of R. C. Smail, notably *Crusading Warfare*, Cambridge 1956; and, on the continent, of J. F. Verbruggen, especially his brilliant summary article, 'La tactique militaire des armées de chevaliers', *Revue du nord* xxix, 1947. Examples could and should be multiplied if this were a full bibliographical note.

[4] London 1960; Fontana paperback 1967.

[5] 2nd. ed., London 1924.

[6] Ed. John H. Beeler, Ithaca, New York, 1953.

[7] Ed. Beeler, 58.

[8] *Die Schlacht von Hastings.*

[9] *Geschichte der Kriegskunst.*

[10] F. W. Maitland, *Domesday Book and Beyond*, Fontana paperback 1960, 363.

[11] *EHR* lxvii, 1952.

[12] *Carmen*, especially Appendix B.

[13] *EHR* xciii, 1978. Cf. *ante* ii, 1979, 1–20.

[14] *The Chronicle of Battle Abbey*, Oxford Medieval Texts, Oxford 1980, 17–23; *ante* ii, 1979, 155–6.

[15] I wish in this note to do public penance and make amends to bishop Odo. I do not

believe he *fought* at Hastings, any more than did Geoffrey, bishop of Coutances. In the famous pl.68 of the *BT* the mace he carries is not an offensive weapon but evidently the eleventh-century equivalent of the field marshal's baton (cf. pls.21, 55–6), and the garment he is wearing is not a hauberk (cf. pl.21).

[16] Wace, *ll*.6423–5. The number given is 696.

[17] *Battle Chronicle*, 44, 45.

[18] *Battle Chronicle*, 40.

[19] For the sources and some commentary upon what follows, see Brown, *Normans*, 145ff.

[20] In a private discussion after this paper had been read, Dr Marjorie Chibnall suggested to the writer that the long delay of the invasion force may even have been at least in part a deliberate feint by William to confuse his adversary.

[21] 'Evidence for a pre-Conquest origin for the chapels in Hastings and Pevensey castles', *Château-Gaillard, European Castle Studies* iii, 1966, London 1969, 144–51.

[22] *ASC*, 142.

[23] *ASC*, 142, 143.

[24] *ASC*, 'C', 143-4; Brown, *Normans*, 156–7.

[25] Glover, *EHR* lxvii.

[26] R. Allen Brown, *The Origins of English Feudalism*, London 1973, 34-43; *Normans*, 94–8.

[27] Freeman, *Norman Conquest*, ii, 2nd. ed., London 1870, 126–7. 'Shield-wall to shield-wall, sword to sword or axe to axe, had men waged the long warfare which had ranged from the fight of Reading to the fight of Assandun.'

[28] *Normans*, 158.

[29] Below, p. 00

[30] *Normans*, 158–60.

[31] Jumièges, 134; *Gesta Guillelmi*, 180; Orderic, ii, 172.

[32] *Gesta Guillelmi*, 180; Orderic, ii, 172; *Carmen*, *ll*.319–20.

[33] *ASC*, 141.

[34] Worcester, i, 227.

[35] *Gesta Guillelmi*, 180.

[36] Jumièges, 135.

[37] Ed. Eleanor Searle, 15, 36; Baring, *Domesday Tables*, 225–6.

[38] *Gesta Guillelmi*, 186–8, 208; Jumièges, 135; Worcester, i, 227. One should perhaps add Freeman's comment here (*Norman Conquest*, ii, 1969, 477 n.2), 'I cannot help noticing the tendency to make the hours of the battles and of other great events coincide with the hours of the Church'.

[39] Eg. Morton and Munz in *Carmen*, 74, 76–7.

[40] Eg. *De Gestis regum* ii 302; Wace, ll.7323 *et seq.*

[41] Jumièges, 134.

[42] *BT* pl.58.

[43] Freeman, iii, 1869, 438ff; C. H. Lemmon, 'The Campaign of 1066' in *The Norman Conquest . . .*, 79–122; Morton and Munz, *Carmen*, 76 n. 3.

[44] *ASC*, 'D', 143.

[45] Worcester, i, 227.

[46] Worcester, i, 227. For desertions see also *De gestis regum*, i, 281–2, ii, 300; Brown, *Normans*, 161; and *ASC*, 'D', 143 ('the king nevertheless fought hard . . . with the men who were willing to support him').

[47] *EHR* lxvii, 2–4.

[48] *Gesta Guillelmi*, 180.

[49] Cf. Freeman, iii, 411–2; D. C. Douglas, *William the Conqueror*, 197. Intentional provocation was accepted by Spatz (*Hastings*, 23, 25) but rejected by Delbrück (*Kriegskunst*, iii, 160). The concentration of Harold's patrimony, *i.e.* the lands of the house of Godwin, in Sussex, however, as shown by Dr Williams (pp. 176–7, 185–6 below), gives a new dimension to this hypothesis of the Conqueror's strategy, for what was at issue in contemporary terms was very much more than the modern and anachronistic concept of the defence of subjects by the king. One wonders, indeed, if William's first intention was to cross from Dives-sur-Mer to Bosham, the eventual crossing from St Valéry to Pevensey (where there were also Godwinson lands) being later substituted.

[50] Brown, *Normans*, 150 n. 47.

[51] I shall continue to use the term until such time as Mr Nicholas Hooper of King's College, London, currently working on pre-Conquest English warfare, tells us what we should mean by it.

[52] Wace, 1.8257; *Chroniques Anglo-Normandes*, ed. F. Michel, i, Rouen 1836, 201.

[53] *De gestis regum*, i, 282.

[54] *Gesta Guillelmi*, 186. Cf. Sten Körner, *The Battle of Hastings, England, and Europe 1035–1066*, Bibliotheca Historica Lundensii xiv, Lund 1964, 220.

[55] Above, p. 3.

[56] *De gestis regum*, ii, 302. 'Rex ipse pedes juxta vexillum stabat cum fratribus, ut, in commune periculo aequato, nemo de fuga cogitaret.'

[57] *BT*, pls. 64–5.

[58] Thus Freeman, iii, 472–6; Spatz, 40–1; Fuller, *Decisive Battles*, 376. For Freeman's dispositions, cf., of course, J. H. Round, *Feudal England*, especially 359ff.

[59] See Brown, *Normans*, 167 n.127, and especially Baring, *Domesday Tables*, 217–20.

[60] Thus William of Poitiers, *Gesta Guillelmi*, 186—'Protinus equorum ope relicta, cuncti pedites constitere densus conglobati'. In the later sources the note of contempt by cavalry for flat-footed infantry already comes echoing across the ages—thus the *Carmen*, *ll*.369–70.

> 'Nescia gens belli solamina spernit equorum,
> Viribus et fidens, heret humo pedibus'

and Wace, *ll*.8623–6

> 'Engleis ne saveient ioster,
> Ne a cheval armes porter,
> Haches e gisarmes teneient,
> Od tels armes se combateient,'

[61] Only one English archer is shown on the Tapestry (Pl. 63), though it should be noted that in the Song of Maldon 'bows were busy' (trans. in *EHD* i, 295).

[62] *Gesta Guillelmi*, 192, 194.

[63] *EHD* i, 294.

[64] Wace, ll.8627–30.

[65] The least ambiguous references to crossbows unfortunately occur in the *Carmen* (ll.337–8, 381–2, 411, and see Appendix C, 112–15). Cf. *Gesta Guillelmi*, 184—'Pedites in fronte locavit, sagittis armatos et balistis.' No crossbow is shown on the Tapestry.

[66] Cf, Burne, 28–9, 30–1; Fuller, 378–9; Lemmon, 106, 108.

[67] *Gesta Guillelmi*, 184.

[68] *Gesta Guillelmi*, 184 ('ipse [Guillelmus] fuit in medio [equitum] cum firmissimo robore, unde in omnem partem consuleret manu et voce'), 190 ('Britanni, et quotquot auxiliares erant in sinistro cornu'). There were, however, also Normans on the right with the French, *e.g.* Robert de Beaumont and his contingent (192). Those modern commentators who place William in some rear 'headquarters' or 'command post' are obviously ignorant of the facts as well as of the spirit of the age and the man (Spatz, 67; Burne, 34; Fuller, 378–9; Lemmon, 104, 106).

[69] Oman, ed. Beeler, 63–4.

[70] *Gesta Guillelmi*, 194.

[71] *Gesta Guillelmi*, 186–8.

[72] 'English Warfare in 1066', *EHR* lxvii, 1952.

[73] *BT*, pls. 70–1.

[74] *Gesta Guillelmi*, 198.

[75] 'L'originalité de "Turoldus": le maniement de lance', *Cahiers de civilisation médiévale* vi, 1963.

[76] Orderic, ii, 30. Cf., perhaps, 132.

[77] The only certain instance I can find, *i.e.* of a lance or spear detached from any (Norman) hand and going in the right direction, occurs in Pl. 62. Cf. perhaps, 64. The circumstance of the attack on the castle of Dinan (pl. 25) is, of course, different.

[78] Eg. pls. 63, 64, 65.

[79] Eg. pl. 62.

[80] *The Alexiad of Anna Comnena*, ed. and trans. E. R. A. Sewter, Harmondsworth 1969, 416.

[81] Eg. pls. 62, 65, 67.

[82] Eg. pl. 55.

[83] Eg. pls. 55, 59, 60, 61.

[84] Pls. 12, 53 and *passim*.

[85] *Gesta Guillelmi*, 202.

[86] *Gesta Guillelmi*, 188–90.

[87] It is generally assumed that they broke orders in advancing, though it is only Wace who makes Harold specifically order his forces to stand firm no matter what (ll.7757 *et seq*).

[88] Pl. 68.

[89] Cf. n. 15 above.

[90] *Gesta Guillelmi*, 192.

[91] *Gesta Guillelmi*, 194.

[92] For the possibility that *BT* pls. 66–7 represent this incident, see p. 20 below.

[93] *De gestis regum*, ii, 302, 303.

[94] *Gesta Guillelmi*, 194.

[95] Thus Spatz, 55ff, 61–2, 67; cf. Delbrück, 165; Burne, 31, 42–3; Lemmon, 108–10; Beeler, 21–2. Fuller (380) is an honourable exception in this company.

[96] Jumièges, 120; D. P. Waley, 'Combined operations in Sicily, AD 1060–1078'. *Papers of the British School at Rome* xxii, 123; A. Fliche, *Le règne de Philippe I, roi de France*, Paris 1912, 258–9.

[97] *Histoire des fils de Louis le Pieux*, ed. P. Laver, Classiques de l'Histoire de France au Moyen Age, Paris 1964, 110–12; *De moribus et actis primorum Normanniae ducum*, ed. J. Lair. Soc. des Antiquaires de Normandie, Caen 1865, 143. In Nithard the two sides at a kind of review or tattoo before Charles the Bald and Louis the German are evidently on foot in spite of current published translations. I owe the first reference to

my son G. P. A. Brown and the second to Professor Eleanor Searle. One suspects that others could be found if looked for.

[98] Here, therefore, cf. Delbrück, 165 and Stenton, p. 587. In general, see J. F. Verbruggen, 'La tactique militaire des armées de chevaliers', *Revue du Nord* xxix, 1947.

[99] *Gesta Guillelmi,* 194.

[100] Huntingdon, 203; Wace, ll.8139 *et seq.* It should perhaps be mentioned that some of the archers in the lower border of the Tapestry hereabouts (pls. 70–1) are apparently shooting high. This is very slender evidence but might conveivably be the source of a legend.

[101] *Gesta Guillelmi,* 200–2.

[102] Jumièges, 135; Orderic, ii, 177 (and in his edition of Jumièges).

[103] *Battle Chronicle,* 38.

[104] *BT.* pls. 71–2.

[105] *Ante* i, 23ff.

[106] *Les Oeuvres Poétiques de Baudri de Bourgueil,* ed. P. Abrahams, Paris 1926, 209, ll.461–4; *De gestis regum,* ii, 303; Huntingdon, 203; Wace, ll.8161 *et seq.*

[107] *Carmen,* 34–6 and Appendix D.

[108] Thus *e.g.* W. H. Stevenson, 'Senlac and the Malfosse', *EHR* xxviii, 1913, 292–303; also the most recent discussion of the Malfosse and its location by C. T. Chevalier, 'Where was the Malfosse? The End of the Battle of Hastings', *Sussex Archaeological Collections* ci, 1963, 1–13.

[109] *Gesta Guillelmi,* 202–4.

[110] Elizabeth M. C. Van Houts, 'Quelques remarques sur les interpolations attribuées à Orderic Vital dans les *Gesta Normannorum Ducum* de Guillaume de Jumièges', *Revue d'Histoire des Textes* viii, 1978, 213–22.

[111] Jumièges, 197.

[112] Orderic, ii, xv.

[113] Orderic, ii, 176–8.

[114] For Engenulf see Dr Chibnall's note 4 to Orderic, ii, 177.

[115] Ed. Searle, 38. See also 8, 15–16.

[116] See above.

[117] *BT* pls. 66–7.

[118] Above, p. 16.

[119] *Anglo-Saxon England,* 584.

[120] The Tapestry's depiction of the terrain on the right of pl.66 is very similar to that of the bay of Mont St Michel in pls. 21–2, with the addition of tufts of marsh grass or other vegetation.

[121] *De gestis regum* 303 and cf. p. 18 above.

[122] Huntingdon, 203.

[123] Wace, ll.6969–72, 7847–8, 8079 *et seq.*

[124] Ed. F. Michel, *Chroniques Anglo-Normandes,* i, Rouen 1836, 197ff.

[125] *Chroniques Anglo-Normandes,* i, 6ff.

[126] Ed. J. A. Giles, *Scriptores Rerum Gestarum Willelmi Conquestoris,* London 1845, 7–8. See Searle, *Chronicle of Battle Abbey,* 19–20.

[127] Ed. Phyllis Abrahams, cxcvi, 207–9, 232. The date is 1099–1102.

[128] Freeman, perhaps characteristically, took both (iii, 490–1, 502–3).

[129] See *Feudal England,* 'Mr Freeman and the Battle of Hastings', 332ff, especially 374ff.

[130] *De gestis regum,* i, 282.

*Les comtes de Champagne
et la 'Normanitas'*　　　　Michel Bur　　　　pp. 22–32

[1] Les descriptions de J. Hugot ont été reproduites par H. d'Arbois de Jubainville, *Histoire des ducs et des comtes de Champagne*, t. 3, Paris 1861, 311–319 (Henri le Libéral) et t. 4, 1ère partie, Paris 1864, 90–98 (Thibaud III).

[2] Pour l'art funéraire en France, voir A. Erlande-Brandenburg, *Le roi est mort. Etude sur les funérailles, les sépultures et les tombeaux des rois de France jusqu'à la fin du XIII° siècle*, Paris 1975. J. Adhemar, Les tombeaux de la Collection de Gaignières, à la Bibliothèque Nationale. Dessins d'archéologie du XVII° siècle. *Gazette des Beaux-Arts*, t. 84, juil.–sept. 1974, p. 3–192. M. M. Gauthier, 'Art, savoir-faire médiéval et laboratoire moderne. A propos de l'effigie funéraire de Geoffroy Plantagenêt', *Académie de Inscriptions et Belles Lettres, Comptes-rendus des Séances*, janv.–mars 1979, 105–131. Sur le tombeau collectif des Saliens à Spire, consulter P. E. Schramm et F. Mutherich, *Denkmale der deutschen Könige und Kaiser*, München 1962 et H. E. Kubach, *Der Dom zu Speyer*, Berlin 1972. On notera que les premiers portraits des rois anglo-normands apparaissent vers 1175 dans les séries généalogiques décorant le manuscrit d'Helmarshausen produit dans l'entourage d'Henri le Lion. G. Swarzenski, 'Aus dem Kunstkreis Heinrichs des Löwens, *Städel Jahrbuch*', t. 7–8, 1932, fol. 334–335.

[3] N. Camuzat, *Promptuarium antiquitatum diocesis tricassinae*, Troyes 1610, fol. 333 v°.

[4] Marie, née en 1173, épouse Baudoin VI de Hainaut en 1186, meurt en 1204. Sa soeur aînée Scholastique est déjà mariée au comte Guillaume de Vienne et Mâcon en 1193. Encore en vie en 1218, elle meurt probablement en 1221 (d'après H. de Faget de Casteljau que nous remercions de ce renseignement).

[5] L'inscription qui le désigne sert de titre à ce paragraphe.

[6] Pour tout ce qui suit et en général pour toutes les indications données sans référence, on se reportera à M. Bur, *La Formation du Comté de Champagne*, Nancy 1977.

[7] Guillaume aux Blanches Mains est né en 1135, année où son père faillit monter sur le trône d'Angleterre. Evêque de Chartres, archevêque de Sens puis de Reims, il fut un des plus farouches défenseurs de Thomas Becket.

[8] Sur le règne d'Etienne, R. H. C. Davis, *King Stephen (1135–1154)*, London 1967, et H. A. Cronne, *The reign of Stephen (1135–1154), Anarchy in England*, London 1970.

[9] Bibliothèque de l'Université de Gand, codex 92, f.239. Edition fac-similée par A. Derolez, *Lamberti S. Audomari canonici Liber Floridus*, Gand 1968.

[10] C. Johnson and H. A. Cronne, *Regesta regum anglo-normannorum*, t. 2, Oxford 1956, n° 1244, 1247, 1249 (année 1121), 1590 (année 1126–29), 1607 (année 1129), 1687, 1692 (année 1131).

[11] Pour replacer ces événements dans le contexte anglo-normand, on utilisera J. Le Patourel, 'The Norman succession (996–1135)', *EHR*, lxxxvi 1971, 225–50; *The Norman Empire*, Oxford 1976; 'The Norman Conquest, 1066, 1106, 1154? *ante* i, 1978, 103–120. A la décharge d'Etienne, il importe de noter que son frère aîné Guillaume avait été déshérité pour sottise au profit de Thibaud II comme Robert Courteheuse l'avait été par Guillaume le Conquévant au profit de Guillaume le Roux. D'autre part, Adèle n'avait pas hésité à soutenir Henri Beauclerc contre Robert en 1106. L'attitude d'Etienne s'inscrit parfaitement dans le contexte familial anglo-normand. Sur le privilège d'ainesse chez les comtes de Blois-Champagne, voir M. Bur, *La formation . . .* 472.

[12] P. Corbet, Les collégiales comtales de Champagne (v. 1150–v. 1230), *Annales de l'Est*, 1977 (3), 198–204.

[13] M. Bur, *La formation* (en particulier le chapitre 3).

[14] Sur le contexte, M. Pacaut, *Louis VII et son royaume*, Paris 1964. Pour la chronologie, A. Fourrier, 'Retour au terminus', *Mélanges J. Frappier*, Genève, 1970, t. 1, 299-311.

[15] W. Heinemeyer, Die Verhandlungen an der Saône im Jahre 1162, *Deutsches Archiv*, t. 20, 1964, 155–189. M. Bur, Recherches sur la frontière dans la région mosane aux XIIe et XIIIe siècles. *Actes du 103e Congrès des Sociétés savantes*, Nancy-Metz, 1977 (1979), 143–160.

[16] K. F. Werner, Die legitimität der Kapetinger und die Enstehung des Reditus ad stirpem Karoli, *Die Welt als Geschichte*, t. 12, 1952, 203–25.

[17] J. Benton, The court of Champagne as a literary center, *Speculum*, t. 36, 1961, 551–501.

[18] B.N. fr. 794, fol. 27 r°. Début du Lancelot de Chrétien de Troyes.

[19] M. Roques, Le ms 794 de la Bibliothèque Nationale et le scribe Guiot, *Romania*, t. 73, 1952, 177–199. Ce manuscrit renferme dans sa première partie les romans de Chrétien de Troyes Erec, Lancelot, Cligès, Le Chevalier au Lion, dans la seconde les Sièges d'Athènes d'Athis et Profilias, dans la troisième Le Roman de Troie de Banoît de Sainte-Maure, le Roman de Brut de Wace, les Empereors de Rome de Calendre et Perceval le Vieil (avec suite) de Chrétien de Troyes.

[20] Une pointe très nettement anti-capétienne dans l'oeuvre de Calendre, *Les Empereors de Rome*, qui assimile les Gaulois vaincus et vantards aux Français et les Bretons, courageux adversaires de César puis fidèles alliés du peuple romain, aux Anglais. M. Schmidt-Chazan, Un Lorrain de coeur, le Champenois Calendre, *Les Cahiers Lorrains*, 1979 (3), 65–75. Calendre écrivait en 1219.

The Romanesque Rebuilding
of Westminster Abbey   R. D. H. Gem   pp. 33–60

[1] F. Barlow, *The Life of King Edward*, London 1962, 44.

[2] M. Bloch, 'La Vie de St. Edouard le Confesseur par Osbert de Clare', *Analecta Bollandiana*, xli, 1923, 130.

[3] Barlow, 44.

[4] F. E. Harmer, *Anglo-Saxon Writs*, Manchester 1952, 294.

[5] Harmer, nos. 73, 75.

[6] Harmer, no. 74.

[7] Harmer, 303.

[8] Barlow, 45–46.

[9] *Pace* Barlow, 45n.

[10] J. A. Robinson, 'The church of Edward the Confessor at Westminster', *Archaeologia*, lxii, 1910, 84.

[11] Robinson, 83.

[12] Robinson, 84.

[13] Cf. W. Stubbs, *Historical Works of Gervase of Canterbury*, RS 1879, vol. I, 27, where Gervase refers to the arcade inclosing the presbytery as being *in chori ambitu*, while the ambulatory vaults are *in circuitu extra chorum*.

[14] Robinson, 84–87.

[15] Barlow, 87.

[16] Barlow, xxxviii–xli.

[17] Bloch, 130–31; *ASC*, sub anno.

[18] Harmer, 560; Barlow, 80.

[19] Barlow, 80.

[20] Barlow, 81.

[21] F. M. Stenton, *The Bayeux Tapestry*, London 1957, 11; N. P. Brooks, H. E. Walker, 'The authority and interpretation of the Bayeux Tapestry', *ante*, i (1978), 18.

[22] L. E. Tanner, A. W. Clapham, 'Recent discoveries in the nave of Westminster Abbey', *Archaeologia*, lxxxiii, 1933, 230–31.

[23] J. A. Robinson, *The History of Westminster Abbey by John Flete*, Cambridge 1909, 140–41.

[24] Robinson, *History*, 140–41.

[25] Robinson, *History*, 84.

[26] *ASC*, sub anno 1077 (*recte* 1076).

[27] R. Widmore, *An History of the Church of St Peter, Westminster*, London 1751, 180.

[28] E. K. Heningham, 'The genuineness of the *Vita Aedwardi Regis*', *Speculum*, xxi, 1946, 450–54.

[29] Bloch, 130.

[30] Bloch, 130.

[31] Bloch, 130.

[32] Robinson, *Archaeologia*, 86.

[33] H. R. Luard, *Lives of Edward the Confessor*, RS iii, 1858, 90.

[34] Harmer, no. 87, pp. 319–20, 509–10.

[35] Harmer (*loc. cit.* in note 34) gives 1057 as the *terminus post quem* for the grant of Sheperton to Westminster, but B. Harvey (*Westminster Abbey and its Estates in the Middle Ages*, Oxford 1977, 354) says Sheperton was one of the estates granted to Westminster by St Dunstan.

[36] F. E. Harmer, 'Three Westminster writs of Edward the Confessor', *EHR*, li, 1936, 98. Following the delivery of the present paper at Battle Miss Cecily Clark has most kindly contributed the following note: 'There is a more recent reference to the name Teinfrith: O. von Feilitzen ("Some Continental Germanic personal names in England", in A. Brown and P. Foote (eds), *Early English and Norse Studies Presented to Hugh Smith*, London 1963, 46–61, esp. 57–8) inclines to agree with Harmer that this probably represents a Continental Germanic original—which at this date could correlate with geographical origins too. But it must be emphasized that any conclusion depends on no more than a balance of probabilities. As a first name-element, *Thegn-* (CG *Thegan-/Thegin-*) is extremely rare anywhere; but in Flanders, Saxony and "Gaul" it is found in several compounds, though not the one under discussion, whereas except for a few moneyers' names (often apparently exotic) it is unexampled in English materials—the examples in Searle's *Onomasticon* are unreliable. On the other hand, our knowledge of Old English personal names other than those of the aristocracy is so poor that it might be rash to assert of any phonologically possible form, such as this is, that it could not have been current in English milieux. As to the further question of whether one would be surprised to find this form specifically in Normandy, I think not. Normandy was full of people with Continental Germanic names like *Robert*, *Godfrey* (another—*fridus* form is *Humphrey*), and so on. In a sense, one is always "surprised" to find a hapax form anywhere at all, but, in the

present state of knowledge, I do not think there is any reason to regard the Thegan-/ Thegin-/Tein—element as characterising any special region. But again it would be unwise to be dogmatic'.

[37] Harmer, *Writs*, no. 90, pp. 322–3, 355.

[38] Harmer, *Writs*, 355; Harvey does not include Wormley in her survey.

[39] Harmer, *Writs*, 566.

[40] Harmer, *EHR*, 98n.

[41] W. R. Lethaby, 'Note on the existing remnants of the Confessor's church', *Archaeologia*, lxii, 1910, 97–100.

[42] J. T. Micklethwaite, 'Further notes on the Abbey buildings at Westminster', *Archaeol. Jnl.*, li, 1894, 1–27.

[43] The apse échelon scheme is the most favoured interpretation today (vid. *e.g.* E. C. Fernie 'Enclosed apses and Edward's church at Westminster', *Archaeologia*, civ, 1973, 235–260), although both Scott and Micklethwaite believed in an ambulatory. Lethaby first introduced the idea of an apse échelon because he thought that Westminster was like Jumièges and that the latter had no ambulatory (a view subsequently proved incorrect). None of Lethaby's arguments is conclusive—anymore than are arguments for an ambulatory. Admittedly the 1220 Lady chapel must have been intended to be approached by an ambulatory, but it is not proved that such an approach existed or was contemplated before 1220 or, if it did, that it went back to as early as the eleventh century (cf. H. F. Westlake, 'Westminster Abbey, the old Lady chapel and its relation to the Romanesque and Gothic churches', *Archaeologia*, lxix, 1917–18, 39).

[44] Tanner & Clapham, 235.

[45] Tanner & Clapham, 232–36.

[46] Tanner & Clapham, 234.

[47] Though Clapham suggested there may have been a wall with a doorway at this point (Tanner & Clapham, 235). The third floor-level was ceiled by the fourteenth-century floor of the present nave. Of the two preceding floors the first, of which only the mortar bedding was discovered, was thought to be the original of the nave. The second floor is important in that it was formed of 'square red tiles (10 in. square)' (Pl. 3) which appear to correspond with the type of tiles used elsewhere at Westminster in the late eleventh century to decorate vertical wall faces (see below p. 59).

[48] Clapham thought that this alteration, like the others, took place before the end of the eleventh century; but he produces no evidence to prove this. A date prior to the opening of the thirteenth-century works anyway seems likely—though as late as the fourteenth century works of repair and alteration were still being carried out to the Romanesque fabric (R. B. Rackham, 'Building at Westminster Abbey from the great fire (1298) to the great plague (1348))', *Archaeol. Jnl.*, lxvii, 1910, 259–78.

[49] Detailed bibliographies for the principal Norman churches will be found in R. Liess, *Frühromanische Kirchenbau des 11. Jahrhunderts in der Normandie*, Munich 1967. Only important additional references will be cited here.

[50] Liess (219–33) disputes the existence of tribunes at Jumièges. His arguments, however, are not convincing, and the surviving fabric is best interpreted in terms of the existence of tribunes.

[51] While Cerisy is clearly related to St Etienne it introduces the use of chevron ornament which must indicate a later date.

[52] The cores are more elongated in an east and west direction at Westminster than at Jumièges.

[53] There are several minor churches—such as Norrey-en-Auge—where alternating supports occur, and these suggest that the form may have been widespread.

[54] M. Aubert, 'St-Hilaire de Poitiers', *Congrès archéol. de France, Poitiers*, 1951, 44–57; M. T. Camus, 'Un chevet à déambulatoire et chapelles rayonnantes', *Cahiers de civilisation médievale*, xxi, 1978, 381.

[55] E. Maillard, 'Le problème de la reconstruction de St-Hilaire au XIe sièle', *Bul. Soc. Antiq. de l'Ouest*, 1934.

[56] W. M. Whitehill, *Spanish Romanesque Architecture of the Eleventh Century*, Oxford 1941, 235–41; S. Moralejo-Alvarer, 'Une sculpture du style de Bernard Gilduin a Jaca', *Bul. Monumental*, cxxi, 1973, 7–16.

[57] A. Mussat 'L'eglise Nôtre-Dame-du-Pré au Mans' and F. Luseur, 'L'église de la Couture au Mans', *Congrès archéol. de France, Maine*, 1961, 100–137.

[58] W. Horn, 'Romanesque churches in Florence', *Art Bul.*, xxv, 1943, 112–31.

[59] R. Krautheimer et al., *Corpus Basilicarum Christianarum Romae*, Vatican & New York 1937 ff., 119, 280, 302–3.

[60] R. Krautheimer, 'S. Nicola in Bari', *Wiener Jhrb. f. Kunstgeschichte* ix, 1934, 5–42; F. Schettini, *La Basilica di S. Nicola di Bari*, Bari 1967.

[61] R. Krautheimer, *Early Christian and Byzantine Architecture*, Harmondsworth 1965, 96–97.

[62] Krautheimer, *Architecture*, 256, 286; S. Guyer, 'Der Dom von Pisa', *Münchner Jhrb. d. Bildenden Kunst*, ix, 1932, 351–76.

[63] A. C. Quintavalle, *La Cattedrale di Modena*, Modena 1964–5.

[64] Detailed bibliographies for the churches in the Empire will be found in F. Oswald, L. Schaefer, H. R. Sennhauser, *Vorromanische Kirchenbauten; Katalog der Denkmäler bis zum Ausgang der Ottonen*, Munich 1966–71: further references are not given here.

[65] *Vita Meinwerci* in *Monumenta Germaniae Historica*, lix, 82.

[66] L. Grodecki, *L'architecture ottonienne*, Paris 1958, 111, 196.

[67] S. Brigode, 'L'architecture religieuse dans le sud-ouest de la Belgique', *Bul. Commission Royale Monuments et Sites*, i. 1949, 115–32; Grodecki, 55–6.

[68] Brigode, 141–55; P. Héliot, 'Les parties romanes de la cathédrale de Tournai', *Rev. Belge Archéol. Hist. Art*, 1956, 70.

[69] Sources *cit.* Liess, 315–16, nn. 353–56.

[70] On the monastic offices in general *vid.*: *Royal Commission Hist. Monuments London*, I, *Westminster Abbey*, London 1924; G. G. Scott, *Gleanings from Westminster Abbey*, Oxford & London 1863; W. R. Lethaby, *Westminster Abbey Re-examined*, London 1925; S. E. Rigold, *The Chapter House and the Pyx Chamber, Westminster Abbey, Official Handbook*, London 1976.

[71] A beautifully preserved example was photographed and reproduced in F. H. Westlake, *Westminster Abbey*, London 1923, plate 9. A surviving example exposed on the east face of the dormitory is now weathered beyond recognition, although its form is preserved in a modern companion (Pl. 8).

[72] Westlake, 25 and plate 5.

[73] This, at least, is what Scott (13) and Lethaby (*Re-examined*, 36) claim: the capitals are now unrecognizable.

[74] G. Black, 'Excavations in the sub-vault of the misericorde of Westminster Abbey', *Trans. London Middlesex Archaeol. Soc.*, xxvii, 1976, 135–78; *Idem*, 'The redevelopment of 20 Dean's Yard, Westminster Abbey 1975–77', *ibid.*, xxviii, 1977, 190–210.

[75] J. A. Robinson, *The Abbot's House at Westminster*, Cambridge 1911.

[76] Robinson, *Archaeologia*, 94.

[77] Robinson, *History*, 85f.

[78] G. Zarnecki, 'Romanesque sculpture in Normandy and England in the eleventh century', *ante*, i (1978), 175–76. I differ from Zarnecki, however, in placing the dormitory range at Westminster before the construction of the Tower rather than after. Also I would not rate it higher than a possibility (cf. *ibid.*, 178, where it is suggested as 'likely') that cushion capitals were used in the Confessor's church.

[79] J. Bilson, *Archaeol. Jnl.*, lxvii, 1910, 401.

[80] The famous *Torhalle* at Lorsch, generally supposed to be of early Carolingian date, achieves a similar visual effect through the use of red and white stone; but it lacks the use of glazed tile which is the essential distinguishing feature of the Westminster work.

*Chichester Cathedral: When was
the Romanesque Church begun?*   R. D. H. Gem   pp. 61–64

[1] R. Willis, *The Architectural History of Chichester Cathedral*, Chichester 1861, 5.

[2] M. Gibson, *Lanfranc of Bec*, Oxford 1978, 114; F. Barlow, *The English Church 1066–1154*, London 1979, 62.

[3] Bede, *Historia Ecclesiastica*, iv, 13, ed. C. Plummer, Oxford 1896, 232.

[4] Barlow, 48.

[5] *Gesta Pontificum*, ed. N. E. S. A. Hamilton, RS 1870, 205: *ubi antiquitus et sancti Petri monasterium et congregatio fuerat sanctimonialium.*

[6] P. H. Sawyer, *Anglo-Saxon Charters*, Roy. Hist. Soc. 1968, no. 616—Whitelock regarded the charter as spurious.

[7] VCH *Sussex*, iii, London 1935, 111.

[8] VCH *Sussex*, i, London 1905, 391.

[9] VCH *Sussex*, i, 391, 421.

[10] Barlow, 66, 68; H. Mayr-Harting, *The Bishops of Chichester 1075–1207*, *Chichester Papers* xl, 1963, 1–2.

[11] Barlow, 68; Mayr-Harting, 2–4.

[12] *Annales Monastici*, ed. H. R. Luard, RS 1864–9, ii, 43.

[13] *Annales Cicestrenses*, ed. F. Liebermann, *Ungedruckte Anglo-Normannische Geschichttsquellen*, Strassburg 1879, 94.

[14] Worcester, ii, 67.

[15] Worcester, ii, 70.

[16] *Gesta Pont.*, 206.

[17] *Gesta Pont.*, 206.

[18] F. Godwin, *Catalogue of the Bishops of England*, London 1601, 384.

[19] Barlow, 48.

[20] *Gesta Pont.*, 183.

[21] Barlow, 48.

[22] Barlow, 48.

[23] F. Hill, *Medieval Lincoln*, Cambridge 1948, 67.

[24] Worcester, ii, 30.

[25] H. W. Saunders, *The First Register of Norwich Cathedral Priory*, Norfolk Record Soc., xi, 1939, 23.

[26] B. Dodwell, 'The foundation of Norwich Cathedral', *Trans. Roy. Hist. Soc.*, vii, 1957, 2–3.

[27] Willis, pl. 1.

[28] *Medieval Archaeol.*, xi, 1967, 282.

The Coming of the Cluniacs   Brian Golding   pp. 65–77

[1] The best account of the Cluniac settlement remains that of David Knowles, *The Monastic Order in England*, Cambridge 1950, 151–8. See also Frank Barlow, *The English Church, 1066–1154*, London 1979, 184–5.

[2] *Monasticon Anglicanum*, ed. W. Dugdale, revised by Caley, Ellis and Bandinel (London 1817–30, v.12–13). For a consideration of this document see *Early Yorkshire Charters*, ed. C. T. Clay, viii, 1949, 59–62.

[3] Barlow, 184–5.

[4] Barlow, 180–82; Knowles, 83–8.

[5] Knowles, 86.

[6] Orderic, ii, 74, 96.

[7] Barlow, 184.

[8] See above, p. 65

[9] Barlow, 185.

[10] *Regesta Regum Anglo-Normannorum, 1066–1154*, i, ed. H. W. C. Davis, Oxford 1913, nos. 179, 192, 232, 325, 353.

[11] David Knowles and R. Neville Hadcock, *Medieval Religious Houses: England and Wales*, revised edition, London, 1971, 96–103.

[12] *Valor Ecclesiasticus*, ed. J. Caley and J. Hunter, 6 vols., Record Commission, 1810–34, i, 332; ii, 60.

[13] Knowles, 154–8. A useful table of affiliations is provided on p. 723.

[14] Knowles, 153.

[15] They were Lewes (£920), Bermondsey (£464), Montacute (£456), Much Wenlock (£401), Pontefract (£335), Lenton (£329), Thetford (£312), Castle Acre (£306), Northampton (£263) and Daventry (£236). *Valor, passim.*

[16] Donald Matthew, *The Norman Monasteries and their English Possessions*, Oxford 1962, 32, 54, 55; Orderic, iii, 142.

[17] See below, pp. 71 ff.

[18] *Complete Peerage*, vi, 641.

[19] *Complete Peerage*, iii, 428; *Annales Monastici*, ed. H. R. Luard, RS 1864–9, iii, 436.

[20] Orderic, iv, 302.

[21] Orderic, vi, 146.

[22] *Monasticon*, v. 153.

[23] Matthew, ch. II *passim*. Also see below, pp. 72, 74

[24] Matthew, 56–8.

[25] On Pontefract castle W. E. Wightman, *The Lacy Family in England and Normandy, 1066–1194*, Oxford 1966, 24.

[26] *Chartulary of St John of Pontefract*, ed. R. Holmes, Yorkshire Archaeological Society Record Ser., xxv, xxx, 1899, 1901, i, I; *Early Yorkshire Charters*, iii, 1486.

[27] *Early Yorkshire Charters*, iii, 1486.

[28] *Monasticon*, v, 197. See also I. J. Sanders, *English Baronies: A Study of Their Origin and Descent, 1086–1327*, Oxford 1960, 104.

[29] *Monasticon*, v, 165–6.

[30] *Complete Peerage*, vi, 640; *Monasticon*, v, 50.

[31] *Monasticon*, v, 178–9. There was also a castle at Newton Longville (Buckinghamshire) where Walter Giffard established a cell of the Norman Cluniac house of Longueville (Derek Renn, *Norman Castles in Britain*, 2nd. ed., London 1973, 257).

[32] See above, p. 66.

[33] Knowles, 723.

[34] *Monasticon*, v, 12, 49–50.

[35] Knowles and Hadcock, 102.

[36] *Two Cartularies of the Augustinian Priory of Bruton and the Cluniac Priory of Montacute*, Somerset Record Society, viii, 1894, 160–2.

[37] *Montacute Cartulary*, 126.

[38] Knowles and Hadcock, 100; for the Ballon family see J. H. Round, *Studies in Peerage and Family History*, London 1901, 181–215.
Winibald also made a grant in favour of the mother-house (*Montacute Cartulary*, 127).

[39] *Monasticon*, v, 178.

[40] *Monasticon*, v, 178.

[41] *Early Yorkshire Charters*, iii, 1665.

[42] Wightman, 39, 41; *Chartulary of Pontefract*, i, 2. In 1166 the family also held a fee of the honour of Skipton (Wightman, 29).

[43] *Montacute Cartulary*, 125–6.

[44] VCH *Dorset*, iii, 85–8; *Somerset*, i, 483; *Devon*, i, 440–1; *Montacute Cartulary*, 125. He witnessed Robert's foundation charter (*Montacute Cartulary*, 120).

[45] VCH, *Somerset*, i, 482; *Montacute Cartulary*, 125.

[46] *Montacute Cartulary*, 125.

[47] *Domesday Book* i, 124; VCH *Somerset*, i, 478, 483.

[48] *Montacute Cartulary*, 120–1.

[49] *Montacute Cartulary*, 125.

[50] *Montacute Cartulary*, 125.

[51] VCH *Somerset*, i, 482–3.

[52] *Montacute Cartulary*, 125–6. In 1086 William *de Lestra* held lands in Bickenhall (Somerset) and Tattiscombe (Devon) of Robert (VCH *Somerset*, i, 476–7; *Devon*, i, 438).

[53] *Early Yorkshire Charters*, iii, 1475.

[54] Wightman, 42–3, 244; *Early Yorkshire Charters*, iii, 1434. The Foliots continued to be benefactors of the priory in the second half of the twelfth century (*Early Yorkshire Charters*, iii, 1527, 1532, 1539).

[55] Wightman, 88, 92.

[56] *Early Yorkshire Charters*, iii, 1541 and note.

[57] *Early Yorkshire Charters*, iii, 1771.

[58] *Charters and Records among the Archives of the Ancient Abbey of Cluni from 1077 to 1534*, ed. Sir G. F. Duckett, 2 vols, Lewes 1888, 44.

[59] *The Chartulary of the Priory of St Pancras of Lewes*, ed. L. F. Salzman, Sussex Record Society xxxviii, xl, 1932, 1934, i, 2–9.

[60] *Chartulary of Lewes*, i, 11–12.

[61] For these grants see *Chartulary of Lewes*, ii, 43 (Falmer); i, 12, 36 (Swanborough); i, 21, 34 (Withdean); i, 31, 35 (Heacham); *The Chartulary of Lewes Priory; the portions relating to countries other than Sussex*, Sussex Record Society 1943, 50 (Walton).

[62] *Valor*, i, 329–31.

[63] VCH *Sussex*, i, 435–43.

[64] VCH *Sussex*, i, 435, 446–7.

[65] VCH *Sussex*, i, 446–7.

[66] VCH *Cambridgeshire*, i, 372.

[67] VCH *Norfolk*, i, 83, 86.

[68] *Calendar of Documents Preserved in France*, i, 439. A member of the Warenne family was a monk at St Evroul (Orderic, iii, 228–30).

[69] *Monasticon*, v, 12; B. L. Harl. MS.2110, f.2.

[70] *Liber Eliensis* ed. E. O. Blake, Camden Third Ser, xcii, 1962, 202. See also E. Miller, *The Abbey and Bishopric of Ely*, Cambridge 1951, 169–70.

[71] The bishops said that such a grant was no great generosity. Since William also had a bad conscience over a claim that the grant of Heacham was his own rather than his father's, he also granted to the monks all his demesne tithes, tithes of rent and property. *Chartulary of Lewes*, i, 16.

[72] *Monasticon*, vi, 729; see also *Complete Peerage*, xii, 497. William granted half of his land in Rottingdean to Lewes in the year in which he went to Jerusalem (*Chartulary of Lewes*, i, 37). His active support of the Crusade may also account for his grant of 40s. *per annum* from his Lewes rents to the Templars (*Early Yorkshire Charters*, viii, 46).

[73] The genealogical notes in the Lewes cartulary record the burial places of the family (*Chartulary of Lewes*, i, 15). The lead cists inscribed *Willēms* and *Gundrada* containing their bones were discovered in 1845 and are now preserved in St John's church, Southover, beneath the late-twelfth century gravestone of Gundreda. Orderic also records William's burial and gives his epitaph inscribed on his marble tombstone (Orderic, iv, 180). Most of the earls' wives between Gundreda and the late fourteenth century were also buried at the priory.

[74] *Chartulary of Pontefract*, i, 1.

[75] Wightman, 48.

[76] VCH *Yorkshire*, i, 243.

[77] Wightman, 231.

[78] *Valor*, v, 65.

[79] *Early Yorkshire Charters*, iii, 1428; *Chartulary of Pontefract*, i, 1.

[80] *Early Yorkshire Charters*, iii, 1486, 1487; Wightman, 67.

[81] *Early Yorkshire Charters*, iii, 1475; *Chartulary of Pontefract*, ii, 535.

[82] *Chronicles of the Reigns of Stephen, Henry II and Richard I*, ed. R. Howlett, RS, 1884–9, iii, 140.

[83] *Early Yorkshire Charters*, iii, 1501; Wightman, 110–2. Dr Wightman suggested that Henry's grants were small 'because of the need to build up the honour once again after the disasters of Stephen's reign, and had to sort out the complications left from the period of his father's banishment'.

[84] VCH *Somerset*, iii, 212–3, i, 483; VCH *Dorset*, iii, 81 and note.

[85] According to Orderic the castle was besieged in 1068 by men of the south-west but was relieved by Geoffrey of Coutances (Orderic, ii, 228).

[86] M. W. Beresford, *New Towns of the Middle Ages*, London 1967, 483.

[87] *Monasticon*, v, 166.

[88] VCH *Somerset*, i, 473–84.

[89] VCH *Somerset*, i, 474, 479, 480, 483.

[90] VCH *Somerset*, i, 438.

[91] *Taxatio Ecclesiastica*, ed. T. Astle, S. Ayscough and J. Caley, Record Commission 1832, 200.

[92] *Valor*, i, 195–6.

[93] *Domesday Book* i, 25 (Bec); *Calendar of Documents preserved in France*, 1208 (Marmoutier); *Monasticon*, ii, 952–3 (Grestain).

[94] R. Graham, *English Ecclesiastical Studies*, London 1929, 93. Her essay 'The Priory of La Charité-sur-Loire and the Monastery of Bermondsey' in *English Ecclesiastical Studies*, 91–118, is the best account of the house. See also C. Brooke and G. Keir, *London 800–1216; the Shaping of a City*, London 1975, 312–4.

[95] *Annales Monastici*, iii, 426.

[96] *Annales Monastici*, iii, 426.

[97] *Annales Monastici*, iii, 427; Graham, 94.

[98] *Annales Monastici*, iii, 426; DB i, 30.

[99] *Regesta*, i, 398.

[100] Brooke, 313.

[101] *Regesta*, ii, 664, 1021; iii, 91, 94, 96.

[102] *Annales Monastici*, iii, 438.

[103] *Valor Ecclesiasticus*, ii, 58–60.

[104] Knowles and Hadcock, 270.

[105] William of Malmesbury several times praised the Cluniacs for their piety (*De Gestis Pontificum Anglorum*, ed. N. E. S. A. Hamilton, RS 1870, 71, 151) and he gave high praise to prior Lanzo of Lewes (*De Gestis Regum*, 513–6). Walter Map spoke of Cluniac hospitality in *De Nugis Curialium*, trans. F. Tupper and M. B. Ogle, London 1924, 301. On Wireker see Knowles, 677–8.

[106] Knowles, 719.

[107] Giraldi Cambrensis, *Opera*, ed. J. S. Brewer, J. F. Dimock and G. F. Warner, RS 1861–91, ii, 102–3.

[108] Giraldi Cambrensis, *Opera*, vi, 43.

[109] Giraldi Cambrensis, *Opera*, iv, 244. See also *Leiston Abbey Cartulary and Butley Priory Charters*, ed. Richard Mortimer, Suffolk Records Society, Suffolk Charters i, 1979, *passim*.

[110] *Monasticon*, v, 63.

[111] See above, p. 65.

[112] M. Gibson, *Lanfranc of Bec*, Oxford 1978, 173; *Monasticon*, v, 12.

[113] Eadmer, *The Life of St Anselm*, ed. R. W. Southern, London 1962, 123.

[114] Monasticon, v, 152; William of Malmesbury, *De Gestis Pontificum*, 151.

[115] *Chronicles of the Reigns of Stephen, Henry II and Richard I*, i, 49.

[116] Peter wanted Henry to be buried at Cluny and several times acknowledged his benefactions (*The Letters of Peter the Venerable* ed. G. Constable, 2 vols., Cambridge, Mass. 1967, i, nos. 49, 56, 60, 88). Henry also helped to reorganize the finances of Cluny and made a loan of 100 ounces of gold to the abbey in 1149 (D. Knowles, *The Episcopal Colleagues of Thomas Becket*, Cambridge 1951, 36; Barlow, 183).

[117] Barlow, 193 and notes.

[118] Peter the Venerable referring to Stephen's grant of a manor worth 100 marks to Cluny said that the monks had it *dono regis sed maxime vestra benevolentia et studio* (*Letters*, i, no. 60). There can be no clearer indication of the role played by Henry in

fostering Cluniac interests at the royal court. Professor Constable has suggested that Stephen's support for Cluny was in order to purchase Cluniac backing for his régime (*Letters*, ii, 256).

The Buildings of
Battle Abbey

J. N. Hare

pp. 78–95

[1] D. Knowles, *The Monastic Order in England*, Cambridge (2nd. ed.) 1963, 702–3.

[2] Based on the figures in, D. Knowles & R. N. Hadcock, *The Medieval Religious Houses: England and Wales*, 1971.

[3] For the history of the abbey and its estates I am greatly indebted to E. M. Searle, *Lordship and Community, Battle Abbey and its Banlieu*, Toronto 1974.

[4] Anon [Catharine, Duchess of Cleveland], *History of Battle Abbey*, privately printed 1877, 245–6, 249.

[5] H. Brakspear, 'Battle Abbey' in *Antiquaries Journal*, xi, 1931, 166–8; *idem*, 'Battle Abbey' in *VCH Sussex* ix, 102–5; *idem*, 'The Abbot's House at Battle', *Archaeologia* lxxxiii, 1933, 139–66. Mr O. S. Brakspear kindly allowed me to study unpublished material about these excavations.

[6] I am extremely grateful to the Department of the Environment for making these excavations possible. The help of Jonathan Coad has been particularly appreciated. Only the hard work of the volunteers and staff have enabled so much to be done. Two of them—Anthony Streeten and Richard Warmington—have suffered more than most from long discussions about the buildings. To all of these, I am most grateful.

[7] *The Chronicle of Battle Abbey*, ed. E. M. Searle, Oxford Medieval Texts, Oxford 1980 (hereafter *Battle Chronicle*) 20; H. E. J. Cowdrey, 'Bishop Ermenfrid of Sion and the Penitential Ordinance following the Battle of Hastings', *Journal of Ecclesiastical History* xx, 1969, 233–42.

[8] Searle, *Lordship*, 22–27.

[9] *Battle Chronicle*, e.g. 180–2.

[10] *Battle Chronicle*, 44.

[11] *Battle Chronicle*, 43.

[12] Brakspear, *Antiq. Jnl.*, 167.

[13] Cleveland, 243–4, 219–20.

[14] Brakspear, *Antiq. Jnl.*, 167–8. The apse of the S. transept has now also been found.

[15] BL LFC vii 4.

[16] R. Graham, 'The Monastery of Battle' in her *English Ecclesiastical Studies*, 1929, 188.

[17] *Battle Chronicle*, 46, 72.

[18] Graham, 191–2; A. Clapham, *St. Augustine's Abbey, Canterbury*, 1977, 17; *Battle Chronicle*, 68.

[19] Clapham, 17; M. Biddle *et al.*, *Winchester in the Early Middle Ages*, Winchester Studies i, Oxford 1976, 310.

[20] *Battle Chronicle*, 44.

[21] *Battle Chronicle*, 96 & note 3.

[22] *Battle Chronicle*, 136–8.

[23] *Battle Chronicle*, 101.

²⁴ *Battle Chronicle,* 108, 116.

²⁵ *Battle Chronicle,* 130.

²⁶ *Battle Chronicle,* 262.

²⁷ H. Brakspear, untitled note in *Proceedings of Society of Antiquaries,* 2nd. series xxviii, 1915–6, 245–50.

²⁸ Searle, *Lordship,* 65–6, 133–8, 141.

²⁹ Searle, *Lordship,* 97–8.

³⁰ Brakspear, *Archaeologia,* lxxxiii. I am grateful to the Headmistress of Battle Abbey Scool for allowing me to examine these buildings.

³¹ Cleveland, 252.

³² Only two of the arches survive fully now, but the others still remained in the eighteenth century, as shown by a drawing on an estate map: East Sussex Record Office (ESRO) BAT 4421 f.12.

³³ I am grateful to the late S. E. Rigold for drawing this to my attention. See also his, *Bayham Abbey,* 1976, 24–5.

³⁴ The steward's accounts for 1685–7 record the sale of building materials—stone, timber, lead and tiles—from the buildings of Battel House, some but not all of the material is specified as coming from the old kitchen (ESRO XA 13—a microfilm of material in the Henry Hungtington Library, California).

³⁵ *Accounts of the Cellarers of Battle Abbey, 1275–1513,* eds. E. Searle & B. Ross, Sussex Record Society, lxv 1967.

³⁶ Ceveland, 245; Brakspear, *Antiq. Jnl.,* 166–7.

³⁷ R. A. Brown, H. Colvin & A. J. Taylor, *The History of the King's Works,* i, 1963, 137–44.

³⁸ As when such a chevet was built at Hailes Abbey in 1271–7—Brown, Colvin and Taylor, 154.

³⁹ I am grateful to Jill Kerr, who is preparing a report on the excavated window glass, for her preliminary comments on the material.

⁴⁰ Cleveland.

⁴¹ PRO E315 f.17, ESRO BAT 269.

⁴² Cleveland, 258.

⁴³ *Calendar of Patent Rolls,* Edward III. 1338–40, 1898, 92.

⁴⁴ *e.g.* on Abbot Odo, see Knowles 305–6.

⁴⁵ Brakspear, *VCH,* 103.

William fitz Osbern and the endowment of his abbey of Lyre

S. F. Hockey

pp. 96–105

¹ Charles Guéry, *Histoire de l'Abbaye de Lyre,* Evreux, 1917; Dugdale, *Mon. Angl.,* vi, 1092; PRO, E315/489.

² Evreux, Archives départementales, H590, fo.337. Cited hereafter as Evreux.

³ *Cartulary of Carisbrooke Priory* (BL, Egerton MS3667, publication forthcoming. Cited hereafter as CC), 11; *Recueil des actes d'Henri II, roi d'Angleterre et duc de Normandie,* ed. Delisle-Berger, Paris 1909–1927, i, 165; *Letters and Charters of Gilbert Foliot,* ed. A. Morey & C. N. L. Brooke, Cambridge, 1967, 331.

⁴ J. Le Patourel, *The Norman Empire,* Oxford 1976, 37.

[5] Daphne H. Gifford, 'The Parish in Domesday Book: a study of the mother-churches and rural chapels in the late Saxon and early Norman periods', University of London, unpublished thesis, 1952; B. R. Kemp, 'Monastic Possession of Parish Churches in England in the 12c.', *J. Eccles. Hist.*, vol, 31, 2 (April 1980), 133–160.

[6] Orderic, ii, 12,282; iii, 130; for the family of fitz Osbern, D. C. Douglas, *William the Conqueror*, London 1964, 90 and App., Table 8.

[7] *Letters of Lanfranc*, ed. H. Clover & M. Gibson, Oxford 1980, 31–33. Cf. below.

[8] Jumièges, 287; Orderic, ii, 317–9.

[9] *Hereford Domesday*, ed. V. H. Galbraith & J. Tait (Pipe Roll Soc., ns xxv, 1950), 77, 68–71, 69.

[10] J. H. Round, *Cal. of Documents preserved in France*, London 1899, 402.

[11] BN, MS lat. 4221, fo.169v.

[12] Guéry, 418; *Rouleaux des Morts du IXe au XV^{e}s.*, ed. Léopold Delisle, Paris 1886, 215.

[13] *Complete Peerage*, vii, 529–530; F. West, *Justiciarship in England*, Cambridge 1966, 35–6.

[14] VHC, *Worcs.*,i, 14.

[15] *Reg. Greg. IX*, ed. L. Auvray (Ecole Française d'Athènes et de Rome), 1896–1910, 1155.

[16] CC, 14, 36, 37, 40.

[17] Evreux, 24, 27.

[18] Hants. R. O., Reg. Orleton, ii, fo.54; PRO, E372/200, rot.7; *Reg. Roger Martival* (Cant. & York Soc.,) ed. K. Edwards & others, 1959, i, 239, 269.

[19] *Reg. Thos. de Cantilupe* (C & Y. Soc.), ed. R. G. Griffiths, 1907, xlvii.

[20] *Thesaurus novus anecdotorum*, ed. E. Martène & U. Durand, Paris 1717; in translation in G. Constable, *Monastic Tithes*, Cambridge 1964, 110.

[21] *EHR*, lxix, 1954, 583–96.

[22] CC, 34, 11.

[23] Hants. R. O., Reg. Stratford, fo.81b.

[24] Evreux, 50; BN, MS lat. 4221, fo.170r.

[25] PRO, SC6/1127/3.

[26] CC, 2.

[27] F. G. Cowley, *Monastic Order in S. Wales*, Cardiff 1977, 57.

[28] *Reg. Richard de Gravesend*, Lincoln Archives Office, 152.

[29] PRO, SC6/Hen. 8/3466.

[30] Emma Mason, 'English Tithe Income of Norman Religious Houses', *BIHR*, 48, 1975, 93.

[31] *Acta Sanctorum Octobris*, t. I (ed. Brussels 1859), 544 (2 Oct.); Guéry, 557.

[32] *Cal. Inquis. Misc.*, ii, 474; *Charters & Records of Hereford Cathedral*, ed. W. W. Capes, Hereford 1908, 121–126, 157–8; R. M. Haines, *Church & Politics in 14c: Adam de Orleton*, Cambridge 1978, 49, 205.

[33] CC, 171; S. F. Hockey, *Quarr Abbey & its Lands.* Leicester 1969, 14.

[34] BL, Cleopatra A VII, fo. 78b–80b (omitted in the chronicle of Tewkesbury); Dugdale, *Mon. Angl.*, ii, 72.

[35] BL, Arundel MS 19 (Cartulary of Tintern), fo.35v.

[36] PRO, E326/8978; Evreux, 64.

[37] PRO, SC1/47/51.

[38] *C.Cl.R, 1327–30*, 546; PRO, SC6/File 123/6109; J. Ramackers, *Papsturkunden, Normandie*, Göttingen 1937, 254.

[39] Evreux 51; BL, Add. Chart. 47150.

[40] *Ann. Mon.* iv, 467; *C. Inquis. p.m.*, 417; PRO, Assize R., 1026, m.59; PRO, Feet of Fines, Worcs. case 258, file 9, 12.

[41] *Cal. Pap. Letters*, ii, 567.

[42] CC, 174, 175; Reg. Orleton, i, fo.57.

[43] CC, 177; *Letters of Innocent III*. ed. C. R. & M. G. Cheney, Oxford 1967, 1133.

[44] PRO, E42/360; CC, app. E.

[45] CC, 184–189; *C. P. R., 1307–13*, 517.

[46] Hockey, 157.

[47] Evreux 102; D. Matthew, *Norman Monasteries & their English Possessions*, Oxford 1962, 124–5; S. F. Hockey, *King John's Abbey, Beaulieu*, Pioneer 1976, 113ff.

[48] Lincoln Archives Office: Reg. John Buckingham, XII B, fo.44 & 50v; K. B. McFarlane, *Lancastrian Kings & Lollard Knights*, Oxford 1972, 192.

[49] Matthew, 168.

[50] Evreux, 103.

[51] Matthew, 169–171.

[52] PRO, C81/665.

[53] BL, MS Cotton Otho B XIV (Cartulary of Sheen), fo.137v; 46v.

[54] L. Courajod, *Monasticon Gallicanum*, Paris 1869, pl.108.

The *Gesta Normannorum Ducum:*
a history without an end

Elisabeth M. C. van Houts

pp. 106–118

I am grateful to Professor Dr L. J. Engels, Drs Jos. M. M. Hermans and Drs Edmé Smits for their helpful criticism. I am greatly indebted to Dr David Abulafia and Drs Annebert Sapir-Abulafia who corrected my English and made useful comments on the text.

[1] *De Moribus et Actis primorum Normanniae Ducum auctore Dudone Sancti Quintini Decano*. Nouvelle édition publiée par Jules Lair, Caen 1865. Drs Gerda Huisman is preparing a study of the manuscript tradition of Dudo's work. I am grateful to her for discussing with me some problems relating to Dudo's history.

[2] *Guillaume de Jumièges, Gesta Normannorum Ducum*, Ed. J. Marx, Société de l'Histoire de Normandie, Rouen-Paris 1914. (Cited: 'Jumièges').

[3] Jumièges, 199–341.

[4] Library catalogues in England mentioning the *GND*:—Durham Cathedral, 12th c. A. J. Piper, 'The libraries of the monks of Durham', *Medieval Scribes, Manuscripts and Libraries. Essays presented to N. R. Ker.* Ed. by M. R. Parkes, A. G. Watson, London 1978, 215–6.

—Reading, 12th c. S. Barfield, 'Lord Fingall's cartulary of Reading Abbey,' *EHR* iii, 1888, 120.

—Saint-Albans, c.1180. R. W. Hunt, 'The library of the Abbey of Saint Albans', *Medieval Scribes*, 270–1.

See for further provenances the checklist of manuscripts of the *GND* (Appendix II). Library catalogues in France:

—Saint-Aubin d'Angers, 12th c. J. Vezin, *Les scriptoria d'Angers au XIe siècle*, Paris

1974, 216 (Dudo of Saint-Quentin), 218 (William of Jumièges). For the library catalogues in Normany, see G. Nortier, *Les bibliothéques médiévales des abbayes bénédictines de Normandie*, Paris 1971, appendix under Dudo of Saint-Quentin and Guillaume de Jumièges. For Fécamp, see B. Branch, 'Inventories of the library of Féamp from the 11th and 12th century', *Manuscripta*, xxiii, 1979, 159–73.

⁵ The manuscript copied furthest from Normandy is now in the University Library of Würzburg, ms. UB M ch f 140. It comes from the monastery of St James at Würzburg and it was copied by order of John Trithemius at the beginning of the 16th century. See H. Thurn, *Die Handschriften der Universitätsbibliothek Würzburg. Handschriften aus benediktinischen Provenienzen*, II, i, Wiesbaden 1973, 136–40. K. Arnold, *Johannes Trithemius (1462–1516)*, Würzburg 1971, 157, 166, 214.

⁶ For the date see Barbara Vopelius-Holtzendorff, *Studien zu Dudo von Saint-Quentin dem ersten Geschichtsschreiber der Normandie*, Göttingen 1967 (München 1970 typescript) 92–7: Dudo, ed. Lair, 20–1 (1015–1026) and H. Prentout, *Étude critique sur Dudon de Saint-Quentin et son Histoire des premiers ducs Normands*, Paris 1916, 14–5 (1015–1026).

⁷ For Adalbero of Laon and his intellectual environment, see *Adalbéron de Laon, Poème au roi Robert*. Ed. and transl. by Claude Carozzi, Paris 1979, ix–xviii.

⁸ The function of the poems has not yet been studied.

⁹ Ms London BL Cotton Nero D viii, fol. 146v: the A redaction of the *GND* has been attributed to Dudo. In the mss London BL Arundel 41, fol. 4v and Paris BN latin 15047, fol. 190v the dedicatory letter and the first book of the C redaction of the *GND* seem to have been attributed to Dudo, because of the fact that the rubric at the beginning of Book II states that the work of William of Jumièges starts there. The *Historia Normannorum* mentioned in the library catalogue of Fécamp has been attributed by modern scholars both to Dudo (see G. Nortier, appendix) and to William of Jumièges (see B. Branch, 171). For the title *Historia Normannorum* see Vopelius, 7.

¹⁰ For some general remarks on the *Gesta* genre, see H. Grundmann, *Geschichtsschreibung im Mittelalter*, Göttingen 1957, 39. R. H. Bautier, 'L'Historiographie en France au Xe et XIe siècles', *La Storiografia altomedievale*, Spoleto 1970, 656–7. Thietmar von Merseburg (975–1018) writing independently from Dudo wrote a history of the Ottonian emperors in Germany. His *Chronicon* consists of eight books. The first four are each devoted to one emperor (Henry I, Otto I, Otto II and Otto III); the last four books describe Henry II from 1004–1018. Ed. R. Holtzmann, W. Trillmich, Darmstadt 1957. I owe this reference to Professor K. U. Jäschke during the discussion following my lecture.

¹¹ Jumièges, vii–xxix.

¹² L. J. Engels, 'De Obitu Willelmi ducis Normannorum regisque Anglorum: Texte, modèles, valeur et origine', *Mélanges Christine Mohrmann, nouveau recueil offert par ses anciens élèves*, Utrecht-Anvers 1973, 250–3. See for some useful comments on Engels' article: A. Sapir, B. Speet, *De obitu Willelmi, kritische beschouwing van een verhalende bron over Willem de Veroveraar uit de tijd van zijn zonen*, Amsterdam 1976 (Werkschrift 10, Historisch Seminarium, Universiteit van Amsterdam).

¹³ R. H. C. Davis, 'William of Jumièges, Robert Curthose and the Norman succession', *EHR* xcv, 1980, 597–606 I am most grateful to Professor Davis for lending me the typescript of his article.

¹⁴ Jumièges, 99.

¹⁵ Jumièges, 2: *Sane genealogiam Rollonis a paganis majoribus nati, et multa etate sua in*

paganismo acta, ad sanctam infantiam saluberrimo fonte renati, necnon somnium ejus cum pluribus id generis ab historica serie desecui, animadvertens ea penitus adulatoria, nec speciem honesti vel utilis pretendere.

[16] Jumièges, xvii. For the *Vita sancti Aichadri*, see J. van der Straeten, 'L'auteur des Vies de s. Hughes et de s. Aychadre', *Analecta Bollandiana* lxxxviii, 1970, 72 n 4. Cf. Jumièges, 11.

[17] Jumièges, 97–8. M. Chibnall, 'Charter and Chronicle: the use of archive sources by Norman historians', in: *Church and Government in the Middle Ages*. Ed. C. N. L. Brooke, D. E. Luscombe, a.o., Cambridge 1976, 6–7.

[18] C. W. David, *Robert Curthose, duke of Normandy*, Harvard Historical Studies 25, Cambridge, Mass. 1920, 89–92.

[19] Mss London BL Cotton Nero D viii and London BL Harley 3742. The third and oldest manuscript of this redaction is ms Rouen BM Y 11 (1173). It is a convolute. The rubric on fol. 160r where the A redaction begins reads *explicit de ricardo primo incipit de secundo*. The *explicit* may point to either a lost Dudo text or the first part of William's work. The manuscript also contains the work of Dudo but it is written by another hand and on codicological grounds it does not seem to belong originally to the part which now contains the A redaction.

[20] Jumièges, 89–91 (Richard II), 107–8, 108–9 (Robert I), 112–3 (Robert I).

[21] Wace, i 234–40, 247, 250–1, iii 139–40. Ranulph Higden, *Polychronicon*, ed. J. R. Lumby, RS 1865–85, vii, 64–6, 118–20, 20, 120, 126–8. The story of Robert I and the smith of Beauvais can be found in J. Taylor, *The Kirkstall Abbey Chronicles*, Publications of the Thoresby Society, 42, Leeds 1952, 27. The story of Robert I and the *miles* is told in the *Cantatorium Sancti Huberti*, ed. K. Hanquet, Bruxelles 1906, 43–4 (although in this version Robert has been replaced by his son William the Conqueror). The story of Richard II and the *philosophus* Bernard is part of the abbreviation of the B redaction represented by the 14th c. mss Cambridge Corpus Christi College 138 p. 167–77 and London College of Arms Arundel 1 fol. 176r–179v.

[22] Engels, 254. The story of Robert I and the *miles* is said to have been told by Isembertus, chaplain of Robert I and later abbot of Sainte-Trinité at Rouen; this implies a date half way through the 11th century, see Jumièges, 108.

[23] E. M. C. van Houts, 'Quelques remarques sur les interpolations attribuées à Orderic Vital dans les Gesta Normannorum Ducum de Guillaume de Jumièges', *Revue D'Histoire des Textes*, viii, 1978, 213–22.

[24] Jumièges, 20.

[25] Jumièges, 17. Add after . . . *de suis navibus submersis: Indeque Fresiam petens ibidem obiit mortem.*

[26] Jumièges, 128: The E redaction does not have the passage on the children of William the Conqueror and Matilda. Thus I reach my conclusion, that E is based on D, with the greatest restriction.

[27] For the Dudo passages, see Van Houts, 221, and Jumièges, 151. For the *Historia Francorum Senonensis*, see Jumièges, 152. Marx does not identify this source.

[28] Jumièges, 153.

[29] Jumièges, 155–98.

[30] F. Lot, *Fidèles ou Vassaux?* Paris 1904, 232. G. I. Lieftinck, *Manuscrits datés conservés dans les Pays-Bas, i: Les manuscrits d'origine étrangère (818–c. 1550)*, Amsterdam 1964, 69. M. Chibnall, 'Orderic Vitalis and Robert of Torigni', *Millénaire Monastique du Mont-Saint-Michel*, Paris 1967, ii, 134.

[31] See for a description of Robert's autograph: L. Delisle, 'Le psautier de Saint Louis et

deux manuscrits de Guillaume de Jumièges conservés à l'Université de Leyde', *Mélanges de Paléographie et de Bibliographie*, Paris 1880, 172–94.

[32] Jumièges, 203–22.

[33] Jumièges, 235–47.

[34] Jumièges, 252–6.

[35] Jumièges, 262–4. M. Mathieu, 'Le manuscrit 162 d'Avranches et l'édition princeps des Gesta Roberti Wiscardi de Guillaume d'Apulie', *Byzantion*, xxiv, 1954, 128–30. M. Mathieu, 'Le manuscrit 162 d'Avranches ou Robert de Torigni et Robert Guiscard', *Sacris Erudiri*, xvii, 1966, 66–70. For the date, see *Guillaume de Pouille, La Geste de Robert Guiscard*, ed. M. Mathieu, Palermo 1961, 13.

[36] Jumièges, 264–5.

[37] L. Boehm, 'Nomen gentis Normannorum. Der Aufstieg der Normannen im Spiegel der Normannischen Historiographie', *I Normanni e la loro espansione in Europa nell'alto Medioevo*, Spoleto 1969, 641–4. It is also in this context that R. H. C. Davis stresses the theme of the Frenchification of the Normans in Dudo's work, see *The Normans and their Myth*, London 1976, 52.

[38] Dudo, ed. Lair, 21.

[39] Boehm, 640. Grundmann, 12–7. Vopelius, 37. Davis, 'The Normans', 50–1.

[40] Dudo, ed. Lair, 125: (Ralph of Ivry) *huius operis relatorem*. Jumièges, 72: *Huc usque digesta prout a Rodolfo comite huius ducis fratre magno et honesto viro narrata sunt . . .*

[41] See note 6.

[42] Chibnall, 'Charter and Chronicle', 6–7.

[43] It is possible that Dudo modelled his history on Suetonius, *De Vita Caesarum* (ed. H. Ailloud, Paris 1961). Suetonius also describes each Roman emperor in a separate book. On the other hand Suetonius' work is mainly seen as biography rather than historiography in the sense of *Gesta* history. See for the typology of Suetonius' work: H. Gugel, *Studien zur biographischen Technik Suetons*, Wiener Studien, Beiheft 7, Wien-Köln-Graz, 1977. See for the influence of Suetonius' work in the Middle Ages: G. B. Townend, 'Suetonius and his influence', *Latin Biography*, ed. T. A. Dorey, London 1967, 79–111; Townend does not mention Dudo of Saint-Quentin.

[44] Davis, 'The Normans', 62–3. K. U. Jäschke, 'Die England-frage in de Gesta Normannorum Ducum des Wilhelm von Jumièges', *Festschrift für Helmut Beumann zum 65. Geburtstag*, ed. K. U. Jäschke, R. Wenskus, Sigmaringen 1977, 236–62.

[45] Jumièges, 137.

[46] See note 15.

[47] Jumièges, 266.

[48] Jumièges, 279–81.

[59] Jumièges, 293–4. Delisle, 'Le psautier', 187–188.

[50] Jumièges, 297–305.

[51] Jumièges, 309–13.

[52] Chibnall, 'Charter and Chronicle', 7 n 39 suggests that some of these stories might have been written in the monastery of Saint-Ouen at Rouen.

[53] See for instance R. H. C. Davis, *King Stephen*, London 1967, 147. Studies of Robert of Torigny as historian are also mainly based on his continuation of Sigebert's Chronicle, see: R. Foreville, 'Robert de Torigni et Clio', *Millénaire Monastique du Mont-Saint-Michel*, Paris 1967, ii, 141–53.

[54] Jumièges, 301. See also K. Leyser, 'England and the Empire in the early twelfth-century', *TRHS*, 5th ser, x, 1969, 67.

[55] Jumièges, 301.

⁵⁶ Robert of Torigny clearly makes a mistake here, although he knows the Life of Saint Margaret well. He cites this work in Book VIII chapter x, Jumièges 280–1: *Quantae autem sanctitatis et scientiae tam secularis quam spiritualis utraque regina Margareta scilicet et Mathildis, fuerint liber qui de vita ipsarum scriptus est, plano sermone describit.* Here again he writes that the book is about both Margaret and Matilda II. The edition of the *Vita* (the long version) is in *Simeonis Dunelmensis opera et collectanea*, ed. H. Hinde, Surtees Society 51, Durham 1868, i, 234–54. An English translation is given by A. O. Anderson, *Early sources of Scottish History A.D. 500–1286*, Edinburgh–London 1922, ii, 59–88. The *Vita* has been attributed to Turgot bishop of Saint Andrews and dated *c*.1108 (again the long version). The most recent article on the *Vita* is that of Dr. Derek Baker who is preparing a new edition and a new translation: 'A nursery of saints: St Margaret of Scotland reconsidered'', *Medieval Women. Dedicated and presented to Professor Rosalind M. T. Hill*, ed. D. Baker. Studies in Church History, Subsidia i, Oxford 1978, 119–43.

⁵⁷ Jumièges, 300: *Quem (sc. librum) propter notitiam rerum gestarum et ad honorem et memoriam matris, de qua editus est, et filiae ad quam editus est, huic operi fortisan adiungemus.* This sentence indicates that Robert has used the long version of the *Vita*. See for a discussion on the two versions of the *Vita*, Baker, 'A nursery', 130–2.

⁵⁸ Jumièges, x, xxvii. Chibnall, 'Orderic Vitalis and Robert of Torigni', 133–4.

⁵⁹ The letter is printed in: *Venerabilis Guiberti Abbatis B. Mariae de Novigento Opera Omnia*, ed. L. D'Achery, Paris 1651, 715–6. Reprinted in: *Recueil des Historiens des Gaules et de la France*, xii, 1781, xliv. *Chronique de Robert de Torigni*, ed. L. Delisle, Rouen 1872–1873, ii, 338–40. D'Achery does not mention the provenance of this letter. By misinterpretation of D'Achery's introduction (p. 715) Delisle says that the manuscript containing this letter is from the monastery of Mont-Saint-Michel. Although the letter seems to be genuine we have to be careful with the interpretation because of possible corruptions in the Latin text.

⁶⁰ *Si autem ad hoc opus manum miseris, volo ut hoc ordine illud exsequaris. In primis omnium comitum Andegavensium scilicet ab Ingelgerio usque ad ipsum Gaufridum breviter et quasi recapitulando, enumeres nomina, genealogias, successiones et quot annis quisque comitatui praefuit, et quae preclara gesta memoriae annalium digna, sive in saecularibus rebus exercuit . . .*

⁶¹ *Cui operi, propter continuationem temporum, illud quod a te postulo, continuari volo, quatenus ea quae in temporibus nostris in nostra provincia gesta sunt, ad notitiam futurorum per scripturam transmittamus. Vale.*

⁶² See for Geoffrey of Anjou as duke of Normandy, L. Delisle, *Recueil des actes de Henri II, roi d'Angleterre et duc de Normandie. Introduction*, Paris 1909, 135–9. Geoffrey used the title duke of Normandy from 1144–5 onwards.

⁶³ It is possible that Saint-Céneri followed the same policy of impartiality concerning the succession as did Saint-Evroult. The attitude of Saint-Evroult and Saint-Céneri may have been due to caution because of their vulnerable position near the frontier of Anjou and Normandy. In this context it is conceivable that a prior of Saint-Céneri would decline an offer to write a history of Geoffrey of Anjou as Duke of Normandy. See for Orderic's attitude concerning the succession, Orderic, vi, 1978, xxv-xxvii. I owe this reference to Dr Marjorie Chibnall.

⁶⁴ *Chroniques des comtes d'Anjou et des seigneurs d'Amboise*, ed. L. Halphen, R. Poupardin, Paris 1913, 172–213. See also the introduction, lxxxiv–lxxxviii.

⁶⁵ I am preparing a new critical edition of the *Gesta Normannorum Ducum* of William of Jumièges including the interpolations and continuations.

Notes to the Appendices: Appendix I gives a scheme of the textual development of the GND. It only contains the interpolations and continuations which are relevant for this article. Appendix II consists of a list of all existing manuscripts of the *GND* known to me.

The Beginnings of the		
Honour of Clare	Richard Mortimer	pp. 119–141

[1] J. H. Round, 'The Family of Clare', *Archaeological Journal* lvi, 1899, 222.

[2] M. Altschul, *A Baronial Family in Medieval England: the Clares, 1217–1314*, Baltimore 1965, 223–4; see also Jennifer C. Ward, The Estates of the Clare Family 1066–1317, London Ph.D. thesis, 1962.

[3] The south-eastern lands of Richard are in *Domesday Book*, i, 3, 4, 4b, 5b–7b, 14, 34b–35b; also 72, 113, 130, 142b.

[4] W. V. Dumbreck, 'The Lowy of Tonbridge', *Archaeologia Cantiana* lxxii, 1958, 138–147.

[5] Jumièges, 289.

[6] F. R. H. Du Boulay, *The Lordship of Canterbury*, London 1966, 85–6.

[7] The Cartulary of Stoke-by-Clare, Suffolk Charters Series, forthcoming, no. 70.

[8] *Domesday Book*, i, 207; Dugdale, *Monasticon Anglicanum* (ed. Caley *et al.*), iii, 473.

[9] J. Le Patourel, 'The Norman Colonization of Britain', *I Normanni e la loro Espansione in Europa nell'Alto Medioevo*, Settimane di Studio, Spoleto 1969, 425.

[10] *Domesday Book*, i, 1.

[11] J. Le Patourel, 'The Reports of the Trial on Penenden Heath', *Studies in Medieval History presented to F. M. Powicke*, ed. R. W. Hunt, W. A. Pantin, R. W. Southern, Oxford 1948, 23; D. Bates, 'The Land Pleas of William I's Reign: Penenden Heath Revisited, *BIHR* li, 1978, 3.

[12] O. von Feilitzen, *The Pre-Conquest Personal Names of Domesday Book*, Uppsala 1937, 170–1; F. Harmer, *Anglo-Saxon Writs*, Manchester 1952, 556; J. M. Kemble, *Codex Diplomaticus Aevi Saxonici*, 6 vols., London 1839–48, no. 824.

[13] *Regesta Regum Anglo-Normannorum*, i, ed. H. W. C. Davis, Oxford 1913, 23.

[14] *Domesday Book*, i, 34, 35b.

[15] *Domesday Book*, i, 36b.

[16] *Domesday Book*, i, 36b.

[17] VCH *Surrey*, i, 283.

[18] *Domesday Book*, i, 35b.

[19] *Textus Roffensis*, ed. T. Hearne, 1725, 149.

[20] *Regesta*, i, nos. 22, 26.

[21] *Regesta*, i, nos. 50, 100.

[22] Kemble, nos. 874, 883, 905; A. J. Robertson, *Anglo-Saxon Charters*, Cambridge 1939, 425.

[23] R. Welldon Finn, *Domesday Studies, the Eastern Counties*, London 1967, 140.

[24] For Richard's East Anglian estate see *Domesday Book*, ii, 38b–41b; 101b–103, 447b–448; also i, 142b, 207, 216. For Finn see also i, 153, ii, 98b, 418b.

[25] *Domesday Book*, ii, 102.

[26] *Domesday Book*, ii, 102, 448b.

[27] *Domesday Book*, ii, 393–4, 352.

[28] Finn, 28.

[29] *Domesday Book*, ii, 448.

[30] *Liber Eliensis*, ed. E. O. Blake, Camden Society 3rd series xcii, 1962, 188; Orderic, ii, 316–8.

[31] *Liber Eliensis*, 188.

[32] *Regesta*, i, nos. 242, 258.

[33] E. Miller, 'The Ely Land Pleas in the Reign of William I', *EHR* lxii, 1947; *Regesta*, i, no. 122; *Liber Eliensis*, 198.

[34] *Liber Eliensis*, no. 122.

[35] *Domesday Book*, ii, 393, 394b.

[36] Dumbreck, 145.

[37] R. Lennard, *Rural England 1086–1135*, Oxford 1959, 51.

[38] *Domesday Book*, ii, 40.

[39] F. M. Stenton, *The First Century of English Feudalism 1066–1166*, Oxford 1932, 79 n3.

[40] *Domesday Book*, ii, 448.

[41] *Domesday Book*, ii, 38b.

[42] E. King, *Peterborough Abbey 1086–1310*, Cambridge 1973, 13 and refs; W. E. Wightman, *The Lacy Family in England and Normandy 1066–1194*, Oxford 1966, 49, 150–3.

[43] Altschul, 19; *Red Book of the Exchequer*, ed. H. Hall, RS 1896, i, 403–7.

[44] *Domesday Book*, ii, 39b; i, 35, 35b.

[45] *Domesday Book*, ii, 396b.

[46] *Domesday Book*, ii, 397, 397b.

[47] Stenton, 18–19.

[48] D. C. Douglas, *Feudal Documents from the Abbey of Bury St Edmunds*, British Academy 1932, no. 168.

[49] L. C. Loyd, *The Origins of Some Anglo-Norman Families*, Harleian Society ciii, 1951.

[50] *Domesday Book*, i, 40b; *VCH* Surrey i, 316 n1.

[51] *Domesday Book*, i, 35; ii, 393b.

[52] Douglas, 4; Du Boulay, 99.

[53] Stenton, 133–5.

[54] Stenton, 153.

[55] Orderic, iii, 96. For the prevalence of coined money see L. Musset, 'A-t-il existé en Normandie au XIe siècle une aristocracie d'argent?' *Annales de Normandie* ix, 1959.

The making of the March:
aspects of the Norman
settlement in Dyfed   I. W. Rowlands   pp. 142–157.

[1] J. G. Edwards, 'The Normans and the Welsh March', *Proceedings of the British Academy*, xlii, 1956, 155–77. The most recent studies are D. G. Walker, *The Norman Conquerors*, Swansea 1977 and R. R. Davies, 'Kings, Lords and Liberties in the March of Wales, 1066–1272', *TRHS* ser. 5, xxix, 1979, 41–61. The best narrative account is still J. E. Lloyd, *A History of Wales from the Earliest Times to* the

Edwardian Conquest, 1911 (and subsequent editions). This is a revised version of a paper read at the Battle Abbey Conference in 1979.

[2] *Brut y Tywysogyon* (Peniarth MS. 20 version), trans. T. Jones, Cardiff 1952, 19. Unless otherwise stated, all references to the *Brut* are to this version.

[3] M. Lapidge, 'The Welsh-Latin Poetry of Sulien's Family', *Studia Celtica*, viii/ix, 1973/4, 89–93.

[4] Giraldus Cambrensis, *Opera*, ed. J. F. Dimock, RS 1861–91, vi, 89–90; *Brut*, 20. The knight Saer lasted only two years as castellan of Pembroke before being removed, *Brut*, 25–6.

[5] Giraldus, *Opera*, i.22; J. E. Lloyd, *History of Wales*, ii, 503.

[6] *The Cartulary of Worcester Cathedral Priory*, ed. R. R. Darlington, Pipe Roll Society, ns. xxxviii, 1962–3, xxxi–xxxiii and charters 252–8.

[7] *Brut*, 58. For Henry I's role, see below pp. 150–3.

[8] T. Jones Pierce, *Medieval Welsh Society*, Cardiff 1972/309–11.

[9] Feuds between settler families are noted in the *Brut*, 55–6 and Giraldus, *Opera*, i. 27.

[10] J. F. A. Mason, 'Roger de Montgomery and his Sons', *TRHS*, ser. 5, xiii, 1963, 1–28; J. H. Round, *Feudal England*, 1964, facing p. 359 for the Clare and Fitz Baldwin branches.

[11] *Brut*, 45, 51 and 54. William fitz Gerald, who succeeded his father as castellan of Pembroke, was one of Earl Gilbert's chief officers, *Worcester Cartulary*, no. 255. See also H. Owen, *Old Pembroke Families*, 1902, though some of the pedigrees are suspect.

[12] Giraldus, *Opera*, vi, 66 and J. Conway Davies, 'Giraldus Cambrensis, 1146–1946', *Archaeologia Cambrensis*, xcix, 1946–7, 85–6.

[13] Giraldus, Opera, vi, 91: '*ut altiores in finibus illis sibi suisque radices figeret, Griphini principis Sudwalliae sororem, cui nomen Nesta, sibi lege maritali copulavit.*' For the De Windsors, see J. H. Round, 'The Origin of the Fitz Geralds', *The Ancestor*, ii, 1902, 91–8 and Appendix ii below.

[14] See J. G. Edwards, 'The Normans', 166–7 and D. G. Walker, 'The Norman Settlement in Wales', *Proceedings of the Battle Abbey Conference*, II, 1978, 224n. 27, for the problem of nomenclature in the *Brut*. There are numerous occasions when French and Flemish are distinguished, the one from the other.

[15] *e.g.* the Bretons Wihenoc and Baderon at Monmouth, the Fleming Turstin at Wigmore and, from Maine, Winebald and Hamelin de Ballon at Caerleon and Abergavenny.

[16] See below pp. 148–50. The monasteries favoured by Wizo the Fleming were both in the West of England, *i.e.* Gloucester and Worcester.

[17] F. M. Stenton, *The First Century of English Feudalism, 1066–1166*, (2 edn.) Oxford 1961, 26–9.

[18] *Brut*, 41–2 and *Cartularium S. Johannis Baptiste de Carmarthen*, ed. T. Phillips, Cheltenham, 1865, no. 10. *Episcopal Acts Relating to Welsh Dioceses* (Historical Society of the Church in Wales, 1946–8), ed. J. Conway Davies, 362. The *chanson* is the basis for *The Song of Dermot and the Earl*, ed. G. H. Orpen, Oxford, 1892, 265; for its probable Dyfed origin, see J. H. Round, *The Commune of London*, 1899, 150.

[19] R. H. George, 'The Contribution of Flanders to the Conquest of England', *Revue Belge de Philologie et d'Histoire*, v, 1926, 81–99; T. Forssner, *Continental-Germanic Personal Names in England*, Uppsala 1916, xxxviii–xiii; W. E. Kapelle, *The Norman Conquest of the North*, 1977, 207, 212–3.

[20] See also G. W. S. Barrow, *The Kingdom of the Scots*, 1973, 289–91, 318, 328–9 and A.

M. Duncan, *Scotland, The Making of a Kingdom*, Edinburgh 1978, 137–8, 141, 476–7.

[21] *Episcopal Acts*, 237 and D. G. Walker, 'The Norman Settlement', 139. The St Evroult chronicler knew that more than one region in Wales had been granted to Flemings, *Orderic*, vi, 443.

[22] For the discussion, see K. Hughes, 'The Welsh-Latin Chronicles: *Annales Cambriae* and the Later Texts', *Proceedings of the British Academy*, lix, 1973, 233–58; reviewed by D. N. Dumville, *Studia Celtica*, xii/xiii, 1977/8, 461–7; D. P. Kirby, 'The Place of Ceredigion in the Early History of Wales, *c.* 400–1170', *Ceredigion*, vi, 1970, 774–6.

[23] *Worcester Cartulary*, no. 252. The most detailed studies are by G. G. Dept, 'Een Vlaamsche Kolonie in Wales', *Annales de la Société d'Emulation de Bruges*, lxxiv, 1931, 16–31 and H. Owen, The Flemings in Pembrokeshire', *Archaeologia Cambrensis*, ser 5, xii, 1895, 103–6. I am grateful to Mrs E. Nicholas for her assistance with the translation. See also T. M. Chotzen, 'Some Sidelights on Cambro-Dutch Relations', *Transactions of the Honourable Society of Cymmrodorion* 1937, 101–44.

[24] *Brut*, 27–8; Worcester, ii, 64; *De gestis regum*, ii, 477 and 477 and *Worcester Cartulary*, no. 252. It is the Worcester tradition that we find in Symeon of Durham, *Historia Regum*, ed. T. Arnold, RS 1855, ii, 245 and Roger of Howden, *Chronica Magistri Rogeri de Hovedene*, ed. W. Stubbs, RS 1870, *s.a.* IIII. The other *Brut* versions are *Brut y Tywysogyon* (Red Book of Hergest Version), ed. T. Jones, Cardiff 1955, 53 and *Brenhinedd y Saesson*, ed. T. Jones, Cardiff, 1971, 105.

[25] *Pipe Roll 31 Henry I*, ed. J. Hunter (Record Commission), 1833, 136–7 and J. E. Lloyd, *A History of Wales*, ii, 424. Earl Gilbert also exercised a measure of authority over the Flemings, *Worcester Cartulary*, nos. 252–5.

[26] *The Song of Dermot*, 35. To Orderic and William of Malmesbury, the Flemings were chosen for their 'shock-troop' qualities, *Orderic*, vi, 443, and *De gestis regum*, ii, 365–6.

[27] *Worcester Cartulary*, no. 252 and J. E. Lloyd, *A History of Wales*, ii, 425.

[28] *Brut*, 34, 164; T. M. Chotzen, 'Willelm von Brabant en Owain ap Cadwgan', *Annales de la Société d'Emulation de Bruges*, lxxvi, 1933, 65–82; J. E. Lloyd, *A History of Wales*, ii, 424, n. 75; B. Howells, 'Pembrokeshire Farming, c. 1580–1620', *National Library of Wales Journal*, ix, 1955/6, 316. See also the distribution map in George, 'The Flemish Contribution.'

[29] *Diplomatic Documents, 1101–1272*, ed. P. Chaplais, 1964, 2 and 6.

[30] Giraldus, *Opera*, i, 28 and vi, 87–8; P. de Keyser, 'Vlaamsche Waarzeggeriz uit de l 12 eeuw', *Annales de la Société d'Emulation de Bruges*, lxxvi, 1933, 39–46; Giraldus, *Speculum Duorum*, ed. Y. Lefèvre and R. B. C. Huygens, Cardiff 1974, 36–7.

[31] *The Song of Dermot*, 193. G. Owen, *The Description of Pembrokeshire*, ed. H. Owen, 1892, i. 177–8 has a thirteenth-century charter whereby Geoffrey de la Roche warrants a grant '*contra omnes homines justiciabiles Francigenas, Flandrenses, Anglicos et Wallenses.*'

[32] B. Coote, *The Triumph of English, 1350–1400*, 1969, 18 and George Owen, *Description* i, 16–17.

[33] B. G. Charles, 'The Records of Slebech', *National Library of Wales Journal*, viii, 1947/8, 180; *The Red Book of the Exchequer*, ed. H. Hall, RS 1896, i, 251 and *Liber Feodorum, The book of fees commonly called Testa de Nevill*, (Public Record Office, 1920–1), ii, 786.

[34] *Pipe Roll 31 Henry I*, 89; *The Red Book*, i, 290 and *Liber Feodorum*, i, 82.

[35] L. C. Loyd, *The Origins of Some Anglo-Norman Families*, (Publications of the Harleian Society, ciii), Leeds, 1951, 70 and 83.

[36] J. H. Round, *Peerage and Family History*, 1901, 215.

[37] J. H. Round, *Family Origins and Other Studies*, ed. W. Page, 1930, 73–102; *Stogursey Charters*, ed. T. D. Tremlett and N. Blakiston, (Somerset Record Society, lxi, 1946), 1–2; G.E.C.'s *The Complete Peerage*, ed. H. A. Doubleday and Lord Howard de Walden, viii 1932, 530–1, and W. Dugdale, *Monasticon Anglicanum*, ed. J. Caley, H. Ellis and B. Bandinel, 1846, iv, 130, for the royal grant of Caldy to Robert. Was his father the builder of *Castrum Martini* near Pembroke?

[38] *Pipe Roll 20 Henry II*, 89.

[39] *Liber Feodorum*, ii, 781–2 and *Baronia de Kemeys*, ed. T. D. Lloyd (Cambrian Archaeological Society), 1861, 48 (Jordan de Hode and St Dogmael's); *Monasticon*, iv, 130 and *Pipe Roll 2 Henry II*, 30 (Hubert de Vallibus). Baldwin de Reviers' charter for St James's (Exeter) was witnessed by Robert fitz Martin, Hubert de Vaux and Roger de Puncardone, *Calendar of Documents Preserved in France*, ed. J. H. Round, 1899, no. 1276; St Nicholas's (Exeter) was also patronised by a Dyfed landowner—Adam de la Roche, H. Owen, *Old Pembroke Families*, 68–9.

[40] *Monasticon*, v, 590 and J. E. Lloyd, *A History of Wales*, ii, 593–4; *Pipe Roll 1 John*, 182 and *Pipe Roll 2 John*, 226, 230.

[41] I. J. Sanders, *English Baronies. A Study of their Origin and Descent, 1086–1927*, Oxford 1960, 15 and n.5; *Calendar of Inquisitions Post Mortem*, 1970, XV, nos. 736–7.

[42] *Brut*, 37; R. F. Walker, 'Tenby', *The Boroughs of Medieval Wales*, ed. R. A. Griffiths, Cardiff 1978, 319–20; Giraldus, *Opera*, iii, 315 for a casual reference to '*miles quidam . . . qui Devoniae partibus illuc nuper advenerat*'.

[43] B. E. Howells, 'The Distribution of Customary Acres in South Wales', *National Library of Wales Journal*, xv, 1967/8, 226–33; J. Beverley Smith, 'The Lordship of Gower and Kilvey', *Glamorgan County History*, iii, ed. T. B. Pugh, Cardiff 1971, 211.

[44] B. G. Charles, *Non-Celtic Place-Names in Wales*, 1938, xxix.

[45] *Orderic*, iv, 101.

[46] J. G. Edwards, 'The Normans', 161–2 and J. Beverley Smith, *Glamorgan County History*, iii, 8–9. For the whole matter, see R. R. Davies, 'Kings, Lords', 53–9.

[47] *Brut*, 20; *Episcopal Acts*, i, 106–114 for the 'concerted and general plan' of 1093.

[48] *Brut*, 42 and 59.

[49] *Brut*, 39 for Henry I's overlordship; see also R. R. Davies, 'Kings, Lords', 53.

[50] *Brut*, 29.

[51] *Pipe Roll 31 Henry I*, 53 and *Brut*, 34 (for Ceredigion).

[52] *Brut*, 38.

[53] *Pipe Roll 31 Henry I*, 136–7; J. F. A. Mason, 'Roger de Montgomery', 18.

[54] T. F. Tout, 'The Welsh Shires: A study in Constitutional History', *Collected Papers*, Manchester 1934, ii, 4–5; *Calendar of the Public Records Relating to Pembrokeshire*, ed. H. Owen, 1918, iii. The subordination of the lord of Cemais to Henry I is asserted in *Calendar of Documents Preserved in France*, i, 353.

[55] J. Beverley Smith, *Glamorgan County History*, iii, 15–24.

[56] J. G. Edwards, 'The Normans', 163–4 and 'The Early History of the Counties of Carmarthen and Cardigan', *EHR*, xxxi, 1916, 90–98.

[57] *Pipe Roll 31 Henry I*, 89–90: J. E. Lloyd (ed.), *A History of Carmarthenshire*, Cardiff 1935, i, 136. As lord of Carmarthen, Henry I had lands at Pentywyn in Llanstephan, *The Chronicle of Battle Abbey* ed. E. Searle, Oxford 1980, 124, 125 n.2; in 1207 land in the lordship of Laugharne was the subject of an assize at Carmarthen county court, *Rotuli de Oblantis et Finibus*, ed. T. Duffus Hardy (Record Commission) 1835, i, 410.

[58] T. M. Charles-Edwards, 'The Seven Bishop-Houses of Dyfed', *Bulletin of the Board of Celtic Studies*, xxiv, 1970/2, 247–62.

[59] Ifor Williams, 'Moliant Dinbych Penfro', *Transactions of the Honourable Society of Cymmrodorion*, Session 1940, 76 'Better are the slaves of Dyfed than the yeomen of Deudraeth'; for the name, see Wendy Davies, *An Early Welsh Microcosm: Studies in the Llandaff Charters*, London 1978, 89–90.

[60] J. Vendryes, 'Le Poéme du Livre Noir sur Hywel ab Gronw',*Études Celtiques*, iv, 1948, 1.11 (p. 287).

[61] R. R. Davies, 'Kings, Lords', 50–2.

[62] *Monasticon*, iv, 130.

[63] J. C. Holt, *The Northerners*, Oxford 1961, chapt. xi. A case has been put forward for the late emergence of the commote in South Wales, by J. E. Lloyd, *A History of Wales*, i, 301 and n.210: 'Penfro, which was originally the name of a cantref could not have become the name of a commote also until Castell Penfro (*i.e.* Pembroke Castle) became known by the shorter title'. The castle and castellany may have had a role to play in commotal formation.

[64] *Monasticon*, iv, 503.

[65] The impact of such raids has perhaps been under-estimated. See the references in the *Brut* for the century preceding 1093; the Welsh rising of 1094 and the punitive harrying of Pebidiog in 1097 by Gerald of Windsor cannot have made for orderly settlement, *Brut*, 19, 20.

[66] B. E. Howells, 'Pembrokeshire Farming', 316–33; 'Customary Acres', 226–33; (editor) *Elizabethan Pembrokeshire*, Pembroke Record Society 1973, viii–x; 'Medieval Settlement in Dyfed', *The Land of Dyfed in Early Times*, ed. D. Moore, Cardiff 1964, 36–9; *The Agrarian History of England and Wales*, ed. H. P. R. Finberg, Cambridge 1972, i, ii, 364–5; W. Rees, *South Wales and the Border in the Fifteenth Century*, 1924, 29, 30 n.i., 65, 136, 144–6.

[67] J. E. Lloyd, *A History of Wales*, i, 347 and ii, 771 (pedigree). Even Rhys ap Tewdwr's brother, Rhydderch, undertook the defence of Carmarthen in 1116.

[68] R. G. Gruffydd, 'A Poem in Praise of Cuhelyn Fardd from the Black Book of Carmarthen', *Studia Celtica*, x/xi, 1975/6, 198–209; for his descendants, J. E. Lloyd, 'Hynafiaid Dafydd ap Gwilym', *Bulletin of the Board of Celtic Studies*, viii, pt. i, 1935, 1–3. *Calendar of Ancient Correspondence concerning Wales*, ed. J. G. Edwards, Cardiff 1935, 48.

[69] Pipe Roll 31 Henry I, 89; C. Bullock-Davies, *Professional Interpreters and the Matter of Britain*, Cardiff 1966, 10–12; W. Rees, *A History of the Order of St John of Jerusalem in Wales and on the Welsh Border*, Cardiff 1947, 113.

[70] *Brut*, 55–6 and 58. See Figure 1, p. 157. See also A. J. Roderick, 'Marriage and Politics in Wales, 1066–1282', *Welsh History Review*, iv, 1968/9, 6.

[71] Giraldus, *Opera*, iii, 432.

[72] Giraldus, *Speculum Duorom*, 71: *Opera*, i, 26, 58–9 and iii, 17–18, 313–5.

[73] Glanmor Williams, 'The Tradition of St David in Wales'; *Links with the Past. Swansea and Brecon Historical Essays*, ed. D. G. Walker, Swansea; 1974, 9. Information on St David's in the period 1073–1148 is brought together in *Episcopal Acts*, 233–70.

[74] Glanmor Williams, 'The Tradition', 9.

[75] Glanmor Williams, 'The Tradition', 4–8.

[76] *The Song of Dermot*, ll.744–53, 986–8, 1936–40, 3432–55.

Women and the legitimisation of succession at the Norman Conquest

Eleanor Searle pp. 159–170

[1] E. Searle, 'Seigneurial Control of Women's Marriage: the Antecedents and Function of Merchet in England', *Past and Present*, no. 82, 1979, 3–43.

[2] *Select Charters*, ed. W. Stubbs, 9th edition, revised by H. W. C. Davis, Oxford 1966, 118.

[3] Professor Milsom, commenting on Glanvill ix, 4, puts the matter clearly: it requires saying that relief is not due from any husband but the first, because the lord's consent, Glanvill assumes, is necessary for all her marriages and his consent will entail payment unless it is specifically denied. S. F. C. Milsom, *The Legal Framework of English Feudalism*, Cambridge 1976, 104.

[4] For a succinct analysis of Orderic Vitalis' evidence concerning the Bellême inheritance, see *The Ecclesiastical History of Orderic Vitalis*, ed. M. Chibnall, ii, Oxford 1969, Appendix I, 362–5.

[5] *Orderic*, iv, 88.

[6] *The Story of England*, 'Robert Manning of Brunne', ed. F. J. Furnivall, RS 1887, i, 230.

[7] Hereward is not the only example of the dangers in complete disinheritance. Earlier, Earl Aelfgar fled to Wales and from there kept the Mercian marches in a state of disruption after his dispossession. *ASC s.a* 1055. In Normandy Arnold of Echauffour for three years 'carried out a furious war of vengeance for the injustice of his banishment' until he was removed by a sudden illness thought to have been poison. *Orderic*, ii, 124. Another feature common to these men's situation is that each had a safe base from which to operate.

[8] In this Edith resembles Cnut's wife Aelfgifu of Northampton. There is no hint that her son was illegitimate, and she ruled legitimately for Cnut in Norway.

[9] Robert of Torigny, in *Chronicles . . . Stephen, Henry II and Richard I*, ed. R. Howlett, RS 1889, iv, 19.

[10] In his interpolations in *William of Jumièges*, ed. J. Marx, Rouen 1914, 191: 'Adelisam filiam suam cum medietati Anglici regni se daturum eidem spopondit'. The Anglo-Saxon Chronicle knows nothing about the supposed marriage, but Orderic speaks of it. *Orderic*, ii, 136; and see William of Poitiers for the story, *Gesta Guillelmi*, 230. See also Eadmer, 8: 'Si de filia sua quam debui in uxorem, ut assevit, ducere agit, super regnum Angliae mulierem extraneam inconsultis principibus me nec debere nec sine grande injuria posse adducere novent'; *De gestis regum*, 297–8; *Huntingdon*, 196–7.

[11] *De gestis regum*, ii, 298.

[12] R. Allen Brown, *The Normans and the Norman Conquest*, London 1969, 206: 'That in the beginning king William had intended to establish a genuine Anglo-Norman state is proved by his patronage of and patience with the aetheling Edgar, earls Edwin and Morcar, Waltheof and Copsi and those other members of the pre-Conquest nobility of England who submitted to him and made their peace after Hastings, as by his maintenance in their positions of English sheriffs and other officials. Yet also (William had the obligation) to meet the claims of those who had supported his invasion on the promise of rich rewards . . .' This, I think, puts William's intentions and dilemma shrewdly and clearly. For the latest treatment of William's not wholly unsympathetic reception by the English thegns, see Eric John, 'Edward the Confessor and the Norman Succession', *EHR* cclxxi, 1979, 241–67.

¹³ *Huntingdon*, 196.

¹⁴ *Liber Monasterii de Hyda*, ed. E. Edwards, RS 1866, 294.

¹⁵ *Orderic*, ii, 214–16 and see 256.

¹⁶ *Orderic*, ii, 260. Orderic puts this *ca.* 1068, but charter evidence does not bear him out. The evidence of the division to which he refers indicates that it was of the early seventies. To this decade or slightly later we may attribute the settlement of Montgomery at Shrewsbury, Beaumont at Warwick, Clare at Pembroke, Avranches at Chester, Count Alan at Richmond, Fitz Hamo in Gloucester.

¹⁷ Worcester, ii, 9–18 (s.a. 1074). *De Gestis Regum*, ii, 313; *Symeonis Monachi Opera*, ed. T. Arnold, RS, London 1882–5, ii, 205.

¹⁸ For Lanfranc's letters to Roger, earl of Hereford, to the king and to Bishop Walcher, see M. Gibson and H. Clover, *The Letters of Lanfranc*, Oxford 1980, 118–26. Domesday Book has evidence to bear out Lanfranc's description of the formality of the procedure. It speaks of land that Earl Ralph forfeited 'postea derationatus est Lanfrancus iussu regis in episcopatum rovensem'. *Domesday Book* i, 381. See also *Orderic*, ii, 316.

¹⁹ *Orderic*, ii, 310, thought that the motive was to replace William with themselves, manifestly an unlikely possibility. Other chroniclers conjectured merely that they had conspired with Waltheof to dethrone the king. *Huntingdon*, 206; *The Peterborough Chronicle*, ed. Cecily Clark, 2nd ed., Oxford 1970, 5; *ADC*, s.a. 1075. Lanfranc's letters, the only contemporary documents, speak of a 'stulto proposito' about which he was fully cognizant before the event, and against which he strongly advised Earl Roger. He subsequently warned the earl to 'lie low' ('ut quiescas') lest he incur even greater royal anger. To the king Lanfranc speaks of the earls as 'periuri', and 'traditori', and of Ralph of Gael's Bretons even as 'spurcicia'. But nothing in the archbishop's letters has any hint of an attempt to overthrow the king, and it is impossible that he could know of such a danger and write to its perpetrator calling it merely 'stupid'.

²⁰ F. M. Stenton, 'English Families and the Norman Conquest', *TRHS* ser. 4, xxvi 1944, 1–17. Stenton mentions the possibility that Normans had married Englishwomen (p. 6), but did not appear to consider inheritance through a woman to be an unbroken lineage. See also Anthony Wagner, *English Geneaology*, Oxford 1960, 47.

²¹ *Charters of the Honour of Mowbray*, ed. Diana E. Greenway, xx and n. 4. Wigot had a son killed fighting for William against Robert in Normandy. *ASC*, 'D', s.a. 1079. The reference enables us to see one Englishman reconciled to the Normans and with a sister married to a Norman. It serves to remind us that he may have had brothers or sons who also made their peace and were allowed to continue holding under their Norman in-law. Such men are almost invisible in our records. But their position was not necessarily humiliating; it may have been acceptable to be represented to the Normans, with their different customs of service, by a Norman. See Stenton, 'English Families', for a reference to an English holder continuing 'at rent heavily and wretchedly', cited in Domesday. The very sympathy of the commissioners might suggest that such exploitation was disapproved.

²² Lucy died in 1138. After Roger's death, their son, William de Roumare, became earl of Lincoln. The barony passed in the late twelfth century to Lucy's heirs by her third husband, Ranulph le Meschin, earl of Chester. *GEC* vii, Appendix J. 743–6. I. J. Sanders, *English Baronies*, Oxford 1960, 18, n. I. Lucy's father was probably the sheriff Thorold and her mother was certainly Beatrice, daughter of William Malet. Beatrice's dowry of Alkborough in Lincolnshire descended to Lucy.

[23] *Carmen*, 38.

[24] For lands that 'William Malet and his father held,' see *Domesday Book*, ii 333. The Malet genealogy is so obscure that we cannot be certain who the mother of Robert and wife of William really was. See C. W. Hollister, 'Henry I and Robert Malet', *Viator* 4 (1973), 115–22. But in 1086 she was a substantial landholder in Suffolk, nearly always of lands once held by the Suffolk magnate Edric of Laxfield or by men who had been commended to Edric *TRE*. In 1086 part of her lands were listed separately as in dispute between herself and the bishop of Bayeux. *Domesday Book*, ii, 450. It would hardly have been a surprising alliance if William Malet had married Edric's daughter, for both men were great landholders and active in government, and Worcester ii, 4, says that in 1069 she was with Malet at the siege of York, with her children. There is some further reason to think that Edric was Robert Malet's *antecessor* in a closer sense than the usual 'predecessor' of Domesday terminology, for lands that Robert had never held could be described as having once been held by Edric and then William Malet, or by Edric, 'Robert Malet's antecessor'. *Domesday Book* ii, 148b, 260a, 332, 332b, 344, 346b, 376. The problem of the Anglo-Norman family is peculiarly complex. The half-English William and his possibly more than half-English son were unswervingly loyal. William fought beside the duke at Hastings, and that he met his death fighting for the Normans can be inferred from the numerous references in Domesday Book to the time when he 'went into the marsh', presumably during the fighting against Hereward. Eg. *Domesday Book*, ii, 133b. Robert Malet was actively loyal at the dispossession of Ralph of Gael in 1074/5. *Regesta Regum Anglo-Normannorum*, i, ed. H. W. C. Davis, Oxford 1913, no. 82 and *Letters of Lanfranc*, no. 35. In spite of this he not only failed to profit from Earl Ralph's fall, but he actually lost lands to the Normans who did profit, and to Count Alan the Red. In 1086 he no longer held the shrievalty that he had once held in Suffolk, and he attested no charters of William II. As Hollister points out, he held important office under Henry I and was a frequent attestor of Henry's charters. But when he died, *ca.* 1106, his heir was not allowed to inherit in England. *ASC* s.a. 1110, merely says he was deprived of his lands; *Huntingdon*, 237, thought that this William, Robert's heir, had somehow 'injured the king', but knew no evidence of such an injury.

[25] J. H. Round, *Feudal England*, London 1895, 324, and his *Studies in Peerage and Family History*, London 1901, 156, 165. Alured's daughter had been married first to Thurstin the Fleming, who died between 1075 and 1086. *Domesday Book*, i, 183b. For 'gener et heres', see *Orderic*, vi, 390, and for his notion that the hopes of alliances through marriage centered upon the children of the marriage, see *Orderic*, vi, 122, 128–30.

[26] *Letters of Lanfranc*, 166. It will be evident that I incline to Dr Clover's choice of Bishop Geoffrey rather than Bishop Gundulph, as recipient, for I think that Lanfranc's ending, 'Et hoc est consilium regis et nostrum' points to the problem as being one for a royal justice rather than a bishop. Eadmer supposes it to have resulted from a council held soon after the first disturbances of the conquest. Eadmer, 129–30. Orderic, without mentioning the letter, puts the story of women dishonoured by Normans with the events of the 1070s. *Orderic*, ii, 268.

[27] *Orderic* ii, 266.

[28] Simeon of Durham, 202–5.

[29] Margaret was probably still a child. Her own first child was born in 1073/4 and she had a numerous family.

[30] G. W. Barrow, *Feudal Britain*, London 1965, 129.

[31] Whether on the Tweed or the Forth is not certain. Orderic places it on the Forth. *Orderic*, iv, 268. The *ASC* and Florence of Worcester say more vaguely that Malcolm came into Lothian. *ASC*, s.a. 1091; Worcester, ii, 28. As Dr Chibnall points out, the armies may have met at the Tweed, *Orderic*, iv, 268, n. 2.

[32] *Orderic*, iv, 270.

[33] Ep. 177, *S. Anselmi opera omnia*, ed. F. S. Schmitt, Edinburgh 1946–61. The incident has been analysed by R. W. Southern, *St Anselm and his Biographer*, Cambridge 1963, 183–5.

[34] Whether she had earlier been at Romsey in the charge of her aunt Christina, a nun there, is unclear. According to Eadmer, Edith herself said that she was raised by her aunt. He also says she was brought up at Wilton. She may well have been taken to Wilton to await her father, who was negotiating a settlement with Rufus. Eadmer, 121–6. See E. A. Freeman, *William Rufus*, ii, n. EE, 598 ff.

[35] Worcester, ii, 30–1.

[36] See E. A. Freeman, *William Rufus*, ii, Note CC, 592–6 for a review of the sources.

[37] 'De Restauratione S. Martini Tornacensis,' *MGH, SS*, xiv, 281. The story is a peculiar one but Anselm's own source was the abbess of Wilton. Rufus rode to the nunnery with a frightening retinue of knights, and demanded entrance. The abbess, fearing for Edith's safety quickly got a veil on the child and while Rufus was pretending an interest in the cloister garden, he was allowed to glimpse her in the company of the other young nuns. Immediately he saw her so dressed he left.

[38] For a summary of the events, see Southern, *St Anselm*, 185–93. Anselm's letters to Gunnilda are epp. 168 and 169.

[39] Southern, *St Anselm*, 188. This brother, Alan the Black, died in 1098.

[40] Southern, *St Anselm* 185, 188.

[41] W. Farrer, *VCH Yorks*. ii, 156. *Reg*. i, 27 is a 'pseudo-charter' from the Register of the Honour of Richmond, conferring all of Earl Edwin's Yorkshire holdings on Alan, and this is borne out of Domesday Book. *Domesday Book* i, 309–13.

[42] W. E. Wightman, *The Lacy Family in England and Normandy 1066–1194*, Oxford 1966, 40–2.

[43] And was hardly necessary for protecting Henry's rear while he dealt with his Norman baronage. That had been already accomplished by keeping the young king of Scots and his brothers at the English Court, which both Rufus and Henry did. Cf. Southern, *St Anselm*, 188.

[44] *De Gestis Regum*, ii, 488. It is interesting to note that while both Rufus and Henry succoured the royal Scots children, Rufus kept them unmarried, while Henry married them into his family/baronage. David married Matilda, daughter of Earl Waltheof and Judith, and received their lands, to the exclusion of her son by Simon of St Liz; Alexander married Sybil, one of Henry's own illegitimate daughters: Mary married Eustace of Boulogne.

[45] *GEC* xi App. D.

[46] Cf. Georges Duby, *Medieval Marriage*, transl. E. Forster, Baltimore 1978, 18–22.

Land and power in
the eleventh century:
the estates of
Harold Godwineson   Ann Williams   pp. 172–187

[1] *Anglo-Saxon Charters: an annotated list and bibliography*, ed. P. H. Sawyer, London (Royal Historical Society) 1968, nos. 970, 1009, 1022 (cited hereafter as S); F. Barlow, *Edward the Confessor*, London 1970, 331. I am grateful to Mr. Nicholas Hooper for reading this paper and commenting upon it. Its remaining defects are my own responsibility.

[2] S.1519, 1535 and see below, p. 5, lines 10–13.

[3] S.1220; A. J. Robertson, *Anglo-Saxon Charters*, Cambridge 1956, 394.

[4] Barlow, *Edward the Confessor*, 155.

[5] Barlow, *Edward the Confessor*, 74.

[6] A. Williams, '*Princeps Merciorum gentis*: the family, career and connections of Ælfhere, ealdorman of Mercia, 956–983', forthcoming.

[7] F. W. Maitland, *Domesday Book and beyond*, Cambridge 1907, 167–8.

[8] F. E. Harmer, *Anglo-Saxon Writs*, Manchester 1952, 563.

[9] VCH *Essex*, i, 336.

[10] C. R. Hart, 'Athelstan Half-king and his family', *Anglo-Saxon England*, 2, 1973, 121.

[11] S.883.

[12] VCH *Hertfordshire*, i, 273, 278: *Domesday Book seu Liber Censualis Willelmi Primi Regis Anglie*, i (London 1783), 133 (cited hereafter as *DB*).

[13] VCH *Buckinghamshire*, i, 209–10.

[14] *Liber Eliensis*, ed. E. O. Blake, Camden Society, 3rd ser. xcii, 1962, xiii–iv.

[15] *DB*, i, fol. 185b.

[16] Swein's earldom included besides Herefordshire, Gloucestershire, Oxfordshire and the West Saxon shires of Somerset and Berkshire (Barlow, *Edward the Confessor*, 91).

[17] Worcester, i, 210; J. H. Round, *Feudal England*, London 1895, 322–4.

[18] *DB*, i, 162b. D. C. Cox (VCH *Shropshire*, iii, 5) considers that Harold's earldom of Hereford included Shropshire also. Hereford and Shropshire together formed the ancient *regio* of the *Magonsæte*, which seems to have been the earldom held by Earl Ranig until 1041 (Robertson, *Charters*, 400).

[19] *Encomium Emmae Reginae*, ed. A. Campbell, Camden Society, 3rd ser. lxxii, 1949, 86–7.

[20] Maitland, *Domesday Book*, 168; *DB*, i, 38b, 75, 101.

[21] F. E. Harmer, *Select English Historical Documents of the ninth and tenth centuries*, Cambridge 1914, 17; VCH *Somerset*, i, 398.

[22] *De Inventione Sanctae Crucis* in *Chroniques Anglo-normandes*, ed. Francisque Michel, Rouen 1836, ii, 227; *DB*, ii, 59.

[23] S.1539, 1535. Ketel was the man of Archbishop Stigand.

[24] *DB*, i, 164.

[25] *DB*, i, 5b.

[26] *DB*, ii, 313; J. E. A. Joliffe, *The constitutional history of medieval England*, London 1937, 142–3.

[27] Maitland, *Domesday Book*, 168; F. M. Stenton in VCH *Leicestershire*, i, 297–8; Barlow, *Edward the Confessor*, 243.

[28] E. Searle, 'Women and the legitimization of succession at the Norman Conquest', above, p. 00; *DB*, i, 189b, 139b–195b passim, 198b, 199b, 200, 201b, 134, 137, 140b, 141b, 146b, 148b, 152; ii, 7b, 284b, 285, 295, 410, 430b; M. Campbell, 'Canute the Great's women: Emma and Aelfgifu of Northampton', *Medieval Scandinavia*, 4, 66–9; *ASC*, 1015; *Charters of Burton Abbey*, ed. P. H. Sawyer, London 1979, xliii.

[29] VCH *Sussex*, i, 370; D. Haselgrove, 'The Domesday record of Sussex', *The South Saxons*, ed. P. Brandon, Chichester 1978, 202. The only member of the family not mentioned in connexion with Sussex is Ælfgifu, Harold's sister, who is mentioned only once in *DB*, in the Buckinghamshire section (fol. 144b).

[30] Godwine is named as a pre-Conquest tenant at Wychbold, Worcs. and Stanton, Herefords. (now Gloucs.); *DB*, i, 176b, 181.

[31] For the death of Aelfgar, see Barlow, *Edward the Confessor*, 210; VCH *Huntingdonshire*, i, 362 note 2. For references to his tenure in Domesday, see Olof von Feilitzen, *The pre-Conquest personal names of Domesday Book*, Uppsala 1937, 172–3.

[32] *DB*, i, 238b, 239, 243b, 244, 252b, 259b.

[33] *DB*, i, 75, 78b; iv (Exon), 28. The Domesday entry for Burton Bradstock states that it was Earl Edwin who had the third oak of Burton's wood, but Exon must be the correct version (VCH *Dorset*, iii, 3).

[34] *DB*, ii, 3b, 106b. In Derbyshire also, the estate at Coton-in-the-Elms is said to have been held *TRE* by Earl Aelfgar, but the Burton Cartulary states that it had belonged to Countess Aelfgifu, Earl Morcar's mother. However, it is possible in this case that the estate had come to her by inheritance and passed to her husband on their marriage (Sawyer, *Charters of Burton*, xliii, xlvi).

[35] D. Whitelock, *Anglo-Saxon Wills*, Cambridge 1930, 16, 22.

[36] It is by no means easy to distinguish between Gytha, wife of Earl Godwine, and Gytha, wife of Earl Ralph 'the Timid' in Domesday: see Feilitzen, *Pre-conquest personal names*, 281.

[37] *Gesta Guillelmi*, 204.

[38] VCH *Bedfordshire*, i, 207.

[39] *DB*, ii, 59; VCH *Essex*, i, 507, note 8. J. H. Round identified *Ehroica* in this entry with Evreux rather than York, but in this instance Freeman must be correct.

[40] *DB*, ii, 67b, 377, 419b, 420; VCH *Essex*, i, 352.

[41] For an example, see the career of Oswold, described by Dr Richard Mortimer on p. 00, above.

[42] VCH *Essex*, i, 351.

[43] *DB*, ii, 86b, 376b, 426b, 427.

[44] *DB*, ii, 377b, 200.

[45] *DB*, ii, 200. Both Blakeney and Bradiston were held in 1086 by William de Noyers of the bishop of Thetford, hence the identification of Eadric of Blakeney with Eadric the steersman of Bradiston (VCH *Norfolk*, ii, 14).

[46] VCH *Norfolk*, ii, 14 n. 6; *Chronica Johannis de Oxenedes*, ed. H. J. Ellis, RS 1859, 291.

[47] *DB*, ii, 219b.

[48] *Chronica Johannis de Oxenedes*, 293; F. M. Stenton, 'St Benet of Holme and the Norman Conquest', *EHR* xxxvii, 1922, 227, 233.

[49] For the distinction between royal and median thegns, see the list of heriots in II Cnut 71 (*Die Gesetze der Angelsachsen*, ed. F. Liebermann, Aalen 1903, i, 356–8).

[50] *Liber Eliensis*, 424.

[51] *DB*, i, 21b, 22b, 26a, 26b, 27b, 28a, 28b. The identification of Azor is by no means

easy. Of Earl Harold, he held the following estates: 2 hides at Shermanbury (fol. 28b), 4½ hides at Wantley, held of Azor by Brihtmær (fol. 28a) and 21 hides at Kingston Bucy (fol. 28b). Azor held two more small estates attached to Shermanbury; ½ hide at Woolfly, held of him by Ælfwine and 2 hides at Sakeham, held of him by Brihtwine (fol. 28b). Two more estates, both held by Azor of King Edward, belonged to Kingston Bucy: 14 hides 1 virgate at Hangleton and 1½ hides at 'Esmerewic' (fol. 26b). Brihtmær held two further estates of Azor: 1½ hides at Cookham (fol. 28b) and 2 hides at Ovingdean (fol. 26a) and Azor himself held 1 hide at Moulstone, attached to Ovingdean (fol. 27b) of King Edward. His lands held of Earl Godwin were: 12 hides at Wiston (fol. 28a) and 8 hides at Tarrant Neville (fol. 21b). Attached to Tarrant Neville were 4 hides at Bevendean, held by Azor of King Edward (fol. 26b) and with Bevendean was associated the manor of Keymer, assessed at 14 hides, and held by Azor of King Edward (fol. 27a), and 1½ virgates at Standen, also held by Azor of King Edward (fol. 22b). His name is very common, and it is not possible to identify him further, but his lands may very well have been much more extensive than this. For other men of the same name, see Feilitzen, *Pre-conquest personal names*, 170–1; Harmer, *Writs*, 556.

[52] *Geþyncðo* (Liebermann, i, 456–8).

[53] *DB*, i, 129b, 136b, 146; VCH *Somerset*, i, 418; Feilitzen, *Pre-conquest personal names*, 232n; VCH *Dorset*, iii, 31–2; *Middlesex*, i, 103; *Hertfordshire*, i, 281.

[54] *DB*, i, 146b, 147b.

[55] F. Ganshof, *Feudalism*, London (3rd ed.) 1964, 165.

[56] *DB*, i, 1.

[57] Worcester, ii, 1.

[58] Feilitzen, *Pre-conquest personal names*, 185–6.

[59] *DB*, i, 2.

[60] *ASC* 1067 (*recte* 1068).

[61] VCH *Somerset*, i, 295; *Dorset*, iii, 32.

[62] *DB*, i, 60, 80.

[63] For Harold's relations with Abingdon, see below p. 183.

[64] *Carmen*, 44–6; for Ansgar (Esgar) the staller, see Harmer, *Writs*, 560–1.

[65] *DB*, i, 21b, 75b, 121, 132, 174, 181b, 182, 182b, 185b; ii, 381a. In Hertfordshire also the sokeman holding a virgate at Hexton 'was a man of St. Albans but Earl Harold attached it to Hitchin by force and injustice as the shire testifies' (*DB*, ii 133b).

[66] Robertson, *Charters*, 226; Harmer, *Writs*, 271, 275. The only surviving writ issued by Harold as King is a confirmation of land and rights to Giso of Wells.

[67] *Hemingi Chartularium Ecclesiae Wigornensis*, ed. T. Hearne, Oxford 1723, i, 275–6 (cited hereafter as *Heming*); *ASC* 1052C, 1065C.

[68] 10 carucates belonging to Rochester, 8 hides 3 virgates belonging to St Guthlac, 8 hides belonging to St Mary Chatteris, 1 hide belonging to St Petroc and a virgate at Parrock belonging to St Johns.

[69] *DB*, i, 75b, 174, 181b, 182, 182b.

[70] Harmer, *Writs*, 275.

[71] *ASC* 1056, 1060. For Walter, see F. Barlow, *The English church, 1000–1066*, London 1963, 83, 157.

[72] E. A. Freeman, *The history of the Norman Conquest of England*, Oxford 1867–79, ii, Appendix E 'The alleged spoliation of the Church by Godwine and Harold'.

[73] *The Chronicle of Hugh Candidus*, ed. W. T. Mellows, London 1949, 67, 70. For Edith's reputation in this respect, see Barlow, *English church*, 114–5.

[74] Harmer, *Writs*, 331–2.

[75] *Heming*, i, 260, 261–2, 265.

[76] *DB*, i, 176; *Heming*, i, 259–60.

[77] D. J. V. Fisher, 'The anti-monastic reaction in the reign of Edward the Martyr', *Cambridge Historical Journal*, 10, 1950, 266–7.

[78] *De Inventione Sanctae Crucis* in *Chroniques Anglo-normandes*, ii, 229. For Waltham's land in 1066, see *DB*, i, 34, 58, 136, 136b, 210; ii, fols 15b, 16, 16b; S. 1036.

[79] *Vita Wulfstani*, ed. R. R. Darlington, Camden Society, 3rd ser. xl, 1928, 13.

[80] For Aelfwig, abbot of the New Minster, see D. M. Knowles, *The Monastic Order in England*, Cambridge 1949, 423; VCH *Hampshire*, i, 417–9. For Aelfwold of St Benet's Holme, see above, p. 179. For Edith Swanneck as a benefactor of St Benet Holme, see *Chronica Johannis de Oxenedes*, 292, where she is recorded as the donor of an estate at Thurgarton.

[81] *Chronicon Monasterii de Abingdon*, ed. J. Stevenson, RS 1858, i, 466–9; S. 1022; M. Gelling, *Early Charters of the Thames Valley*, Leicester 1979, 141, 142 argues that the charter of Edward granting Sandford to Abingdon is based on the earlier one granting the same estate to Earl Godwine.

[82] *Chron. Abingdon*, i, 474, 484; ii, 283; *DB*, i, 59.

[83] *Chron. Abingdon*, ii, 3.

[84] *Chron. Abingdon*, i, 103, 457–9, 475; Harmer, *Writs*, 121–3, 131. Harold also appears in his character of Earl in Robertson, *Charters*, 212, a confirmation by the shire-court of Hampshire of Queen Emma's bequest to Wulfweard White and the Old Minster.

[85] *DB*, i, 59.

[86] *Chron. Abingdon*, i, 484.

[87] For the benefactions of Aelfhere and Aelfheah, see S. 1216, *Chron. Abingdon*, i, 157–9; S. 564. For Eadric's relationship to Aelfheah, see Robertson, *Charters*, 339. For Eadwine of Sussex, see *ASC* 982; Robertson, *Charters*, 365–6.

[88] *Chron. Abingdon*, i, 484–6; ii, 283.

[89] *Chron. Abingdon*, i, 482.

[90] *DB*, i, 298.

[91] VCH *Yorkshire*, ii, 219, note 10.

[92] VCH *Yorkshire*, ii, 193; for the battle, see F. W. Brooks, *The Battle of Stamford Bridge*, East Yorkshire Local History Society, 1956.

[93] *DB*, i, 18b.

[94] *DB*, i, 16a.

[95] *ASC* 1049.

[96] *ASC* 1051.

[97] F. M. Stenton, *The Bayeux Tapestry*, London 1957, pl. 4.

[98] *DB*, i, 24a, 25b; VCH *Hampshire*, i, 427.

[99] *ASC* 1066.

[100] *ASC* 1052, 900.

[101] *DB*, i, 21, 22.

[102] *ASC* 1052.

[103] *DB*, i, 86.

[104] *ASC* 1009. 'F' a manuscript associated with Christchurch, Canterbury (*ASC* xii, xvii) states that Wulfnoth *cild* was Earl Godwine's father. Since one of Godwine's kinsmen, called Aelfric, was a monk of Christchurch and almost archbishop (*Vita Edwardi Regis*, ed. F. Barlow, London 1962, 18) there may have been some special knowledge of the family history preserved there.

[105] Only three ealdormen of the tenth century can with any confidence be assigned to the eastern shires; Aethelwold (940 × 46), Aelfric (957 × 9) and Eadwine (977 × 83). See C. R. Hart, 'Athelstan Half-king', *Anglo-Saxon England*, 2, 1973, 119, 123, and *Early charters of Northern England and the North Midlands*, Leicester 1975, 267, 332; Robertson, *Charters*, 365. Since no ealdorman is recorded for the south-east between the disappearance of Aelfric in 959 and the appointment of Eadwine in or after 977, it seems likely that the south-eastern shires were administered from 959 to 971/2 by Aelfheah ealdorman of central Wessex, and were perhaps thereafter either administered by his brother Aelfhere, ealdorman of Merica, or were in the king's hand (A. Williams, 'Princeps Merciorum gentis').

[106] D. P. Kirby, 'The church in Saxon Sussex', in *The South Saxons*, ed. Brandon, 172–3.

[107] The raids of the 980s affected mainly the south-west (Devon and Cornwall in 981, Dorset in 982, Devon again in 988). The 990s saw attacks on the east coast from East Anglia to Bamburgh (the Maldon campaign in 991, Lindsey and Northumbria ravaged in 993) and later in the same decade an army entered via the Severn and campaigned all over Wessex until it left England for Normandy in 1000. Whether this army used Normandy as a base is unclear; Aethelred II's campaign against Cumberland and the Isle of Man in 1000 suggests rather that it came from the Norse settlements in the north and west (P. Stafford, 'The reign of Aethelred II' in *Ethelred the Unready*, ed. D. Hill, *British Archaeological Reports*, lix, 1979, 30). Exeter was stormed in 1003 and Swein Forkbeard appeared off Norwich in 1004, but after this it is Sandwich which begins to figure as the gateway to England (*ASC*, 1006, 1009, 1013, 1014, 1015, 1040). For the assembly of the English fleet at Sandwich see *ASC* 1044, 1045, 1049, 1052, 1066.

[108] H. R. Loyn, *Harold son of Godwin*, Historical Association (Hastings and Bexhill Branch) 1966, 29 note.

Danish Kings and England in the late tenth and early eleventh centuries: economic implications
David M. Wilson   pp. 188–96

[1] H. R. Loyn, *The Vikings in Britain*, London 1977, 63.

[2] F. M. Stenton, *Anglo-Saxon England*, 3rd ed. Oxford 1971, 375.

[3] Translation adapted from Bernhard W. Scholz, *Carolingian Chronicles*, Ann Arbor, 1970, 89.

[4] *Skalk* No. 3, 1980, 18–26.

Index